HANDBOOK OF PSYCHODIAGNOSTIC TESTING

The Analysis of Personality in the Psychological Report

Second Edition

HENRY KELLERMAN, Ph.D.
Training Analyst and Senior Supervisor

ANTHONY BURRY, Ph.D.
Director, Psychology Internship Training

Postgraduate Center for Mental Health
New York, New York

ALLYN AND BACON
Boston   London   Toronto   Sydney   Tokyo   Singapore

To Linda

To Veena

 Copyright © 1991, 1981 by Allyn and Bacon

A Division of Simon & Schuster, Inc.
160 Gould Street
Needham Heights, Massachusetts 02194

Library of Congress Cataloging-in-Publication Data

Kellerman, Henry.
    Handbook of psychodiagnostic testing : the analysis of
personality in the psychological report / Henry Kellerman,
Anthony Burry. — 2nd ed.
        p.   cm.
    Includes bibliographical references.
    ISBN 0-205-12526-3
    1. Psychodiagnostics.   2. Personality assessment.   3. Re-
port writing.   I. Burry, Anthony.   II. Title.
    [DNLM: 1. Personality Assessment.   2. Psychological
Tests.   WM 145 K29h]
RC469.K44   1990
616.89'0075 — dc20
DNLM/DLC
for Library of Congress   90-495
                                                            CIP

Printed in the United States of America

10   9   8   7   6   5   4   3   2   95   94   93   92

Contents

— INTRODUCTION

This handbook is designed to offer to psychology students as well as professional psychologists a central resource for the construction and organization of psychological test reports. Rather than using a workbook approach and presenting sample reports for study, this text aims to help the reader conceptualize the theory of psychological report development by carefully examining the integration of the concepts and data of personality analysis and the logic of effectively communicating psychological results. The rationale of each section of an effective, well-aimed psychological and psychodiagnostic workup is analyzed in detail so that the writing of the report can be organized section-by-section to reflect a clear and synthesized view of the patient. The psychodiagnostic report is a communication between the tester and the referring person and can play a vital role in the ultimate treatment or intervention plan for the patient. Because personality analysis is vitally connected to report writing, the distinctiveness of each person tested is stressed. Use of this book, therefore, should help both students and psychologists formulate reports based on the particular needs and conflicts of the individuals under consideration. In sum then, this handbook is a guide to transforming the referrer's understanding of the person under study into logical, integrated written communication.

Directors of university and internship programs in psychology recognize that their doctoral students often perform well in all aspects of their training with the exception of constructing meaningful and cogent psychodiagnostic reports. The effectiveness of the student's write-up is very often impaired by incomplete conceptionalization, a lack of planning, the overuse of jargon, and adjective stringing. This relatively uneven development reflects a striking feature of report writing based on psychological testing: Formulating the report requires the student to synthesize all training in personality theory, differential diagnosis, psychodynamics, psychotherapy, testing, and hypothesis formation—a formidable task indeed. The internship usually represents the first full professional experience in which these students are actively required to implement this comprehensive knowledge of psychological evaluation, and report writing thus becomes a key point of stress in these students' professional functioning.

The array of data generated through testing can readily produce a sense of being overwhelmed in both experienced and student testers. For students, report writing requires an integration of virtually everything they have learned with respect to clinical material, creating a sense that each report represents a major task and requires a correspondingly intense effort. Understanding the proper construction of the write-up can help students transform this task from an enormous and sometimes overwhelming job into one of manageable proportions. The writing then can become an opportunity to demonstrate one's skill and talent in the interest of the patient.

The genesis of this volume is inextricably tied to two significant experiences for each author. First is the responsibility for conducting, for nearly 25 years, both a major clinical psychology internship approved by the American Psychological Association and a psychodiagnostic testing program at the Postgraduate Center for Mental Health in New York City. The high quality of these programs is derived from an emphasis on standards, depth of training, and scientific and professional values. In maintaining a universal set of criteria for psychological training, the American Psychological Association reinforces a uniform structure within which students in various geographical locations receive instruction that is of equally high caliber. Consequently, should these students come together at a later time, they can expect to share similar comprehensive and professional expertise. It is this consistency in professional background that facilitated the collaboration of the authors of this volume.

The second significant experience is the internship each author underwent in entering the profession of clinical psychology. Both internships were clearly formative periods in which professional role models and peer interaction were crucial in establishing a serious climate for study and learning. Each author was a member of a small cohesive peer group that became a crucial aid in helping to meet the demanding scientific and professional challenges set by the internship requirements. Departmental conferences, interdisciplinary activity, case presentations, supervisory contracts, peer exchanges, therapy efforts, and especially the particular focus on psychodiagnostic testing and evaluation comprised the overall training format. This structure in turn provided a framework for the ultimate understanding and appreciation of the vicissitudes of personality, its shifts, symptoms, strengths, and diagnoses. This training in psychological testing and evaluation yielded a basic professional skill that is still relevant to current work in individual, group, and family psychotherapy, as well as in research. The importance of the role of psychological testing and evaluation in psychology training is the reason that this area of study has become one of the central foundations of the current internship program at the Postgraduate Center.

Each author remembers with continued appreciation certain professional colleagues who influenced him during his internship training. These psychologists deserve particular appreciation for their generous and unfailing support.

Special thanks go both to Ms. Karen Machover and to the late Dr. Soloman Machover, former Directors of Psychology at Kings County Hospital. For more than 50 years they inspired hundreds of students to continue a standard of excellence that they themselves exemplified. It is particularly rewarding to be able to represent these multitudes of former students in thanking Karen and Mac for their sterling contribution. All interpretive references to figure drawings in this volume are essentially based on the Machover Figure Drawing Test. Of the many other important influences at Kings County Hospital, the professional and personal interaction with Dr. Gerald Yagoda and Dr. Stanley Silverstone is especially warmly remembered.

Dr. David T. Johnson, Director of Clinical Training at the Veterans Administration Hospital in Lexington, Kentucky, is also remembered. He provided psychology interns with steady professional support and expert instructional involvement, in a gifted and devoted manner. Special appreciation is also extended to Dr. Ehrling Eng, who taught the sensitivity to human and scholarly qualities that is essential for the effective clinician.

In our past efforts to contribute to psychology internship training at the Postgraduate Center under the leadership of Dr. Kellerman, and in our current efforts to sustain and further enhance this training under the leadership of Dr. Burry, our collaboration has generated several training components of the program as well as several books. Thus, the model that has been created for psychology interns at the Postgraduate Center affords them the opportunity to develop their professional identity with reference to a clinical, scientific, and scholarly foundation.

We would like to express our appreciation to the many colleagues, including supervisors, faculty, and administrative personnel of the Post-graduate Center for Mental Health, who have been exceedingly helpful in the development of the psychology internship training program. Their collective efforts have contributed to the national reputation enjoyed by this training program during its span of 30 years.

PREFACE TO THE SECOND EDITION

This *Handbook of Psychodiagnostic Testing* was originally designed to provide the reader with a model for constructing a psychodiagnostic report that integrates and synthesizes personality data derived largely from the standard projective battery. In the second edition of this volume, various aspects and vicissitudes of the personality relevant to evaluation are expanded in several already existing chapters as well as introduced in new material. To this end, material is provided that amplifies diagnostic considerations, the assessment of reality testing, the evolution of character, and the construction of the psychological report for readers such as psychiatrists, psychotherapists, counselors, teachers, and parents. For example, with the advent of the third edition of *The Diagnostic and Statistical Manual* and its revision (*DSM-III* and *DSM-III-R* leading to *DSM-IV*), the differential diagnostic nomenclature has been revised; consequently, the material presented in the second edition of this present volume on characterological development and differential diagnosis reflects the latest advances in the understanding of such psychopathology.

Yet, despite these newer formulations of personality vicissitudes, the *Handbook* still rests on the model provided by the basic projective battery with the addition of contributions from intelligence tests. This basic projective battery consists of the Rorschach Inkblot Test, the Thematic Apperception Test (TAT), and the Machover Figure Drawing Test. The use of this projective battery is inextricably related to the development of the entire field of clinical psychopathology and the study of personality.

This particular aspect of the field of clinical psychopathology and personality—that of projective psychology—was a direct outgrowth of efforts to expand the domain of the field of psychology to include a broader clinical base. In the history of the development of projective psychology this clinical base intersected with and drew richly upon the clinical field of psychoanalysis. From the 1920s to the 1950s, an exceptional ferment occurred in thinking, psychological experimentation, and observational methods; essentially, it was the time when the field of projective psychology crystallized and matured.

The three projective tests, the Rorschach, TAT, and Machover Figure Drawing Test, have for almost 50 years comprised the clinician's core projective assessment technology for the distillation of information on the infrastructure of emotions, personality, and thinking. Although clinicians have also utilized other tests such as word association, sentence completion, the Bender Gestalt, and animal metaphors to fill out the basic battery, these other tests have been used quite selectively. Simply by the power of their clinical usefulness it was the Rorschach, TAT, and Machover that became the generally agreed upon basic projective battery. Together, it was observed that these tests could, by projective means, elicit a picture of the person's emotions, defenses, psychodynamic arena of conflict, personality configuration or type, unique psychopathology, symptoms, and diagnostic state. In addition, the power of this projective battery generated a proliferation of general interest in the development of projective psychology, as well as in the development of other tests.

The configuration of psychodynamic psychology in its applied form with its presumed scientific base rested especially on the use and validation of these three projective tests. It can even be claimed that projective psychology was born with the advent of the Rorschach but that projective psychology, as an aspect of clinical work with a purported scientific foundation, was crystallized more fully with the amalgamation in clinical use of the Rorchach, TAT, and Machover Figure Drawing tests.

The use of these tests began to generate a prodigious amount of clinical data. It was the clinical use of this basic projective battery that led to the gradual surfacing of the person's emotional landscape in greater detail. This emotional landscape also included aspects of personality, cognitive processes and diagnostic considerations. Thus, this *Handbook* has its basis and rationale in a history that includes technology that was developed to reveal both the inner life as well as the unconscious aspect of that life.

This technology was, of course, created in the form of the basic projective battery. The rationale of this volume is in an empirical context in which the technology of the projective battery presents the psychologist with general personality data and which also reveals expressions of many specific aspects of the personality. The uncovering of these multiple facets of personality tends in itself to confirm that the personality is composed of many components, and is not simply an amorphous configuration. For example, the projective battery yields data that includes behavioral samples, information on reality testing and cognitive functioning, indicators of anxiety, the vicissitudes of impulse versus control in the personality, information on the defense system and its effect on emotions, patterns of interpersonal behavior, and diagnostic information including the infrastructure of character formation.

With this profusion of information, the clinical psychologist first needs to compartmentalize such a body of data into the various aspects of personality described above, such as *impulse versus control* or *nature of reality testing*, and then needs to organize this data into a meaningful report. Insofar as such a process of compartmentalization and organization corresponds exactly to the scientist's requirement of analyzing and then synthesizing data and phenomena, then we may declare that the construction of the psychodiagnostic report is a unique and distinctive clinical operation where the art of the clinical psychologist is fused with the science of clinical psychology.

Thus, this *Handbook of Psychodiagnostic Testing: The Analysis of Personality in the Psychological Report* becomes an instrument or a template that can be used by the clinician to analyze the personality and to synthesize the resulting data so that the final psychodiagnostic report becomes an integrated and faithful representation of the person's inner life with respect to the central ingredients of the personality.

1
The Referral

A psychological testing referral is usually made when a specific problem appears in a person's behavior. Such behavior or experiential symptoms call attention to the fact that something disturbing has happened and a personality conflict or disorder has appeared. The behavioral difficulty that the person displays is usually the point at which a psychologist may be called upon to utilize psychodiagnostic expertise to clarify and localize the underlying cause of the problem.

Children showing acting-out problems in school, teenagers demonstrating suicidal or depressive behavior, sexual problems in a marriage, an employee with an emotional difficulty interfering with work, a person suddenly confused and disoriented, an individual experiencing a state of panic or free-floating anxiety, or an elderly person becoming progressively more withdrawn are some examples of the ways in which problems show up in behavior. These symptoms or problem behaviors need to be understood within the context of the personality of the individual. This is the essence of the task before the psychologist who has received a testing referral. The psychological test report is an organizational aid in understanding such problems.

WHAT IS A PSYCHOLOGICAL TEST REPORT?

The psychological test report reflects a process that starts with a referral source. Since the referral source can originate from different professional areas and levels of expertise, the psychologist needs to keep in mind that the final report must be written in a manner that is understandable to the person who will be reading it. This means that the same report cannot be sent to a parent, a therapist, or a school counselor. The problem of the

1

patient may be critical, and the referral person helping with the problem must be able to utilize the psychologist's input. Thus, the psychologist responsible for the testing and report must always respond to the needs of the patient as well as to the needs of the particular referral source.

What is a psychological test report? A psychological test report is a communication. Therefore, it must be written in a way that corresponds to the reader's level of understanding and training. The report must meet the criteria of clarity, meaningfulness, and synthesis.

Clarity of the Report

The report should be written in specific language. The writing should be cogent and free of statements that are uncommunicative because they are too general. Since the data to be presented can be extensive and elaborate, students and professionals alike may feel overwhelmed with the task of clarifying and ordering this material. This hurdle frequently leads to reliance on a style that does not facilitate clearly communicated ideas. Clarity requires understanding and appreciation of the reader's concerns, which is then transformed into presentation of the report. The writer of the report must be considerate and help the reader by presenting digestible material. One way of doing this is to use shorter rather than longer sentences. While this is a good method in all professional writing, it is especially useful for achieving clarity in psychological test report writing.

The raw data of the protocol reflects a complex and mysterious world. The test report turns the mystery of data and symptoms into a recognizable form that has been constructed out of clear rather than diffuse statements. In addition, a logical progression of ideas is instrumental in making the report a meaningful communication between tester and referrer. In reporting about patients, it is important to remember that we are dealing with real people whose problems need to be meaningfully understood.

Meaningfulness of the Report

The report is a meaningful communication if the reader finds that it is clear and understands it. Understanding occurs when the level of discourse and use of language is based upon the level that the particular referrer can utilize. For example, a parent cannot understand a report written to a psychiatrist; similarly, a psychiatrist may not derive enough meaning from a report directed toward a parent. A more sophisticated audience for the report does not mean more precision, however, just because an audience is less sophisticated should not mean less precision in the report.

The goal of the report as a vehicle of communication is always to transform mystery or confusion into meaningfulness. Consequently, the words and ideas must be clear at whatever level the report is written. The use of jargon, adjective stringing, and generalization are handicaps to clarifying precise ideas; therefore, the use of these contrivances interferes with and reduces meaning. Instead of relying on such inefficient devices, it is essential to keep a sharp focus on the subject's specific problem. By detailing the exact factors involved in the person's functioning, a portrait that has clear meaning will be developed. The uniqueness of the person being tested emerges in the synthesis of the report. Thus, clarity and meaningfulness should guide the organization of the presentation of findings.

Synthesis of the Final Report

A relevant synthesis or integration of a report means that the initial behavior or experiential problem of the patient has been given a context that serves as a sort of map in which the relevant details of the problem can be made visible and related to each other. These fundamental details are encapsulated into large concepts, which are then organized in relation to one another. This integration demonstrates that a presenting problem is only part of a larger system that includes all aspects and levels of personality, which are not immediately evident or understood only from the presenting symptoms. As a result, mapping out this system in a report reveals the meaning of the presenting symptoms and provides information as well as guidelines in the management and treatment of the overall problem.

Thus, a psychological report can be viewed as a communication about the logic of a specific personality. Aspects of personality are logically related, and thus the structure of the report must form a relevant synthesis; that is, the parts of the report will reflect different aspects of the same personality. In the final report, the presenting complaint is no longer a random, unexplained, or inexact phenomenon.

For the report to have value, it needs to be written in a way that includes sections logically and relevantly related to each other. In addition, the report is a coherent synthesis that directly bears upon the meaning of the original presenting symptom and its context.

Before outlining the various salient sections of a psychological report, it is necessary to discuss the kinds of referrals made to psychologists and how such referrals relate to the kinds of reports that are written.

WHY A PSYCHOLOGICAL REPORT MAY BE REQUESTED

Referral to a psychologist for psychodiagnostic testing represents a profound moment in the process of help. This referral becomes a pivotal event in the life of the person who displays the symptom as well as to those intimately related to the person. Why should the referral be described as representing a "profound moment" or a "pivotal event?" The answer to this question can only be appreciated by understanding the sequence of events surrounding the referral.

Context of the Referral

The reason for the referral is the symptomatic behavior that the subject displays. This may be acting-out behavior in school, at home, or on the job; grossly bizarre behavior; or behavior reflecting anxiety conditions. The point is that either the problematic behavior may be causing personal difficulty, or its effects may be disturbing a larger system such as the classroom, family, or workplace. The psychologist must constantly focus on the nature and extent of the tension that is involved with the symptom.

The problem behavior is a statement of anxiety that is either visible and directly experienced by the subject, or disguised and expressed in particular behavior. The disturbance of the person who is displaying difficulty or the disruption to those who are affected by it lead to contact with a person whose role is to help in some way. This helping person may be a teacher, counselor, nurse, therapist, or hospital staff person who then refers the patient to a psychologist for evaluation.

The fact of this referral already implies that significant concern is being registered by the referring party and involves a signal of recognition of distress. The referrer starts a process that eventually will lead to a profound intervention in the person's life in the form of a therapeutic intervention, a remedial learning program, neurophysiological procedures, or some other application, depending on the nature of the problem. The psychological report is frequently the first step in this process; also, it contributes to the foundation for the intervention to follow.

Thus a psychological report is requested so that relevant information can be marshalled. This information leads to the implementation of therapeutic helping procedures of further diagnostic measures; for example, a psychopharmacological consultation, neurological assessment, or learning disabilities evaluation.

Focusing the Report

A psychological report can provide many kinds of information. A psychiatrist attempting to decide a differential diagnostic problem, for example, would seek one type of information. A guidance counselor helping a withdrawn student would require something else. The teacher of a student with a learning disability needs information clarifying the source of the student's particular problem. The therapist of a patient troubled by frequent loss of jobs has another question in mind. Sometimes even the person making the test referral is confused about the problem and potential solutions and requires help in conceptualizing the issues that need to be addressed.

It is important for the psychologist to realize that all these circumstances lead to a variety of referral problems. The psychologist's response must be to help resolve the issue that stimulated the referral in the first place. A request for a psychological report is an inherent part of this helping process and may play a variety of roles in furthering the process. Depending on the referral question, the psychological report furnishes information, recommendations, diagnostic and prognostic considerations, clarification of the patient's life context, and specific recommendations to the referral source, all of which deeply influence the helping process.

At this point, a serious issue arises. It would most likely be agreed that projective testing always produces a psychological profile of the person that can highlight maladaption, insufficiencies, underdevelopment, and aspects of overall maladjustment. In this sense, the findings produced by any person subject to psychological testing cannot be "normal." Therefore, a distinction needs to be made between those subjects whose functioning lies within the normal range in spite of areas of weakness, and those in whom pathology plays a more central role. While this distinction between weakness in the normal range and psychopathology can prevent a pejorative use of the psychological report, the fact remains that diagnosis of personality is ubiquitous; it may, for example, be a character diagnosis, since all individuals have character trait dispositions. Thus, a child who is referred for testing can reveal psychopathological data whether or not actual symptoms exist. One task of the examiner is to be able to distinguish clearly between the idiosyncratic psychological data in the average range of functioning and the psychopathological data relevant to a presenting symptom.

As can be seen in Table 1.1, pathology needs to be identified that ties into the referral problem. It is not sufficient simply to describe all pathology that surfaces in the data. *All persons will yield material that*

TABLE 1.1   The Referral and the Psychological Report

- Identify the presenting problem with respect to symptoms, relationships, and events.
- Problem behavior reflects anxiety. The psychologist must be aware that this anxiety can be managed in a number of ways; frequently, tracing such anxiety can be a guide to understanding the coherence of the personality and its disturbance.

---

reveals conflict, defense, particular psychodynamics and diagnostic information. Yet, not all people require testing or referral. Thus, the pathology of the subject under consideration that surfaces in the test protocol needs to be targeted toward the referral symptoms in the test report.

Because the psychological report can be so varied in its influence and in the information it provides, there are different kinds of reports as well as various discrete but related sections. The following chapter delineates important sections relevant to the construction of a psychological report, as a model for therapeutic and diagnostic purposes. Later chapters deal with sections appropriate to psychological evaluations used for other purposes. Table 1.1 presents a thumbnail sketch of salient issues in the referral itself.

SUMMARY

This chapter outlined the way in which the referral for a psychodiagnostic test evaluation arises, the importance of its communicative nature, its place in the referral and helping process, and the fact that it can be focused in various ways. It was also pointed out that any pathology uncovered by the test data needs to be related to the referral problem.

2

Sections in the Typical Psychodiagnostic Report

It is important to understand the anatomy of the psychological report by the sections that comprise it. Although these sections seem to reflect discrete aspects of personality, they actually serve to unify data so that a comprehensive picture emerges of the person under evaluation.

Students sometimes have difficulty synthesizing psychological test data because working on different sections of the report evokes the experience in them of dealing with several people instead of a single individual. This sense of fragmentation can be ameliorated if the student remembers that each aspect of personality and each corresponding section of the report are about one individual. Although each section is a discrete analysis of a different aspect of personality, it nevertheless must be logically and coherently related to and reflect the total personality. Even when pathology is manifested, it relates to the overall personality in a logical and coherent manner. When a student or professional psychologist approaches the task of report writing from this point of view, then the data can be organized and the total person will be centrally visible, even though different aspects of functioning are focused on in various sections of the report.

With this organizational principle in mind, a sequence of sections in a typical diagnostic report can be proposed. Following this outline can help to integrate the development of a coherent personality profile, and endless fragmentary discussions of personality can be avoided. The sections start with the clinical interview, range through analyses of aspects of personality, and conclude with a diagnostic and prognostic statement.

It is important to remember that the areas to be analyzed and reported are being presented in a logical sequence of sections. Each section has a central focus corresponding to an aspect of personality functioning. Section titles are stipulated for purposes of clarity in presentation, as an aid in organizing, focusing, and sustaining the writing process, and as a help to the reader of the report. Of course, whether specific section titles are included in the final written report depends on the judgment of the writer regarding their value to the referral source and other readers of the report.

SUGGESTED OUTLINE OF SECTIONS

The Clinical Interview

The first section of the report concerns an evaluation of the behavior of the subject. As discussed previously, the patient's behavior calls attention to a problem that creates anxiety, suffering, and distress for the patient or those around the patient. Thus, the observation of behavior by the psychologist in both the interviewing and testing phases of the psychological evaluation is an essential source of highly pertinent information. The behavior that the tester observes is a sample of the patient's overall behavior and can reveal the problems that led to the referral and evaluation in the first place.

The test situation may reflect in microcosm the psychological and behavioral functioning of the patient in daily life. Consequently, the psychologist's conversation with the patient has a special purpose and is not idle and random. Both the test material and the interview stimulate responses from the patient that can be analyzed to provide insight and understanding about the patient's internal conflicts and problems in interpersonal relating. Thus, the interview is designed in such a manner that the first hypotheses about the patient's particular personality construction are distilled from it.

These initial hypotheses generated from the interview material relate to basic or fundamental dimensions within the personality that emerge from consideration and are constantly evaluated throughout the various sections of the report. In this way the hypotheses are confirmed, invalidated, or modified as they are scrutinized in terms of the increasing data that accrue as the analysis progresses.

A particularly important aspect of the clinical interview is that it enables firsthand observation and evaluation of the interpersonal style of the patient. Direct opportunities to observe the manner, responsiveness, direction, and orientation of the patient as that patient relates specifically to the tester are generated. These psychological features of the subject as well as the impact of such qualities on the tester provide essential and immediate data that may be used to assess and analyze the patient's input and reactions in a social and purposeful context. The patient's spontaneous comments as well as reactions to the test material and directions are significant sources of observational data that can be utilized in the analysis of functioning.

Above all, the clinical interview section is a discussion of the patient's coping and relating style. This information is vital in understanding the patient's problem behavior because it relates social functioning to the presence of undercurrents of anxiety. The next section of the report considers how attuned the patient is to external perceptions of reality. Thus, the next section deals directly with the issue of reality testing and the framework in which it is embedded, namely cognitive functioning.

Cognitive Organization and Reality Testing

A fundamental consideration of behavior concerns the extent to which it is realistic and, accordingly, in the best interest of the individual. If the behavior is not logically related to external reality, then the patient will have basic difficulties in fulfilling aims and interests. In addition, significant problems can develop in managing and coping with the broad range of circumstances that have to be faced in life. Thus, an inherent behavior or experiential problem is screened by the tester at the clinical interview and then is examined for its appropriateness with respect to reality considerations.

The statement that behavior is examined for its appropriateness with respect to reality testing means that it can be analyzed to determine if external reality, including an understanding of the individual's place in it, is known and appreciated. The psychologist constructing the report needs to evaluate the patient's behavior, broadly speaking, in terms of whether it respects the confines or boundaries of external structure or is derived from more subjective and idiosyncratic sources. This is a determination of whether reality testing is impaired, as in a psychotic patient, and if so, to what extent. Whether the patient's behavior is problematic but fundamentally related to a grasp of external reality also can be determined.

In order to make this reality determination, the psychologist focuses on various aspects of cognitive processes, including ascertaining the state or condition of the subject's ability to discriminate the subjective world from objective conditions. The patient's capacity to keep reality in the forefront and to control irrationality is the main issue. In addition, it is necessary for the psychologist to evaluate the nature of the subject's perceptions of external structures. Perception is inexorably tied to thought and meaning and consequently reflects the deepest structure of cognition. One of the ways that the psychologist focuses on the nature of perception is to use the raw material of the interview as well as the patient's test responses to assess the patient's judgment, logical coherence, rationality, and even empathic capacity.

The importance of the cognitive apparatus as a groundwork for understanding personality functioning is reflected in the appearance of this section early in the report. This placement is logical because the question of reality testing bears so heavily on the meaning of the patient's presenting problem. It is necessary to begin to discriminate between psychotic and nonpsychotic functioning at an early point.

Second, further cognitive factors having to do with thinking, logic, judgment, memory, abstraction, and rational planning are explored. The manner in which these capacities function forms the basis of the person's intellectual structure. This structure is reflected in the analysis of intelligence test results, which is sufficiently important in the overall analysis of cognitive functioning to require a separate section.

Intellectual Functioning

The intelligence test is a special measure that primarily helps to assess a wide spectrum of cognitive features. The manner in which such cognitive features operate for the patient needs to be delineated. Departures from sound reality testing often are reflected in quantitative and qualitative results of the overall findings of the intelligence test, as well as in scores of particular subtests of the scale. A substantive and clinically meaningful use of the intelligence test would be one in which cognitive analysis was as important as reporting the I.Q. figure.

No aspect of the data from intelligence testing can stand alone. In this sense an I.Q. score must be integrated in the report in a way that brings focus to the development of personality hypotheses, deepening and amplifying emerging themes. The same principle of integration is true for the components of cognitive structure and their implications in relation to reality testing. The I.Q. score, therefore, does not exist in a vacuum.

Evaluation of component aspects of cognitive and intellectual functioning also must be related to hypotheses about personality dynamics being developed in the test report. Thus, evaluations of memory, planning, judgment, frustration tolerance, the influence of anxiety on performance, abstraction capacity, reasoning, and degree of empathy can all be assessed independently. These components also need to be integrated and related to the core understanding of the person and his or her difficulties that the overall report explains. A crucial aspect of this integration concerns the way in which anxiety is managed in the personality, since cognitive and intellectual skills are strikingly sensitive to interference from anxiety.

Thus, anxiety and its vicissitudes are evaluated as a logical next step, because frequently anxiety is largely responsible for the initial problem behavior or experience. The nature of the anxiety, its quality and quantity, is important for understanding both the immediate problem and the relative intactness of the cognitive structure.

The Nature of Anxiety

Just as anxiety can impair cognitive and intellectual functioning, it can similarly interfere with the manner in which a person handles problems. This fact underscores the central role that anxiety plays in personality functioning, and its particular link to the presenting symptom complaint. If the anxiety is managed through somatization, for example, the patient tends toward preoccupations with problems of physical health. If the anxiety were to be impulsively acted upon instead, then it would lead to traumatic behavioral and social problems, such as those frequently encountered in school settings. If the anxiety cannot be channeled, panic and extreme discomfort can result in distressing personal experience, such as the development of phobic behavior or free-floating anxiety. On the other hand, intense, diffusely global anxiety may be experienced in connection with fragmentation accompanying a psychotic break. Clarifying the nature, intensity, and management of anxiety, therefore, is an important communication to the person who will be reading the report. Such analyses facilitate the hypotheses about the subject's personality which evolve as the report continues.

Anxiety is a fulcrum at this point in the sequence of the report because it connects sections dealing with the clinical interview and cognition to those dealing with personality considerations, such as emotions and defense mechanisms. Therefore, the section on anxiety appears before the discussion of personality dynamics, emotions, and the defense mechanisms established for emotional regulation and control.

Thus far, the sequence of the report stresses the behavior of the patient during the clinical interview, the patient's reality testing and cognitive organization. This sequence leads to consideration of the role of anxiety and the part it plays in such behavior. After discussing the nature of anxiety and its management, an opportunity exists to evaluate impulse-control problems, emotions, defenses, and intrapsychic structure.

In broad terms the following section of the report should help to clarify the relative balance in the personality between impulse and control. This balance is inextricably bound to the issues of behavior and anxiety.

Impulse versus Control

Consideration of the issue of impulse versus control brings focus from a new perspective to the presenting behavior problem. This point of view provides an elaboration of the patient's dynamic forces through an analysis and discussion of the interplay between impulse and controls. Consequently, conclusions from the section on cognition and reality testing can be linked to broader aspects of the individual. For example, problems with issues of judgment, perception, and thinking can be related to strains in the relative balance between impulse expression and the extent of control over such expressions. Findings regarding the way in which anxiety operates in the functioning of the personality can now also be applied to the mechanisms that regulate impulses. Cognitive elements, anxiety, and control over impulse constitute an important sequence in understanding the struggle or conflict that underlies the more superficial and obvious problem behaviors and experiences of the patient.

Another major feature in analyzing and reporting the nature of the dynamic interplay between impulse and control concerns the level of maturation in the structure and makeup of the personality. For example, extremely poor controls that enable powerful impulses to initiate immediate behavior sequences reflect a relatively primitive maturational level. On the other hand, the presence of stronger inhibitions indicates other clinical implications. The relation of impulse-control features to maturational aspects of the personality also has a direct bearing on intrapsychic functioning and on diagnostic considerations. Because of the more detailed discussion permitted by analysis of issues stemming from impulse-control findings, the initial broad, differential diagnostic concern with reality testing and the possibility of psychosis can be developed, and narrower categories of diagnostic possibilities can be established.

Thus, in the sequence of sections within the report, a refinement takes place in the communication about the meaningful details of the person's essential makeup, starting with the problem behavior and leading to a rich and clear elaboration of the framework in which this behavior is embedded. The problem behavior is gaining context and meaning. It is apparent that even the most bizarre behavior or experience can be clarified through the interpretive steps in the developing sequence of the report.

The dynamics of impulse-control as they relate to behavior, cognition, reality testing, and anxiety can be further understood through an analysis of the specific, characteristic defense operations and defense mechanisms that permit such dynamics to operate.

Defensive Structure

Defenses in the personality are employed to manage emotionality, anxiety, and tension. The role of defenses is important because it bears on the issue of whether emotions are overtly acted upon with weak or poor governing mechanisms, or if they are overcontrolled, or if emotions are well managed and controlled more adaptively. Defense mechanisms, which comprise the basic elements of the defensive structure, are periodically mobilized to regulate or govern emotions and the anxiety surrounding these emotions.

In psychodiagnostic formulations, the usual concern of the psychologist is with the defenses that play a part in the management of emotional conflict. An analysis of defense structure leads to a better understanding of the entire personality. An analysis of defense operations also illuminates the behavior involved in the original distress of the patient. Thus, one important aspect of the evaluation of defensive operations involves an analysis of specific emotional conflict.

A second element of importance in the exposition of defensive operations concerns the character style of the individual. Character style is more than a consideration of individual defenses; it encompasses an individual's personality trait configuration. Character style is a person's unique personality fingerprint, reflecting that person's trait pattern. It is an enduring configuration, and although it may be a pathological and maladaptive pattern in some people, it is nevertheless resistant to change, and therefore quite consistent.

Defensive operations are analyzed with respect to both individual defenses and characteristic defensive patterns which are inextricably tied to behavior. Although individual defenses may not be easily discerned because of their subtle interplay with emotion, characteristic styles and patterns of behavior are, on the other hand, consistently visible in all spheres of the person's relating.

These issues of defensive operations tie together behavior and diagnostic considerations. One feature of defenses is that the variety of mechanisms are systematically related to character trait formations, and clusters of defenses consequently tend to be associated with particular diagnoses. Thus, in this section of the report a detailed analysis of the subject's defensive structure will provide essential data conveying diagnostic information.

The most dramatic manner in which defensive operations and character traits reveal themselves is through the individual's functioning and relationships with people. Consequently, an understanding and description of the patient's interpersonal reactions, behaviors, and relationships are needed. This kind of description is presented in the following section on interpersonal behavior, and it includes an analysis of the person's psychosexual development and identification.

Identity and Interpersonal Behavior

The major focus of each section of the report after the referral and interview has been largely on intrapersonal concerns, including reality testing, cognitive functioning, anxiety, impulse control, and defensive structure. At this point it is necessary to crystallize the information so that its impact on the person's life can be appreciated. Thus, the conflicts within the personality must be viewed as they affect relations with others. Another way of saying this is that what was previously analyzed in terms of intrapersonal organization will now be viewed in terms of interpersonal expression.

There are two basic subsections to be considered here. The first concerns problems of self-image, self-esteem, and sexual identity. Second, the nature of the individual's personal development needs to be ascertained because it will be used to explain the interpersonal conflicts.

Identity Concerns.   The primary consideration of identity revolves around one's psychosexual identification. The extent of maturation in the personality determines the clarity of identifications. Ambivalence in psychosexual identification correlates to immature and diffuse psychosexual development. Some derivatives of a relatively immature psychosexual identity of a subject involve the extent of dependency; sexual acting-out (whether heterosexual or homosexual); the nature and management of frustration tolerance; overall ability to sublimate impulses for constructive purposes; and the ways in which ambition, achievement, mastery, and gratifications are worked out. In addition, identity refers to the nature of parental identifications and to the manner in which these have been internalized and accepted. When the internalizations are not acceptable, then psychosexual problems will exist.

The nature of an individual's identity is an integral part of that person's ego. A report that discusses a patient's ego structure and identity concerns also should discuss the strength of the ego, including whether the ego is brittle, rigid, flexible, or fragile. This discussion of the ego in turn leads to a clearer understanding of the person's problems with respect to self-image and self-esteem.

All of these issues having to do with the self and the strength of the subject's ego become determinants of interpersonal relations and constitute the point at which the intrapersonal and the interpersonal intersect. Thus, the intrapersonal features of identity and ego can be viewed as they are expressed interpersonally. This leads to discussion in the report of the interpersonal strains, conflicts, aims, and disturbances of the subject.

Interpersonal Behavior.   Interpersonal difficulty is primarily determined by the nature of intrapersonal development in relation to ego strength and identity. The idea is that the subject's intrapersonal conflicts and deficiencies lead to corresponding interpersonal problems. In the report, this connection has to be clearly maintained. Previously, implications may have been drawn about the potential for interpersonal difficulties in terms of discussions of frustration tolerance, impulse control, maturational level, and overall reality testing. In this section of the report, the psychologist considers the prior implications about interpersonal behavior; those that can be confirmed need to be elaborated, and those that need revision are further explored. For example, based upon characteristic defensive operations, anxiety, and the nature of the ego, interpersonal behavior may now be more readily understood and explainable. Interpersonal behavior usually refers to how well one manages any personal relationship, such as a marital relationship, one's relationship with an employer, a teacher-student relationship, or a sexual liaison.

What are the important features about relationships to include in the report? First, it is significant to ascertain the extent to which relationships can be sustained and deepened. It is also important to assess whether the patient can be accommodating to the needs of others, or whether under stress he or she becomes explosive, depressed, or withdrawn. In analyzing these features, the psychologist can refer to the previous discussions of the patient's reality testing and defense mechanisms to amplify these problems of interpersonal relations.

On a more detailed level, one's behavior in interpersonal relations can be formulated in terms of highly specific, overt trait behavior. The characteristic role taken by the patient in a relationship, for example, may have very specific consequences for the relationship's long-range quality and viability. Characteristic trait or role behaviors can be seductive, autocratic, passive, obedient, dependent, aggressive, or depressive. The essential point, however, is not simply to provide an endless string of adjectives about the patient. Instead, it is imperative to realize that all role characteristics revolve around only a few possible needs. Examples of such needs or themes include power, security, and control. The role that is assumed reflects such basic needs of the personality.

Thus, the interpersonal role played by the patient is based on underlying needs from which the problems arise. Disturbances in meeting these needs were undoubtedly directly concerned with the problem or symptom behaviors stimulating the referral. Problems such as depression, withdrawal, confusion, or acting-out can now be diagnosed on the basis of internal needs.

In this way, the clinical picture becomes an integrated analysis that includes behavior, experience, and the clarification of internal functioning. When all of these aspects of personality analysis are sufficiently integrated, diagnostic and prognostic conclusions can be formulated. The final diagnosis and prognosis represent the culmination of a clear and concise communication between the psychologist and the referrer.

Diagnosis and Prognosis

The final diagnosis is valuable as a summarizing and integrating statement of the patient's personality, and it also provides information about any pathology. The diagnosis is formed by understanding the personality in terms of a clinical synthesis. Understanding the structure of the personality and the clinical nature of the disturbance clarifies areas for change, improvement, correction, and stabilization. The diagnosis becomes an important tool in any treatment strategy or remedial plan. Furthermore, the diagnosis also helps in assessing the relative merit of one treatment plan over another. The important point here is that the diagnosis helps to reveal the most effective means of treatment among the alternatives, no matter how guarded or pessimistic the prognosis may seem.

Generally speaking, the diagnosis consists of fine discriminations following broader ones. The first consideration is whether the individual's functioning reflects an organic disturbance or psychosis, character disorder, or neurosis. Once the broad area is defined, the specific diagnosis within that area can be evaluated. If a particular disturbing symptom

TABLE 2.1   Sections of the Report

- *Clinical Interview.* Generate hypotheses regarding the person's functioning based on the initial observations and data.
- *Cognitive Organization and Reality Testing.* Assess the subject's capacity to appreciate reality and to control irrationality; ascertain the nature of judgment, logic, and empathic capacity; attempt to distinguish between psychosis and nonpsychosis.
- *Intellectual Functioning.* Integrate I.Q. scores and intellectual functioning to contribute to a greater focus and understanding of the emerging salient factors of personality, anxiety and distress. Cognitive and intellectual functions assessed include: memory, planning, judgment, frustration tolerance, relations of anxiety to performance, abstraction capacity, reasoning, and empathy.
- *Nature of Anxiety.* Assess how the salient signal of anxiety is managed and expressed: is it somatized; acted-out; expressed in panic, phobic, or free-floating states; or expressed in fragmentation of the personality?
- *Impulse vs. Control.* Relate issues of judgment, perception, and thinking to strains in the balance of impulse versus control. This balance is also related to the degree of maturity in personality.
- *Defensive Structure.* Assess whether defenses can manage emotional pressure, whether pressures are too strong or defenses too weak and therefore permit breakthroughs of anxiety. Try to specify particular defense patterns. Identify the character style of the individual. The character imprint is the person's distinctiveness, and portraying this imprint with precision is, therefore, important. Defense clusters are directly tied to diagnostic considerations.
- *Identity and Interpersonal Behavior.* Discuss problems of self-image, self-esteem, and sexual identity. Ascertain the level of maturity and of psychosexual development. How are gratifications managed? Are they sublimated, mastered, or impulsively sought? What are the parental identifications like? Is the ego brittle, rigid, flexible, or fragile? How are personal relationships managed? Can they be sustained or deepened? What are the patient's characteristic role behaviors (passive, obedient, dependent, aggressive, depressive) that revolve around basic themes such as power, security, or control?
- *Diagnosis and Prognosis.* Distinguish broadly between organicity, psychosis, character disorder, and neurosis. The specific diagnosis follows: it implies the problem behavior, underlying character structure, and the particular diagnosis in which symptoms are embedded. The prognosis depends on diagnostic statements that imply the probability of repair.

---

such as an addiction, a sexual dysfunction, or a phobia is affixed to the specific diagnosis, then it also can be defined.

This method implies a system of diagnostic levels which are used for increasing refinement. Diagnostic understanding is developed from broader levels to deeper, latent dimensions. Thus, the diagnosis starts with a problematic behavior that may be specified as a clinical syndrome such as a phobia, sexual disturbance, or compulsion. If manifestations of anxiety are associated with these symptoms, a neurotic level of difficulty such as an anxiety neurosis or obsessive-compulsive neurosis can be specified. Underlying this level is the character formation in which the symptom is embedded. At this point the diagnosis is addressed to the character organization that produces symptomatic outgrowths. If there is a stable, deeply ingrained maladaptive pattern, a personality disorder can be specified; for example, a schizoid or passive-aggressive personality.

When psychosis is present in either manifest or latent terms, another diagnostic level must be addressed. This level is important when the character structure has the potential to weaken, and a deeper level of pathology may be manifested. If neurological impairment has become apparent, that also allows for diagnosis at this basic level of pathology.

Approaches to diagnosis that follow this multidimensional plan broadly depict the complexity of personality and provide a fuller assessment of the potential for repair. Consequently, the prognosis may be based on needs for support, treatment of the character disturbance, or the amelioration of disturbing symptoms. The successive sections of the report now conclude with this prognostic indicator, which relates directly to the original problem behavior.

One of the main accomplishments of a report following this sequence is that it reveals the essence of the original presenting behavior, how it fits into the total personality, and the strengths that may be mobilized to modify the presenting disturbance.

An elaboration of each section of the report will now be presented. Table 2.1 presents a distillation of key issues to be covered in each section of the psychological report.

SUMMARY

In this chapter, the particular importance of each section in the psychological report was defined, and a rationale was presented to reveal the logical interconnections and sequence of the various sections. The need to compartmentalize various aspects of functioning was emphasized as a means of systematically covering the essential dimensions of personality. Finally, the coherence and unity that need to characterize the final report derive from the organization imposed by maintaining focus on the whole person under evaluation.

3

The Clinical Interview

In this chapter, an approach to evaluating and formulating clinical observations in the first section of the report is discussed. This section of the report is based largely on data obtained during the clinical interview with the patient. When writing this section, the psychologist also will have data available as noted from other sources, such as the patient's behavior and spontaneous comments and questions throughout the test session. In addition, of course, the psychologist will have observed the patient's responses and productions (as opposed to behavior and spontaneous remarks) in connection with the tasks of testing.

All of these sources of information, as well as any historical, social, and developmental material the tester learns about, will naturally contribute to the psychologist's impressions. The impressions gained during testing have an immediacy and firsthand validity that make them especially valuable. The impressions gained specifically during the clinical interview also have special value since the psychologist is probing in a purposeful, directed manner to uncover necessary material.

The section of the report that corresponds to the clinical interview presents findings derived from several sources. Nevertheless, the careful and coherent clinical interview that the psychologist conducts provides core data and valuable impressions about the patient. The impressions are essential to begin interpretation of the psychological dimensions appropriate to the analysis of the patient. Support and assistance for these beginning interpretations are naturally provided by other sources of data that play a special role in connection with components of the personality which are evaluated, interpreted, and written up in subsequent sections of the report.

MEETING THE PATIENT

You meet the patient for the first time. What do you personally notice first? What qualities of the patient are immediately striking? What will you do with these impressions? Do you notice posture, voice quality, dress, handshake, energy level, and overall responsiveness? Why are such impressions important to you?

All people have first impressions, but those of the psychologist are special because they serve a clinical purpose. The crucial difference is that the psychologist's impressions of style, quality, and behavioral details can be utilized to generate diagnostic hypotheses. Furthermore, these impressions can be coordinated with the content material secured through testing to assess the validity of the hypotheses. Thus, the clinical interview will ultimately produce some statement of a diagnostic nature.

The diagnostic formulation extends beyond a description of the underlying framework that classifies the nature of the patient's psychopathology. Diagnostic evaluations can also be made concerning the intensity and character of the patient's anxiety, defenses, interpersonal relating qualities, handling of emotions, and maturation level.

The clinical interview is unique in terms of broad diagnostic considerations because the examiner can observe the patient and directly interact, without an intervening instrument or task. It is the most natural, spontaneous part of the testing sequence. As such, the interview enables diagnostic impressions to arise regarding a wide range of the patient's functioning. Observations can be made and conclusions determined about the behavior and experience of the patient as they are viewed directly by the psychologist. Consequently, the clinical interview affords an opportunity to examine a unique sample of the patient's overall functioning.

SAMPLES OF BEHAVIOR

Throughout the testing sequence, different samples of the patient's behavior are generated in response to questioning, conversation, and test administration. Each approach taken with the patient, including those afforded by different testing techniques, evokes samples of the patient's ways of responding, defending, and functioning. What this unequivocally reveals is that the behavior of the patient during the clinical interview is not random or extraneous information. Rather, the interview is a purposeful way of obtaining a sample of the patient's behavior in order to develop a beginning understanding of the patient's total experience.

As can be seen from these considerations, the different approaches that the patient adopts throughout the testing situation are a microcosm of the patient's overall functioning. By studying and evaluating the details of this microcosm, the tester is able to assess the entire spectrum of the patient's functioning. Included in this spectrum are, for example, the patient's strengths, weaknesses, conflicts, and coping styles, as well as diagnostic implications. These samples of behavior lead to an understanding and description of the life of the patient. This model of evaluation is distinctly different from one suggested by an accumulation of or search for data as evidence. The psychologist neither seeks nor accumulates evidence about the patient.

Samples versus Evidence

What is the difference between evaluating samples of the patient's behavior versus the accumulation of evidence about the patient? Clearly, the role of the psychologist is to support or refute hypotheses. This task requires objectivity and scrutiny of information in order to develop a picture of the patient's personality. The psychologist is not interested in proving anything for or against the patient. Instead a focus is maintained on strengths and weaknesses, abilities and incapacities, and resources and their development, among other qualities, rather than on judgments of good and bad or guilty and innocent behavior.

The patient is not on trial. The psychologist's goal is to utilize samples of behavior to understand, describe, and logically present hypotheses pertinent to diagnostic considerations. For example, a person with offensive body odor would not prompt condemnation, but rather an indication as to what this might imply regarding the patient's overall functioning, personality integration, self-image, or the presence of depression.

The distinction between the process of gathering samples of behavior as opposed to the accumulation of judgmental evidence is important because it helps to clarify the psychologist's role in the overall communication of findings. This manner of thinking about samples of behavior in the psychodiagnostic report applies also to the evaluation of all data accruing from the tests that are employed. By dealing with the samples of the patient's behavior in this way, a unified description of the patient's overall functioning can be derived and constructed.

Thus, the psychologist's role is to bring coherence to the samples of behavior stimulated by the different test techniques and the interview method that the psychologist employs. In addition, the initial problem behavior that led to the test referral is also an important sample of behavior. Therefore, the clinical interview and the presenting referral problem must be taken together as sample elements pointing to important underlying personality dimensions which ultimately will be analyzed in detail.

THE REFERRAL AND THE CLINICAL INTERVIEW

The questions asked by a referring source may not faithfully reflect what needs to be considered as the central concern about the patient. For example, a psychiatrist asking for a differential diagnosis between endogenous character depression and psychotic depression may be avoiding his or her own anxiety about the patient's potential for suicidal acting-out. The referring person frequently needs help in sorting out and clarifying such major issues. This implies that the psychologist need not necessarily be constrained by the initial limits set by the referral source.

In the clinical interview, the differential diagnostic referral cannot be taken at face value. It is therefore desirable for the psychologist to hear firsthand, from the patient whenever possible, the details leading to the referral. This attitude of information gathering enables the psychologist to remain sensitive to other possibilities that may be important to the patient, although they may have been poorly formulated or avoided by the referral source. The thrust of these considerations is that the psychologist needs to remain open to concerns outside of those established by the referral source.

The clinical interview often provides a circumstance in which the patient's problem behavior or associated functioning can be observed. The interviewer assesses the presence, absence, or shifts of problem behavior, and then formulates tentative first hypotheses about symptoms, personality, and diagnosis. With a patient who problematically drinks on the job, for example, tension, uneasiness, and the elaboration of self-defeating patterns may emerge in connection with the pressure of having to answer the psychologist's interview questions. Similar responses may be observed in the tasks of testing. Excessive anxiety may relate to dependency needs that threaten the patient. The patient's need to drink to calm this sense of threat can be seen firsthand in the interview and by observing test behavior.

The patient's overall coping and relating style emerges out of the interaction between examiner and patient in the interview. This sample of interpersonal characterological patterns can be utilized to develop hypotheses about symptoms, personality, and diagnosis. Tentative conclusions about the patient's behavior and its probable meaning can be pointed out in this section of the report. An important caution in this connection is that the behavior which is noted and the meaning it implies should be limited to features that will add to both the understanding of the patient and the clarity of the report. Therefore, in writing this section, a random or unfocused catalogue of observations is not helpful. What is beneficial and illuminating to those who rely on the report in dealing with the patient is the accumulation of relevant and pertinent observations that add up to meaningful, if tentative, hypotheses. Such formulations require careful thought and conscientious decisions about the irrelevant data that are omitted as well as the observations selected for inclusion.

Tentative diagnostic formulations are useful in organizing observations related to coping and personality style that emerge from the clinical interview.

DIAGNOSTIC FORMULATIONS BASED ON THE CLINICAL INTERVIEW

Partial diagnostic steps may be taken prior to the refined diagnostic statement offered at the conclusion of the report after all of the relevant findings have been considered. One practical consideration in connection with the partial diagnosis that appears early in the report concerns locating the patient's observed behavior within a relatively broad diagnostic class. While not yet establishing a final, refined, and specific diagnosis, this preliminary step does establish a definite clinical diagnostic impression that can be systematically tied to the presentation of additional data and to the subsequent development of more refined diagnostic hypotheses. A progressive diagnostic sequence continues until the end of the report, when the final and sharpest diagnostic impression is offered.

A convenient approach to establishing a first, tentative diagnostic statement is to locate the samples of behavior observed in the interview and testing session within one of four broad diagnostic categories. This approach involves a discrimination among psychosis, organicity, character disorder, and neurosis.

Locating the patient in one of these four sectors on the basis of interview formulations allows for later refinements and additional diagnostic details as further data is considered in the write-up of the report. In writing the clinical interview section of the report, the psychologist has the advantage of observations of the patient's behavior, response style, and test productions. Impressions from all of these sources can play a part in the early diagnostic formulations which are communicated in the context of this section of the report.

Since a discrimination among four major categories of diagnosis is being considered, the first step is to rule out or establish the existence of psychosis. Following this, the nonpsychotic alternatives of organicity, character disorder, or neurosis can be considered. At later points in the report, appropriate subtleties of overlapping and tandem associations among these divisions are clarified and presented.

In order to evaluate the clinical interview and report the findings in the corresponding section of the report, it is useful for the psychologist to rely on a few organizing principles. These principles provide a way of parsimoniously viewing the sampling of behavior amassed during the clinical interview. One useful approach is to consider the so-called four "A"s proposed by Eugene Bleuhler nearly a century ago.* His diagnostic elements are still valuable today, particularly in determining the presence or absence of a psychotic process. They are *autism, affect, ambivalence,* and *association.* The need to evaluate the patient's functioning in terms of these four qualities was emphasized by Bleuhler because of his interest in securing an accurate diagnosis of schizophrenia. He was dissatisfied with the unreliability of depending on the presence of hallucinations or delusions in the diagnosis of schizophrenia, since these phenomena could also occur in other diagnosis, such as organic disorder and episodic hysterias.

A discussion of each of the four "A"s introduced by Bleuhler follows, along with suggestions indicating the role these dimensions can play in evaluating pathology and organizing the material in the clinical interview section of the report.

Autism

This key diagnostic concept is based in a general sense on the degree to which the patient is withdrawn and the effects of the withdrawal on functioning, especially with respect to how the subject relates. The phenomenon of autism and its implications for relating always seem to impress the clinical observer. When autism is seen, the psychologist should be concerned with estimating its extent. Autistic relating appears somewhat unusual or strange. The responses of a person who displays autistic relating are predominately governed by internal factors, because

*Bleuhler, E. (1950). *Dementia Praecox or the Group of Schizophrenias.* New York: International Universities Press. (Originally published 1911.)

pressure toward withdrawal is its main characteristic. The internal regulators include fantasies, wishes, impulses, and other idiosyncratic subjective signals that become predominant and flood the person's inner world. Depending on the extent of autistic withdrawal, such a person is organizing a determinable proportion of behavior around these compelling internal signals. By noting deficiencies in the patient's interpersonal contact and corresponding manifestations of internal determinants, such as wishes and fantasies, the psychologist can estimate the possible extent of autism in the patient's functioning.

The predominance of idiosyncratic or autistic determinations of behavior necessarily implies that the subject minimizes the importance of external reality as a guide for behavior. Consequently, during both the clinical interview and the entire testing session, the patient who displays autistic responses will be consistently withdrawn from the interpersonal nature of the contact. Instead, such a person maintains a relatively consistent inner focus.

The patient's autistic quality can be perceived by the tester because of the distinct impression conveyed of an absence or void with respect to the patient's responsiveness. This sense of absence is engendered because the autistic patient is absorbed to a greater or lesser extent in personal inner processes. Therefore, it is exceedingly difficult for the patient to give full, realistic attention to the interpersonal situation. Most noticeable is the lack of attention given to the examiner's attempts to approach the patient. In some instances the testing materials may be easier for the patient to approach, but even then the patient's task involvement is characterized by a largely self-absorbed style.

Somewhat more difficult to pin down is a labile or fluctuating process in which the patient shifts some attention to external factors but invariably returns to an internal focus. It is during these periods of the patient's inner preoccupation that the tester's impression of the patient's interpersonal avoidance will signal a problematic autistic phenomenon.

Implications of Autistic Response. As previously noted, the first general diagnostic consideration in the clinical interview section of the report is the possible existence of psychosis. Since autism bears directly on the capacity for reality testing, it is especially important to evaluate. The patient's autism or withdrawal must contain an unreal quality to count as a psychotic indicator. This sense of unreality derives from the urgency of inner preoccupations and consequent lack of attention to the interviewer.

In nonpsychotic diagnoses, withdrawal and avoidance may derive instead from the patient's characterological manner of achieving security by living with reduced interpersonal contact. This may occur for instance in the schizoid character disorder, in which the individual demonstrates a bland, aloof quality rather than a strange quality. Withdrawal during the interview may also be observed in an extremely passive patient with dependent or passive-aggressive qualities as main features of character disorder withdrawal.

Another example in which nonpsychotic behavior avoidance of the interviewer may be prominent is the withdrawn, absent quality indicative of a patient who is depressed and self-preoccupied. As in all of these nonpsychotic alternatives, the strange, unreal quality of autism which frequently characterizes psychosis usually is absent. Instead, a hopeless quality may emerge.

In order to proceed with evaluating gross diagnostic possibilities, affect or emotion must be explored thoroughly in conjunction with autism, because severe disturbance of affect also can be associated with indicators of psychosis.

Affect

The quality of the patient's mood and handling of emotion is directly observable during the clinical interview; thus, the psychologist can evaluate the patient's expressions of emotion in comparison with the normal expression of affect. In order to ascertain this normalcy of emotion, the psychologist needs to assess the patient's mood, modulation of affect, appropriateness of affect, and degree of emotional lability.

In determining psychotic indicators, the observation of unusual qualities of emotion in the patient is a key finding. Affect in a psychotic patient may be uniformly flat, inappropriately labile, silly, or even bizarre. These disturbed affect states can be readily tied to the autistic posture of such patients since their mood is regulated by internal phenomena to a greater extent than by realistic external features. Determination of affect disturbance includes the reaction to the presence of the interviewer and whether the patient's questions and comments during the interview are realistic.

Observations of the patient's quality of mood can assist in differentiating psychotic potential from a mood of depression. In depression, autistic withdrawal and self-preoccupation appear, but there is a distinct mood either of helplessness and hopelessness or of agitated pressure that points to a diagnosis of depression without psychosis. Other indicators, to be considered in the discussion of association, can offer further diagnostic refinement regarding the possibility of psychotic depression.

Lability of emotion as a diagnostic indicator offers the psychologist a first glimpse of the nature of ego controls. In psychotic individuals, lability is a function of external reality factors since the presence of fragile internal controls makes external focusing difficult. Lability, therefore, can reveal fragile ego processes and weak ego controls. Such information can be useful in evaluating the likelihood of psychosis, since severe ego deficiencies form a crucial part of psychotic pathology.

Constriction of affect, in which the patient's mood uniformly reflects only a limited range of emotion, is another indicator of a pathological process. In the weakened or decomposing ego controls that appear in psychosis, constriction of the range of affect as well as blunting or flattening of affect can be utilized to reduce pressure on fragile ego mechanisms. The presence of these kinds of affect disturbances provides information pertinent to assessing the patient's difficulty in maintaining adequate contact with reality.

Where the range of mood is distinctly limited or unusually flat in nature, the interviewer may also detect an unreal, strange, empty, or possibly even bizarre quality. Again, such findings can help to determine psychosis and are valuable to report. The unreal quality may also derive from an agitated, pressured, manic elation that reveals marked inappropriateness in its sustained, unrelenting nature. These impressions contribute to the interviewer's assessment of psychotic process with an element of mood disorder. Other indicators of the intactness of reality testing and thought processes can help to clarify whether a hypermanic, agitated quality is related to a nonpsychotic diagnosis or to a manic psychosis.

Sometimes a psychotic patient's weakened ego controls are expressed through mood and affect that are inappropriate to the conversation taking place with the interviewer. For example, inappropriateness of affect may involve laughter in connection with a discussion of sad events, a display of noticeably bizarre features in the patient's emotional expression, or the previously described sustained hypermanic enthusiasm and pressure. Such affective disturbances can provide broad diagnostic discriminations as to whether a psychotic process exists.

Shallowness of affect or labile emotions can also indicate possibilities of organic impairment. Another disturbance of affect that can relate to organic disorder is outbursts of irritability. Irritability may especially occur at points in the interview and test administration when the patient feels frustrated, pressured, and overwhelmed by the demands inherent in the test requirements. In contrast, irritability conveyed in a blaming manner may represent the externalization and shifting of responsibility often seen in character disorders, particularly if passivity, dependency, or passive-aggressiveness are attendant features.

In summary, an analysis of the appropriateness of affective expression involves an estimate of mood, handling of emotion, range, modulation and lability of emotion, and bizarre or inappropriate aspects of affective expression; constriction, flatness, and shallowness of affect; and temporary irritability. In composing the clinical interview section of the report, findings related to these estimates of affective expression must be analyzed and communicated as part of a beginning, gross diagnostic formulation. Evaluation of these factors assists in the differential diagnosis between psychotic possibilities and mood disorders of sadness, helplessness, and hopelessness that are more often linked to depression. As previously noted, indicators of organicity and characterological problems may also be detected in disturbances of affect. Thus, in the diagnostic formulation of this section of the report, it is extremely important to analyze and communicate the forms, aspects, and appearances of affect.

The Special Problem of Anxiety. One of the most important affect features for the psychologist to assess is the nature of anxiety as it appears in the interview situation. The interviewer must determine whether the anxiety shown is appropriate and consistent with the fact that, under ordinary conditions, the testing situation is highly stressful. The patient's behavior and relatedness should reflect this fact. Although the problem of anxiety is treated at length in chapter 8, the issue to consider in this section of the report is its appropriateness in the interpersonal setting of the clinical interview.

Anxiety is generally an internal warning signal for the individual; that is, it alerts the person that something either is not going right or feels terribly wrong. Thus, the analysis of anxiety is important in connection with its bearing on reality considerations. The psychologist observes whether the patient's anxiety appears to be excessive, or if it is hidden or otherwise avoided. An inappropriate expression of affect in psychotic patients can be the avoidance of the expected anxiety of the testing situation. In another instance when a patient seems thoroughly traumatized with anxiety, a process of depersonalization and corresponding panic may be occurring. These kinds of phenomena need to be considered in relation to the overall handling of affect being assessed and reported at this point.

In contrast to the expressions of disturbed anxiety that have just been cited, anxiety may be well managed and appropriately expressed. This finding would contraindicate psychosis and would be a positive strength to report about the patient. Nonpsychotic but pathological anxiety also may be expressed in the interview.

In patients with character disorders, anxiety is usually absent or inhibited through the mechanisms associated with character defenses. Thus, patterns of impulsivity, withdrawal, passivity, compliant-dependency, and other personality styles ward off anxiety. These global characteristics are experienced in *ego-syntonic* terms. An ego-syntonic phenomenon involves an impulse, feeling, behavior, or symptom that the subject accepts comfortably; such an experience is not sensed as strange, alien, or uncomfortable, as is the case with *ego-dystonic* or *ego-alien* phenomena. The causes of difficulties and problems are externalized to others, who need to be manipulated or distanced as a means of handling problems. A characterological diagnosis may be established for a person with a consistent avoidance of anxiety and a relatively rigid character style who perceives the source of difficulties to be external. This diagnosis is one nonpsychotic possibility in forming a first, broad diagnostic impression.

On the other hand, in neurotic patients the anxiety and underlying conflict are incompletely contained. Symptoms are produced, and anxiety and discomfort are closely associated with them. These symptoms are experienced as ego-alien and neurotic patients typically regard themselves as being troubled by internal problems.

The role of anxiety is central in neurotic functioning. Thus, the appearance of anxiety associated with ego-alien symptoms and a sense of personal conflict suggests a neurotic diagnosis. This diagnostic impression can then be used as an organizational aid in the construction of the report.

Thus, the way in which the patient's anxiety is revealed in the clinical interview has significant diagnostic implications. These features of the patient's anxiety can be indicated in the report as part of the broad diagnostic discrimination that is being formed in the clinical interview.

Another element to be considered in the analysis of affect concerns the patient's ability to express, in a clear manner, specific emotions toward others. This ability is a positive indicator of interpersonal relatedness. When the patient's emotional responses to others are uncertain, or the patient needs to retract or to qualify the responses after they are made, then this sort of behavior would be indicative of ambivalence.

Ambivalence

Ambivalence refers to a person's indecisiveness, fear of directness, confusion within a broader context of doubt, and strong need for balance. On a practical and immediate level, indecisiveness refers simply to a person's inability to choose among alternatives. Fear of directness is a form of ambivalence insofar as it reflects a person's avoidance of expressing a clear preference, which underscores a difficulty in making commitments of any sort. In addition, ambivalence reflects problems in self-assurance and self-esteem and frequently relates to dependency problems. Ambivalence may affect the spheres of ideas or emotion, and especially refers to the ways in which a person's will and motivation are challenged; ambivalence, therefore, persists in calling into question the person's will — a debilitating and exhaustive experience. A person with intense ambivalence needs to rely upon others for decision making and direction. Many manifestations of ambivalence problems can be noted in evaluating the content of the patient's responses in the interview. The style of indecisiveness can also be noted in the nature of the patient's responses to questioning by the psychologist.

Confusion in the context of self-doubt occurs because the patient feels greatly protected by familiar surroundings and acutely troubled by possibilities of change. Confusion therefore occurs with respect to all change conditions and is amplified when there is an expectation that the person should function more independently. Such confusion can reflect a psychotic process. Consequently, this form of ambivalence must be evaluated in conjunction with features of autism, affect, and disturbances in the associative process.

A deeper level of pathology may be discerned in another kind of ambivalence-confusion when there is a loss of clarity between what emanates from within and what properly belongs to external reality. In this case, use of psychotic projection and ideas of reference may be discerned. If autistic phenomena are present, the patient's over-reliance on inner processes can lead to confusion between inner and outer states because inner determinants are indiscriminantly substituted for external reality. This kind of ambivalence is distinctly characteristic of increased primary process operations and appears in developing psychotic problems.

Ambivalence may also be expressed by the patient in connection with sexual feelings and problems. If these issues are discussed in the interview, the nature of the patient's ambivalence regarding sexual and personal identity factors can be assessed. Generally, ambivalence in the person's identity is seen along with a focus on symmetry and balance in the test responses. The patient's over-concern with balance, symmetry, or order may reflect varying levels of pathology from psychosis to characterological or neurotic problems in which identity confusion may play a central role. This concern with balance and symmetry also reveals that the central concern expressed through ambivalence refers to the person's need to sustain and preserve the safe, typical internal equilibrium.

When the patient expresses clear response samples of ambivalence, then these become important for diagnostic consideration. Ambivalent confusion on the part of the patient may also indicate an associative disturbance.

Association

The fourth principle, association, actually refers to an attempt to ascertain whether any disassociation occurs. The intactness of this vital dimension relates to the patient's abilities to be cogent, logical, clear, incisive, and relevant, qualities that the psychologist can evaluate in the interview.

Association is the most important of the four organizing principles considered because it relates most directly to confusion about the essence of reality. The relative integrity of the associative function is the most visible sign of intactness or disorder. This function bears on the capacity to construct and appreciate reality in a logical way, to relate to it adaptively, and to conceptualize about it coherently.

During the clinical interview, the psychologist needs to observe and evaluate signs of disturbance in the patient's language construction and coherence. Associative integrity is ascertained through the patient's verbal productions and language usage, where any psychotic rumination or process is readily reflected. As the patient responds to the psychologist and interacts in the interview, it is possible to determine whether the associations that follow each other are tangential, or illogical to any noteworthy degree. These samples of behavior can form a basis for establishing a thought disorder. The patient's production of bizarre or clang (rhyming) associations or of neologisms (made-up words) are similarly signs of a psychotic process in the patient's functioning.

Persons with milder disturbances, though perhaps feeling confused, anxious, and uncomfortable in discussing their problem, still express themselves in a largely reasonable and orderly manner. In contrast, persons in whom a psychotic process is present (reflected, for example, by a thought disorder) express thoughts in a tangential manner. The essence of a confused thought disorder is that these thoughts relate to each other obliquely rather than in a natural and logical sequence. This is quite different from a patient whose anxiety, for instance, interferes with adequate articulation and who may not be able to state the precise nature of what is feared, but nevertheless communicates at an acceptable level of coherence and relevance.

When autistic elements exist in addition to an associative disturbance, intrusions of idiosyncratic or emotional material may further confuse the associative process and result in such a strain in cognitive functioning that consistent, logical thinking becomes virtually impossible. Associative disturbance also can appear as a confusion of cause and effect, which is known as correlational, syncretistic, or paralogical thinking. It means that the person attributes cause and affect to any two events that have occurred together, instead of understanding that these events may not be inherently connected. The person's thinking, therefore, has an illogical and unrealistic quality.

Another associative disturbance that the psychologist may detect is circumstantial thinking, or the inability to maintain a basic theme. In relating an incident or problem, the patient introduces lengthy and unnecessary digressions, preambles, subthemes, and circumlocutions which are endlessly strung together so that the patient is unable to complete what he started out to convey. This disassociative symptom is considered pathognomonic of psychosis. Circumstantial thinking can be noticed immediately because its net effect is to render the patient's narrative pointless and mostly irrelevant.

Thus, the four "A"s of autism, ambivalence, and association (along with an additional "A," namely anxiety) comprise an essential structure in which all the material observed and gathered in the clinical interview may be understood, and the broad question of psychosis versus nonpsychosis may be addressed.

Along with the "A"s there are special but more obvious symptoms that can be diagnostically important. The patient's indication or retelling of any strikingly unusual or bizarre experiences bears on the possibility of psychosis and can be included in the clinical interview section of the report. Additional samples of behavior revealing delusions, hallucinations, and disorientation with reference to time, place, or person also need to be considered.

Orientation to Time, Place, and Person

During the interview, the extent to which reality orientation is intact can be noted from the patient's responses, questions, mannerisms, and answers to questions from the examiner. In the conventional psychiatric interview, this data is analyzed in terms of the patient's relationship to the important reality and cognitive factors of *time, place,* and *person,* which presumably provide estimates of the patient's current state of consciousness, stability, and reality testing.

The patient's overall state of consciousness can be clear, clouded, confused, or even stuporous. Clouding, for example, occurs in alcoholism, drug intoxication, delerium, head trauma, and other organic involvement. Stuporous behavior may be seen in forms of schizophrenia such as catatonia, depression, and even hysteria. Detecting and evaluating the patient's state of consciousness during the interview enables the psychologist to discriminate between psychosis and nonpsychosis in this section of the report. In addition, findings regarding the patient's state of consciousness may indicate a preliminary diagnostic hypothesis of organic brain syndrome.

Time Orientation. One possible impairment that would derive from a patient's pathology is a distorted sense of time, a particularly common occurrence in mood disorders. In depression, for example, the patient's sense of time seems to lag, while in manic states it can seem to speed up to such an extent that its passage does not consciously register. The psychologist can evaluate the patient's more precise awareness of time by questioning his knowledge of specific dates, years, and current time. The psychologist specifically needs to assess the patient's awareness of the current date and year, either through questioning or by conveniently requesting that the patient date any of the projective drawings or other graphic material required in the test battery.

Place Orientation. In place disorientation, reality strains in the form of adaptational demands disrupt the patient's knowledge of personal location. It is important in the clinical interview that the patient is encouraged to express an understanding of where the interview is taking place, and why, so that this measure of reality contact can be assessed. Confusion as to one's personal location and, similarly, confusion about the purpose for being there clearly reflects the possibility of psychosis.

Person Orientation. This crucial and most basic cognitive awareness of personal identification is disrupted only in very severe psychotic disturbances, in which projections and hallucinations impair one's fundamental self-identity.

These fundamental orientations are important cognitive reference points and bear directly on an estimate of the patient's reality testing. When these reference points are disrupted, the more serious disorders, such as organic impairment and overt psychosis, immediately become diagnostic possibilities. The following two chapters present an analysis of approaches to assessing reality testing and corresponding cognitive organization. Table 3.1 outlines some of the salient focuses of the clinical interview.

TABLE 3.1   The Clinical Interview

- All expressive behavior gathered from the clinical interview is utilized to formulate diagnostic impressions and to generate diagnostic hypotheses.
- First impressions, even upon first greeting, can be valuable to the psychologist and should not be minimized, as they are samples of the patient's personality pattern. These samples of behavior constitute a microcosm of the patient's overall functioning.
- Clinical data is not collected as judgmental evidence. Clinical data is an accumulation of samples of behavior that affords the psychologist an opportunity to understand possible conflicts in the personality.
- The psychologist should address the referral problem but not be limited by the main referral question. Frequently, it becomes necessary for the psychologist to clarify or augment the referral problem. Thus, the psychologist should obtain information regarding the referral problem directly from the patient.
- Tentative conclusions about the patient's behavior and its probable meaning can be pointed out in this section of the report.
- Random observations are not useful here. Rather, tentative hypothesis building is relevant. Thus, general diagnostic statements may be made as, for example, in the distinction between organicity, psychosis, character disorder, or neurosis.
- It is useful, in the general diagnostic discrimination for the clinical interview section, to ascertain a diagnostic domain by assessing the psychosis-nonpsychosis dimension. To clarify this dimension, an evaluation of Bleuhler's four "A"s—autism, affect, ambivalence, and association—can be a useful assessment tool. Evaluation of anxiety is also especially important with respect to its appropriateness, conscious affect, or symptoms it may produce.

  Autism. Indicated by withdrawn interpersonal contact.
  Affect. Assess the normalcy of mood, modulation of affect, appropriateness of affect, and degree of lability.
  Ambivalence. Apparent from the need to balance responses, fear of directness, approach-avoidance conflicts, surfacing of severe self-doubt and indecision, and need to maintain typical internal equilibrium.
  Association. The patient's capacity to be cogent, logical, clear, incisive, and relevant as opposed to exposing disassociative ideation and tangential thoughts. Involves an assessment of the degree to which thinking is structured within the context of cause and effect as opposed to thinking that is circumstantial and irrelevant.
- Phenomena of delusions (fixed, false beliefs) or hallucinations (gross misperceptions of reality) need to be noted along with disorientation with reference to time, place, or person—an assessment, essentially, of the patient's state of consciousness.

  Time Orientation. The patient's sense of time is distorted.
  Place Orientation. The patient is confused about current defining aspects of location.
  Person Orientation. The patient's self-identification is confused.

SUMMARY

This chapter considered the clinical interview that takes place during the testing of a patient. A parsimonious structure of psychological and psychiatric organizing principles was presented as a guide to synthesizing the impressions, observations, and conclusions that the psychologist forms. The aim of this synthesis was to formulate a preliminary, broad diagnostic hypothesis with respect to discriminating psychosis from nonpsychosis. Further described were the remaining broad diagnostic possibilities of organic, characterological, or neurotic psychopathology, completing a four-level diagnostic discrimination that begins to form during the interview and observational phase of testing.

4

Reality Testing and Cognitive Functioning
Psychosis

In the previous chapter, issues of diagnosis with respect to broad conceptions of psychosis, organic impairment, character disorder, and neurosis were discussed. At this point it is important to estimate the central concern inherent in formulating such diagnoses, namely reality testing and the nature and qualities of cognitive functioning. Problems with the intactness of reality testing and the integrity of cognitive functioning relate to diagnostic issues concerning psychosis.

In this chapter and the next, reality testing is discussed in relation to cognitive organization, with an emphasis on impairments that interfere with various cognitive functions. In psychodiagnostic terms, cognitive organization is the manner in which a person is able to integrate and synthesize the complex demands emanating from the environment, including inner as well as external forces. Cognitive functions generally include the mental activities involving such facilities as thought, planning, memory, judgment, and organization as well as the various intellectual qualities, such as abstraction, concept formation, learning, and appropriate appreciation of detail.

An individual's cognitive functioning can be assessed by evaluating the various cognitive and intellectual capacities as revealed by interview and test functioning. In addition, the state of a person's overall cognitive organization may be inferred by the person's capability to unify personal perceptions, thoughts, and feelings. In addition, it is important to assess the way in which a person pursues tasks and goals and the style of the individual's approach to the task. The psychologist is fundamentally concerned with gauging how external demands are met in connection with the person's inner resources.

ASSESSING REALITY TESTING

In estimating reality testing, it is possible to conceive of three steps that take place. The first is a global impression, which is referred to as the estimate of overall cognitive organization. The second step involves understanding the constituent elements of cognitive organization and the way in which they are unified. This attempt to unify the components of cognitive organization also involves consideration of the elements of perception, thinking, and feeling and their overall coordination. Third, in order to examine these elements and their integration in detail, it is necessary to understand the state of ego functions in the personality. Analysis of ego functions clarifies how a person has managed to align perception with thinking and feeling to develop a particular cognitive approach which becomes visible in behavior and directly reflects the person's cognitive organization.

Thus, cognitive organization as a reflection of reality testing is analyzed by evaluating all test results that bear upon ego functions. In addition, the integrity and intactness of these ego functions and, therefore, the capacity for reality testing can also be assessed through test results and interview data that reflect the dyscontrol and intrusiveness of emotionally driven responses. Therefore, data from projective material and intelligence testing as well as interview impressions need to be analyzed to formulate the level and quality of the patient's ego functioning.

Just as Bleuhler's four dimensions were helpful in organizing the testers clinical impressions, Heinz Hartmann's five ego function elements are similarly useful in ascertaining the strength and resilience of the patient's ego. These are the *primary autonomous* ego function, the *secondary autonomous* ego function, the *integrative* ego function, the *synthetic* ego function, and the *adaptive* ego function.* Analyzing ego strength and the relationship to reality, through the perspectives afforded by the various ego functions that Hartmann described, enables the reporting of a diagnostically meaningful assessment regarding the patient's level of reality involvement.

*Hartmann, H. (1958). *Ego Psychology and the Problem of Adaptation.* New York: International Universities Press.

Primary Autonomous Ego Function

The primary autonomous ego function, when intact, encompasses basic contact with reality and realistic integration of percepts, thoughts, and feelings. Impairment of this function involves the level at which distinct and gross perceptual distortions appear. On the psychological test material an aggregate of such properties as poor form level on the Rorschach, lack of coherent stories on the Thematic Apperception Test, severe body breaks or bizarre transparencies on the projective drawings, and other similar broad distortions of reality are reflected in the test responses. This function is the most basic of all ego functions, and if it is found to be impaired the existence of a psychotic process is definitely indicated.

The psychologist can report specific information regarding the impairment of this ego function by citing findings that indicate fragmentation among perception, thinking, and feeling. Such findings convey that the patient does not appreciate what exists in an integrated and coherent manner; instead, the person operates from a disintegrated and highly distorted perspective. For example, a patient with a defect in this function probably cannot bring thought processes to bear adequately on perceptions. Consequently, both perceptions and thinking are isolated from each other as well as from other ego strengths. Instead of unity and integration among perception, thinking, and feeling, there are gaps and isolations. This is specifically what is meant by a psychotic break or thinking disorder. When such a break or thought disorder occurs, this ego resource—the primary autonomous function—reflects the disintegration of the cognitive organization.

Similarly, the feelings that would be appropriately associated with the individual's perceptions and thoughts are disjointed. This disturbance reflects the mood impairment aspect of psychosis and may be more or less prominent than the thought disorder component. This thinking-mood distinction leads to diagnostic discriminations among types of psychoses. For example, in psychoses such as manic-depression and psychotic depression, designated among major affective disorders in the third revision of the *Diagnostic and Statistical Manual* (*DSM-III* and *DSM-III-R*), mood disturbances reflect the predominant aspect of difficulty. In schizophrenia, disordered thought is the most disturbed component.

Communicating Findings. The psychodiagnostic report should not actually contain the technical phrase "primary autonomous ego function." Clarity and communication are better served by focusing on terms relating to judgment, perception, thought, and feeling. What needs to be detailed is the extent to which these ego functions are impaired, distorted, and idiosyncratic. In this way, the particulars of the psychotic process are communicated in a manner that is simple and clear and specifically relates to the particular individual being evaluated.

A discussion in the report of impairment of the primary autonomous ego function necessarily means that the psychologist is committed to the diagnosis of psychosis. Therefore, the remainder of the report, as well as the material discussed in the previous clinical interview section, must be consistent with the establishment of a psychotic diagnosis. If any inconsistent findings are noted, they need to be discussed and explained, as, for example, data related to residual strengths that continue to be present. Outside of such residual strengths, some data from the observed behavior of the patient in the clinical interview, as well as the test data results, must confirm the diagnosis of psychotic impairment.

When the primary autonomous function of the ego is impaired, the patient is not, then, in contact with reality. Consequently, overt psychotic behavior may be readily identified by the presence of hallucinations and delusional material. This behavior is not usually subtle and is readily visible during the clinical interview. A patient who has such an impairment can be described in the report in terms of gross judgment lapses, perceptual distortions, hallucinations, delusions, and illogical thinking. Further descriptive material may also refer to thoughts and perceptions that are unrealistically dominated by emotional turbulence. In all probability, a patient of this sort will be in need of hospitalization because of the extent of disorganization or else is likely to be already hospitalized. The testing is usually conducted in order to confirm the presence of psychosis, to determine its diagnostic type, or to detect if additional complications, such as organic problems, are present.

Drug-induced psychoses also involve impairment of the primary autonomous function of the ego. In the case of a floridly psychotic patient, testing may be undertaken in the hospital setting not only to help differentiate among manic, schizophrenic, and depressive psychoses, but also to assist in making decisions about the management of the patient and choice of chemotherapy.

Intellectual functioning will fail to register anywhere near its potential in the test data of the psychotic patient, even if the premorbid I.Q. was within average limits or higher. Most subtests of the intelligence scale with such individuals will reflect severe impairments because of the patient's disorganization, even to the extent that scores of zero appear consistently. On the projective data, form level and content will be significantly distorted and idiosyncratic. All of these data reflect the fundamental disintegration of ego resources basic to the primary autonomous ego function. Thus, when this function is impaired, gross fragmentation of the unity among perception, thinking, and feeling results. A global cognitive disorganization is reflected, in which virtually all behavior is determined by the patient's internal needs instead of by reality factors.

Secondary Autonomous Ego Function

The secondary autonomous ego function relates specifically to the capacity for directed thought. In evaluating this ego function, the tester is interested in determining if any impediments are interfering with directed thought. The presence of directed thought, even if impaired, differentiates the secondary autonomous function from the primary autonomous function. Patients demonstrating processes of decompensation or depersonalization, persons who are ambulatory schizophrenics, borderline patients, individuals in profound general crisis, or incipiently schizophrenic or prepsychotic patients are likely to show impairment of this ego function.

The major issue for the psychologist to evaluate in assessing the secondary autonomous ego function is whether primary process thinking appears in directed thought in a strong, interfering manner. The following case is presented as an example of the effect of impairment on this level:

> A hospital pathologist began to feel compelled to visit the hospital morgue more often than his job needs dictated. He began to think that he would dissect or do something else to the corpses, something that he thought would be inappropriate. Yet the impulse to do "something" at times dominated him.

This clinical vignette demonstrates a vital question the psychologist can ask with respect to gauging the state of this ego function: To what extent is the patient impulse-dominated? In this case, primary process urges were clearly beginning to break into consciousness and to become increasingly uncontrolled. Such pressure of impulse usually refers to the inability to control these urges directly. Thus, under conditions of the presence of pervasive impulse, an impairment of the secondary autonomous function of the ego—in which directed thought is impeded— becomes more apparent. Consequently, a thought disorder is a primary diagnostic possibility.

Another interesting feature of this case was that the hospital pathologist did not experience tension or express anxiety about the specific appearance of his urges, although he thought that they were inappropriate. This aspect of the example suggests that the unity among perception, thought, and feeling was disrupted and reflects a cognitive organization characterized by a growing propensity for acting-out. Thus, this man's cognitive approach was becoming unduly influenced by an impulse-dominated action-orientation.

The issue of anxiety versus a propensity for action indicates another aspect of the secondary autonomous ego function, concerning whether or not the person experiences anxiety about the new behavior and actions that are emerging. When an impairment in this function becomes evident, the patient generally does not experience anxiety in connection with the accompanying new aspects of overt behavior. Thus, such behavior is ego-syntonic (that is, behavior the subject accepts comfortably) and clearly reveals why an impairment of this ego function is so serious. When primary process breaks into directed thought, dire consequences can result without anxiety necessarily being experienced in connection with the new behavioral tendencies toward impulse expression.

In addition to the elements of primary process material breaking into consciousness and the relative lack of anxiety explicitly associated with such primary process material, impairment on this level reveals a cognitive approach that can be characterized as highly ideational in style. That is, as such patients become impulse dominated, they may show ideational over-concern by overtalking, overthinking, and ruminating. These types of obsessional features reflect both the activity of the intruding impulse as well as efforts toward containing or controlling the impulse through this ideational compensation.

Diagnostic Application.   How does impairment in the secondary autonomous function of the ego appear in patients who are seen for testing?

> In the example of the hospital pathologist, his growing preoccupation with doing something with bodies in the morgue reflected an increasing breakthrough of unmanageable impulses which was probably a process of disintegration of the secondary autonomous ego function. As this ego function broke down further, more obvious psychotic thoughts and behavior became evident, confirming the diagnostic impression of incipient schizophrenia that was made largely on the basis of psychological test results, before the complete breakdown occurred. The patient's breakdown was eventually characterized not by an acting-out of impulse-dominated behavior, but by a highly idiosyncratic ideational cognitive organization. The development of this ideational cognitive ap-

proach served the purpose of limiting the pressure that was accumulating to act-out and the inherent thought that he might actually do something with the corpses.

On the projective material and intelligence testing in such a case, the psychologist would obtain samples of test data reflecting perhaps the breakthrough of unusual impulses along with the patient's particular ideational organizing approach. The presence of both extensive samples of impulse material and compensatory ideational material can reflect fragmented alignment of thoughts and ideas with perceptions and feelings, all revealing primary process infiltrations.

Secondary autonomous ego impairment may also be visible in the borderline personality. Here, the intrusion of primary process impulses appears in the form of abundant themes and percepts reflecting anger and hostile impulses and, perhaps, sexual identity confusion as well. This kind of response pattern reflects the strain on the patient's ego resources and the flimsiness of cognitive controls.

Thus, when secondary autonomous ego functions are impaired, the patient's cognitive organization shows disturbances in the form of infiltration of impulses affecting thought. Consequently, the question of good versus poor reality testing is extremely important to discuss. With such impairment, reality testing is certainly at least strained, tenuous, and somewhat inadequate. In contrast to impairment of the primary autonomous ego function, however, florid hallucinations and pervasive delusional organization do not typically characterize the existing cognitive organization of this secondary autonomous ego function.

Communicating Findings. The writer of the psychodiagnostic report should not actually refer to the technical phrase "secondary autonomous ego function." Reporting the impairment of this ego function commits the psychologist to a discussion of interference with directed thought, the appearance or breakthrough of primary process thinking, and the relative lack of anxiety about the specific nature of these impulses. The lack of anxiety is qualified as relative because the patient may experience a sense of inappropriateness or doubt as the acting-out propensity strengthens. Such impairment reveals a cognitive approach that is idiosyncratic and highly ideational in style and not solidly or consistently governed by reality factors. Thus, the impairment of this ego function also commits the psychologist to a diagnosis that reflects some process of deterioration or significant ego deficiency. In cases in which substantial anger is seen, a borderline state may be diagnosed.

Patients with some organic involvement may also show impairment of secondary autonomous ego functions that are expressed as disturbances of directed thought as well as by virtue of the display of periodic impulse episodes. The broad diagnostic categories encompassing character or personality disorders and neuroses are not involved in impairment at this level and, consequently, should not be referred to when disorders based upon impairment of this ego function are described. However, an exception may occur in the instance of borderline personality organization which is regarded as a character or personality disorder by some diagnosticians, as in *DSM-III* and *DSM-III-R*. The aim of the secondary autonomous ego function is specifically designed to guard against the breakthrough of primitive and morbid primary process impulses. Persons of neurotic and character disorder types might exhibit the appearance of acting-out behavior, ideational ruminating, or inappropriately limited manifestations of anxiety; however, such acting-out would not include the appearance of primitive primary process material.

The challenge to the psychologist in reporting these phenomena is to be able to convey the basic idea that profoundly pathological material of a serious and primitive sort is beginning to emerge. The central treatment concern is to recognize the labile nature of an ongoing process, because such a process generally means that further deterioration is a definite possibility. Although cohesive cognitive intactness may still be obvious in such patients, once impairment of the secondary autonomous ego function appears, the integration or cohesion of the cognitive structures of perception, thinking, and feeling is surely weakening. Such weakening allows feelings to influence other functions disproportionately, impairing directed thought. One consideration in view of this weakening of cognitive integration is the prediction of its rate. Thus, it is important to assess how rapidly the disintegration of cognitive functions is proceeding, and if it will stabilize or persist further.

It should be realized that patients who show infrastructural impairment are frequently those whose behavior is beginning to perplex family, friends, and teachers as well as referring sources such as psychiatrists and social agency personnel. Such patients will at times behave normally and function and engage in reasonable social interaction; yet, at other times, they also show seemingly aberrant behavior or behavior that is so idiosyncratic as to be quite striking and strangely ambiguous. Thus, there is an inconsistency between coherence and aberration that confuses others involved with these patients.

Since the referral source may be puzzled by the patient's inconsistency, the psychologist can be helpful in explaining the paradox of the patient's behavior by presenting an analysis of the precise nature of the problem. This analysis takes the form that new, aberrant behavior, strongly characterized by primitive and morbid impulses, is emerging in the context of a weakening or breakdown of certain ego functions. It is helpful to the reader of the psychodiagnostic report to learn about the specific cognitive impairments through a discussion and careful analysis of the relation among perception, thinking, and feeling. This discussion serves a useful communicative function in contrast to merely indicating that "there is a breakdown of the secondary autonomous function of the ego." A careful analysis, simply described, is helpful; reliance on overly condensed, technical jargon can be limiting.

The psychologist will want to clarify the nature of the patient's judgment, control and sense of discrimination between fantasy and reality. In this case, the psychologist may have to say that the patient is sometimes disturbed and sometimes not disturbed, but in so doing, the patient's cognitive organization with respect to the relative cohesion of perception, thinking, and feeling can be clarified. Conclusions drawn about the extent and quality of fragmentation will bear directly on the evaluation of reality testing. As fragmentation progresses, perception, thinking, and feeling, as well as their relation to each other, tend to become increasingly dominated by impulses. For this reason, reality testing is impaired if fragmentation continues. Because of the disturbing nature of this process in the patient, it is important to assess and report whether fragmentation is persisting in an ongoing fashion or if it is in a more stable state.

The importance of assessing whether the fragmentation is progressive is exemplified by the differential diagnosis between incipient and ambulatory schizophrenia. In incipient schizophrenia, the fragmentation process may be progressive; in the diagnosis of ambulatory schizophrenia, the fragmentation and inconsistency in behavior are usually of a relatively stable nature.

The Special Problem of Anxiety. When impairment in the secondary autonomous function exists, directed thought is repeatedly intruded upon by morbid primary impulses as a result of the fragmenting process that interferes with perception, thinking, and feeling. The underlying impulses begin to dominate ideation in an unrealistic manner, putting a strain on reality testing and adding an overideational style to the patient's approach. The patient may talk or think excessively. These highly ideational increasing preoccupations reflect the nature of the impulses that are being contained.

Although noticing these increasing urges, the patient may not experience the anxiety that would be expected in view of the seriousness of what is occurring. Thus, as previously mentioned, the tension or anxiety associated with such urges tends to be limited or not experienced. Whenever anxiety does appear, as in the case of pseudoneurotic schizophrenia, it is displaced to concerns of proficiency, competence, social approval, and general feelings of inferiority, rather than reflecting the morbid quality of the emerging primary process impulse and its derived behavior. In the previous clinical example of the hospital pathologist, he experienced concern related to the fact that there was an unfamiliar shift in his thinking pattern and interests. This concern was not related to his specific behavior with the bodies or the consequences that could ensue if he were to act-out upon the impulses that were emerging.

Another example of displaced anxiety in persons who show behavior and test samples of impairment of the secondary autonomous ego function is demonstrated by the following case of a male music teacher in a boys' high school.

> This man became preoccupied with possibilities of homosexuality and was absorbed by corresponding ideation. He was not at all anxious about homosexuality or homosexual impulses; his only tension concerned maintaining satisfactory job performance. Thus, he shifted his anxiety away from the emerging impulse to questions of competence. On the projective tests, this sort of impulse breakthrough was clearly indicated in his productions, but his thematic content was concerned with perfection and achievement. As a result of cognitive fragmentation, form quality on the projective material was at lower than average levels, reflecting strains in reality testing. Corresponding cognitive impairment was also seen in the results of intelligence testing, where responses were contaminated by overideation and by a focus on needs to be excessively thorough, which clearly reflected the ongoing impairment of his reality testing. Previously well-integrated cognitive organization could no longer adequately serve him in the test situation because of the problem of fragmentation. This man, although not anxious about his homosexual feelings, showed a pananxiety about virtually all other aspects of life, work, marriage, friendships, and the future. This clinical picture remained stable for some time without signs of further deterioration or fragmentation. The diagnostic impression of pseudoneurotic schizophrenia was based on his pananxiety among other determinants.

This case is an example of the relationship between the diagnosis of pseudoneurotic schizophrenia and impairment of the secondary autonomous ego function. Reality testing and cognitive organization in such cases can be strained although not deteriorated. Directed thought exists, but there can be occasional interferences from primary process impulse breakthrough such as the homosexual preoccupations in the example presented. In addition, primary process breakthroughs in pseudoneurotic schizophrenia can also appear in the form of depressive or suicidal feelings, severe energy depletion creating profound fatigue experiences, or in actual disorientation.

In the following chapter, an evaluation of the remaining ego functions is presented. The discussion concerns impairment of each ego function, its relation to reality testing and cognitive organization, and implications in terms of the diagnoses of character disorders and neuroses. Table 4.1 presents the salient references to the section of the report reflecting reality testing and cognitive functioning in terms of the primary and secondary autonomous ego functions.

TABLE 4.1 Primary and Secondary Autonomous Ego Functions as Related to Cognitive Organization and Reality Testing

Primary Autonomous Ego Function. Impairment in this function is marked by:
• Gross perceptual distortions
• Fragmentation among perception, thinking, and feeling, reflecting a diagnosis of psychosis
• A breakthrough of primary process material
• An impulse-dominated record along with compensatory ideational material
• The presence of hallucinations and delusional material
• Illogical thinking
• Judgmental lapses, perceptual distortions, and highly idiosyncratic responses
• Impaired intellectual functioning
Diagnostic possibilities include overt psychosis such as schizophrenia or manic depression.

Secondary Autonomous Ego Function. Impairment in this function is marked by:
• Disturbances in directed thought; a constant threat of impulse breakthrough is present although reality testing may be strained and impaired but not deteriorated
• The processes of decompensation and depersonalization experiences are apparent
• The presence of primary process colors cognitive processes, including loss of control of direction of thought and a propensity for acting-out
• The experience of anxiety is reduced because of acting-out and/or an overideational style, apparent as a compensatory device to manage excessive impulses
Diagnostic possibilities include ambulatory schizophrenia, pseudoneurotic schizophrenia, incipient psychosis, and borderline personality organization.

SUMMARY

In the preceding sections, reality testing and cognitive functioning from the point of view of ego boundaries were discussed and instances were cited in which the ego boundary is violated so that reality testing does not remain viable. In addition, the cognitive integration of perception, thinking, and feeling does not remain fully integrated. Thus, any disturbance in the ego boundary or ego integrity raises the issue of impairment of the primary or secondary autonomous ego functions. So far, this discussion has considered in detail how such boundary violations appear with respect to the primary and secondary ego functions, and the effects of such impairment in terms of diagnosis, mostly concerning psychosis.

5

Reality Testing and Cognitive Functioning
Character Disorders and Neuroses

Additional material relevant to the cognitive organization section of the psychodiagnostic report is presented in this chapter. The ego functions described here pertain to the analysis of cognitive organization involving diagnostic formulations of nonpsychotic character problems, neuroses, and normalcy.

INTEGRATIVE FUNCTION OF THE EGO

The integrative function of the ego regulates anxiety, thought, perceptions, and feelings to promote effective pursuit of goals. The integrative function involves the level of cognitive functioning at which—even if impaired—essential ego integrity and the capacity for reality contact are no longer in question. In terms of reality testing and cognitive organization, the assumption of nonpsychosis has been established and reality testing is considered intact. In considering this ego function, it is important to evaluate the regulation of instinctual drives and feelings, the management of anxiety, and the extent to which there is adaptation to realistically perceived, external demands. Impairment of the integrative function of the ego means that the person, although essentially intact and in touch with reality, may nevertheless misapprehend, distort, act-out, and become labile. Such distortions can occur on the basis of less than adequate defensive control over impulses and needs, but not out of the direct breakthrough of primary process primitive urges.

The problems in connection with impairment in the integrative function of the ego occur in personality disorders and neurotic pathology, that is, in those disorders in which the issue of anxiety is a major concern. In personality disorders, undue energy is devoted to the promulgation of rigid character styles as a means to control anxiety. In neuroses, energy is expended in the formation of symptom patterns as a response to the experience of anxiety. In both cases, the extra expenditure of energy diminishes the person's capacity for goal-directed achievement. Thus, the characterological and neurotic problems reflecting impairment of the integrative function of the ego include difficulties in regulating anxiety, distortions that interfere with constructive interpersonal relating, reduced efficiency in working toward the achievement of aspirations, and inhibitions in goal direction. A person with impaired integrative ego functioning displays the capacity and interest as well as sufficient reality intactness to master all of these challenges. However, flaws in the cognitive regulation of perception, thinking, and feeling interfere with progress toward mastery and achievement in these areas. Such deficiencies in cognitive regulation occur because energy is deflected away from external goals in the service of regulating internal impulses, conflicts, and anxiety.

An example of insufficiency in the integrative function of the ego can be seen in the case of a bright student who intensely desires academic and career achievement but cannot study unless forced. In such a case, there is impaired regulation of the ability to manage anxiety constructively because instinctual drives, internal conflicts, and inefficient defenses absorb the energies that the student needs for achievement. Impersonal tasks related to external interests and goals are relegated to a secondary position. Accordingly, when this student is forced by authority figures to study, inner resources can be utilized because anxiety about the work is now made threatening in a personal way.

From this example it can be seen that the person's defenses in regulating anxiety, conflicts, and instinctual drives do not serve long-range interests or even short-term obligations. This example illustrates that the central feature of the integrative function of the ego is its regulatory function—the way in which the individual's energies and efforts are regulated. Thus, in the previous illustration, the student reveals an impairment in the regulatory integrative ego function.

In terms of cognitive orientation and practical functioning, the integrative function of the ego affects the adaptive involvements and strategies that are required for effectiveness and success in the important areas of life such as relationships, school, and career development. When there is a disturbance at this level, personal conflicts of a neurotic or characterological type reduce the cognitive strengths needed for gratifying, goal-directed functioning. Furthermore, anxiety is experienced in an unregulated manner, so that energies and volition cannot be shifted by means of cognitive direction to ensure accomplishments and cope with everyday demands. Internal worry, distress, guilt, and tension, and the symptoms these emotions produce, take the place of constructive and effective application of energies to realistic problem solving. The psychologist must be alert to the specific qualities of pathology associated with impairment of the regulative, integrative cognitive function so that they can be conveyed appropriately in the psychodiagnostic report.

Communication Findings.　The psychologist can convey the nature and effects of impairment in the integrative ego function by discussing the patient's absorption in and over-focus on personal concerns and inner conflict material. Such conflict undermines efficient involvement in realistic, external goal-directed achievement. Patients with cognitive impairments at this level have great difficulty in focusing in a constructive manner on impersonal, external, and task-oriented requirements or on the realistic activities required to develop satisfying personal relationships. Rather, personal worries, narcissistic preoccupations, and unsettling inner conflicts replace action and drain significant energy away from external challenges and opportunities. These inner conflicts may appear as sexual preoccupations, masturbatory compulsions, dependency needs and avoidance of anxiety associated with risk-taking, and the involvement in fantasies related to these preoccupations. Such findings are appropriate to discuss in reporting the impairments related to the patient's integrative aspect of cognitive functioning.

It should be clear that impairment of this ego function does not involve gross or basic impairment of the patient's capacity for reality testing, or fragmentation of the patient's cognitive organization. Instead, extra demands are placed on the integrative, regulatory mechanism of the ego to keep urgent personal inner preoccupations and priorities less central in the individual's overall functioning. When the integrative function is under strain, its regulatory capacity is compromised. There follows, therefore, an over-concern with utilizing the ego's full repertoire of controls, including defenses, ruminations, and fantasies, for purposes of the management of personal anxiety. Because of this inner focus, there is marked interference with the achievement of success in the range of opportunities that present themselves in the external world. Since this impairment centers around difficulties in achievement, one way for the psychologist to communicate deficiencies in cognitive strength is to report findings specifically related to the issue of underachievement.

The Regulatory Aspect in Relation to Underachievement

The regulatory component of the integrative ego function bears on problems of underachievement because of its role in the patient's inability to shift energies from egocentric or personal concerns to the external challenges and opportunities that are desired. The underachievement occurs, in part, because of defenses that are poorly adaptive in managing tensions and conflicts. Accordingly, the ability of the person to implement goal-directed activity is adversely affected. Success will be impeded in any number of areas, including school achievement, career advancement, and even interpersonal relating. One example of interference in interpersonal relating is the difficulty encountered in the establishment of substantial companionable or other deep and close relationships. The individual's concerns become so self-centered that commitment of energies to others is minimized.

As personal concerns absorb more energy, a relation appears between a decreased level of achievement and a corresponding inefficiency in efforts devoted to fulfilling external requirements. The greater the underachievement, the more inventive and ingenious (although relatively ineffective) the person becomes in efforts to meet ordinary requirements of reality. This phenomenon accounts for cramming tactics employed before examinations, extra efforts required to do ordinary tasks, and other ineffective routines established when a defective regulatory function of the ego impairs efficient activity toward achievement.

Test material indicating problems in the regulation features of the integrative ego function suggest egotistical preoccupations and an immature, adolescent-like fantasy life. Fantasies are characterized by grandiose and compensatory features, and there is an intuitive or magical approach to problem solving rather than one that emphasizes information and learning. An intuitive, noninformational cognitive style is consistent with the presence of fantasy preoccupations because tasks are approached primarily through feelings and personal concerns. As a derivative, this style lends itself to all-inclusive optimism along with a magical approach to problem solving that is adopted in reaction to external demands. Optimism and magical fantasy take the place of instrumental activity that would appropriately lead to the accomplishment of goals. A typical finding is the presence of high expectations with reduced accomplishments, that is, a marked discrepancy between aspirations and achievements. In addition, even though such a person is focused on internal concerns, nevertheless, acting-out within an overall action-orientation is often seen. This pattern of action-orientation is an attempt by the person to engage in activities requiring limited learning, and stressing play instead. This component of play is a disguised passive approach—that is, an approach that comprises doing without effort.

On the results of the intelligence test, the scatter of scores between subtests may reveal well-developed abilities for passive comprehension tasks in contrast with poorer capacities for informational tasks or those requiring more objective and active functioning. These findings often imply defensive functioning involving obsessive rumination and high repression, with diagnostic implications suggestive of hysteric, narcissistic, or obsessional dispositions. Projective material often includes stories in which magically achieved success is presented with little emphasis on realistically detailed efforts. Projective responses may also reflect an immature level of development as suggested by a limited capacity for delay and a corresponding need for action. Inclinations toward dependency and needs for affection often appear in keeping with the immaturity that influences the response approach, although reality testing is essentially sound.

In reporting on the deficiencies of regulatory, integrative cognitive functioning as it is involved in a patient's underachievement, it is appropriate to indicate that estimates of reality testing and cognitive organization reflect intactness. It should be stressed that in terms of utilization of the capacity for reality testing, application of resources is impaired and compromised by conflict and inefficient regulation of anxiety. Functioning then appears immature and inappropriate. Thus, the integrative ego function is poorly developed in terms of allowing for the application of resources toward external goal orientation and realistic accomplishment.

In this way, the reader of the report can understand the basis for the patient's inadequate and immature reactions as related to deficiencies in the integrative function of the ego and the presence of personal conflict and its derivative anxiety. This finer discrimination in reporting the difficulty that interferes with the patient's utilization of an intact capacity for reality testing serves more than one purpose. It communicates a lucid, meaningful description of the specific nature of the patient's problem, and it can enable the referral source to devise a more helpful treatment plan for the patient. The recommendation of a treatment plan that includes tutoring and relationship building is one example.

The integrative ego function is closely related to a fourth, and higher-order function of the ego, called the synthetic function, which plays an important part in cognitive capacity and the utilization of reality.

SYNTHETIC FUNCTION OF THE EGO

In this synthetic function of the ego, the basic integrity of the ego also is no longer in question, in terms of the essential intactness of reality testing. The synthetic function of the ego involves the capacity to manage the inconsistencies and ambiguities of goal pursuit in an active, energetic fashion. Consequently, the analysis of this particular ego function does not concern impaired reality; instead, its focus is on the degree to which the ambiguity of reality circumstances can be tolerated, and on the nature of securing goal achievement. The synthetic ego function centers on the energy available to the person to deal with the inconsistencies, ambiguities, and uncertainties of reality conditions in the active pursuit of goals. The synthetic ego function is the capacity of the individual to utilize resources in an active way, as opposed to succumbing to passivity and fantasy under the pressure of a lack of specific guidelines or structure in external circumstances.

The essential issue of the integrative ego function discussed in the previous section was the regulation of energies to enable activity directed toward external goals. The central concern in the closely related synthetic ego function is that, given an accurate perception of reality, the realistically appreciated external goal can be approached in an active, unambiguous manner. A decisive, active approach to reality involves the person's capacity to implement steps to achieve specific goals. Such goals are not set or regulated by passive fantasies, but are approached instead in an assertive manner involving an array of necessary cognitive capacities, including planning, attention, concentration, consideration of detail, and the active, effective channeling of energy. Therefore, in discussing the synthetic ego function, the psychologist needs to be able to appreciate clearly the combined factors of tolerance for ambiguity within the context of reality testing and cognitive organization.

Diagnostic Implications

When the synthetic ego function is intact, the individual engages in goal-directed fantasy that is only minimally compensatory in nature because this fantasy exists along with goal-directed behavior. The fantasy serves as a means of promoting and assimilating the ongoing activity.

When the synthetic ego function is impaired, however, the fantasy no longer accompanies ongoing activity, and goal achievement becomes restricted. Thus, the fantasy assumes a compensatory role. It retains and partially gratifies the wish for achievement in the absence of a full application of instrumental activity. When this occurs, the person may be quite lucid, intelligent, and striving, but is essentially passive in the sense that the person is not applying energy consistently toward achievement and is, therefore, unable to fully achieve personal goals. In certain cases in which there is impairment of the synthetic ego function, the test protocol responses may indicate intense frustration, aggressive fantasy, and difficulty joining unconscious urges with goal-directed behavior. In addition, the person's ability to tolerate ambiguity and incongruous ideation is diminished. The breakdown in the capacity to tolerate ambiguity bears directly on the nature of the person's cognitive organization of perception, thinking, and feeling, which is strongly imbedded in a passive framework.

Since the synthetic ego function enables a person to implement goal-directed behavior, tolerate ambiguity, and synthesize fantasy with instrumental activity and aspirations, impairment of this function leads to several consequences. These consequences include impaired implementation of goal-directed behavior, reduced ability to tolerate ambiguity, and a clear discrepancy between aspiration and achievement. The discrepancy between aspiration and achievement occurs because the tendency is to fulfill goals through fantasy. Thus, the impairment of the synthetic ego function amplifies a passive framework. When desired goals are not actually and realistically attained, a number of disturbing reactions and problems in personality functioning are generated, including frustration, irritability, and aggressive preoccupations, as well as overtly passive-aggressive behavior or unpredictable outbursts of angry frustration.

Another phenomenon that develops within the framework of insufficiency of the synthetic ego function includes preoccupation with aggressive themes characterized by rumination and corresponding anxiety resulting from the poor assimilation of the person's wishes. Thus, passive-aggressive as well as obsessional behaviors are generated by such anxiety, rumination of aggressive themes, and poor integration of wishes. In the instance of passivity with covert hostility, a passive-aggressive approach is characteristic. In contrast, when rumination and ambivalence are characteristic ways of managing ambiguity, obsessional tendencies develop.

A third diagnostic possibility is the manifestation of dependency characteristics which occur because of a tendency to rely on other people to handle the reality challenges that the individual may feel inadequate to manage. Thus, in terms of diagnostic implications, impairment of the synthetic function of the ego may be manifested in terms of passivity, obsessional ruminations, or dependency problems.

On the projective material, the protocol responses may reveal passive yearnings, such as a preponderance of relatively immature responses or those showing a passive experience of anxiety with themes of dependency in interpersonal imagery. In addition, obsessional rumination may appear in the form of aggressive themes and preoccupations with symmetry and ambivalence.

Communicating Findings.   When impairment of the synthetic ego function occurs, the psychologist can report the existence of passive, compensatory fantasies instead of active goal pursuit. Intact synthetic function would reflect goal-directed instrumental activity—the ability to implement and apply energies decisively and unambiguously to practical and concrete accomplishments. It is also important to report an assessment of the patient's capacity to utilize planning, judgment, and commitment in spite of the uncertainties and ambiguities of reality.

These findings regarding passive, compensatory fantasies and incapacities for handling ambiguity can be formulated in terms of the concepts of reality testing and cognitive organization. The psychologist can indicate that although reality testing is adequate, cognitive organization reveals certain problems. These problems are detailed in terms of the patient's tendencies to be passive rather than goal directed; to be preoccupied with thoughts that cannot be translated into productive work; to experience passively compensatory fantasies in place of instrumental action toward meeting the challenges presented by important goals; and to experience undue anxiety whenever the uncertainties of reality cannot be immediately clarified.

Often associated with these disturbances may be findings indicating a component of frustration, a preoccupation with reactive aggression, or an inability to deal with feelings related to these reactions. These problematic findings reflect impairments in the patient's capacity to combine perceptions, thoughts, feelings, and fantasies in well-synthesized activity which is directed toward meeting definite goals. The psychologist can also indicate the nature of the difficulties that the patient may be experiencing in utilizing cognitive capacities for planning, judgment, attention, concentration, and the general management of frustration. Impairment of the synthetic ego function can be seen both on the projective material and on the subtests of the intelligence test that require successful application of cognitive capacities such as planning, judgment, and concentration. In presenting material that relates to the nature of this ego function, the major concern is to focus on the degree to which ambiguity, passivity, and fantasy interfere with goal achievement.

When the synthetic ego function is reasonably intact, enabling successful coping, the question arises as to how well the person is managing. Coping constructively with the strains and ambiguities of reality relates to the degree of adaptation that the individual presents. Thus, the final ego function to be considered concerns adaptational operations.

ADAPTIVE FUNCTION OF THE EGO

A discussion of the adaptive function assumes that all other ego functions are intact. For this reason, referrals made for behavior disturbances, personality impairment, or crisis problems will generally not be concerned with an analysis of this particular ego function. However, testing referrals that are made to determine acceptance into special progress classes or to assist in determining job promotions all require estimates of the degree to which this function is operating. The adaptive function of the ego involves flexible cognitive organization with the capacity to utilize inner resources and energy creatively. Integration of thinking, feeling, fantasy, and behavior predominates with only limited interfering anxiety. In reporting on this ego function, the focus is on evaluating the extent to which one's coping experience is successful. Behavior in school, on the job, and in relationships are the criteria to be considered.

On the tests that are administered, the psychologist who reports positive findings of a sound adaptive function of the ego will necessarily also find reasonably intact cognitive organization and good reality testing. The psychologist can then report a variety of highly adaptational strengths, including flexibility in problem solving, the existence of creative and inventive resources, the ability to change set when appropriate, a sense of originality that may especially be seen on the projective material, stability and evenness of functioning reflecting a strong, adaptive assimilation of unconscious fantasy, and an evenness of scores on the subtests comprising the intelligence test. The positive qualities reflect stability and an overall resourcefulness that reveal an eagerness to seek out and master a variety of challenges.

In terms of diagnostic implications, the successful operation of this ego function reflects a well-integrated personality. In such an adaptive personality, ego functioning involves a cognitive organization that is integrated, consistent, and cohesive with respect to the manner in which thinking, feeling, fantasy, and behavior operate. Anxiety appears to be free rather than bound to symptoms. The person shows great strength in the ability to deal constructively and productively with anxiety, rather than neurotically diverting it or being inappropriately driven or over-whelmed by it. This quality frequently is apparent in the evenness of the subtest components of the intelligence test, reflecting the fact that all abilities are developed to full strength and that the various capacities present are expressed to near their full potential.

The entire ego function system can now be recognized as hierarchical. This recognition helps the psychologist to organize concepts around the basic themes of *diagnosis,* such as in the overall distinction between psychosis and nonpsychosis; *intrapsychic phenomena,* such as the manner in which impulses and tensions are regulated and unconscious urges are channeled into acting or fantasy; and *interpersonal activity,* as in the individual's ability to achieve goals, manage relationships, and function autonomously. From an evaluation of these themes, the psychologist can describe and make inferences about reality testing and cognitive functioning. In addition to these basic dimensions, specific traits that coincide with various cognitive and ego operations can be presented and discussed from an analysis of the results of the I.Q. subtests. Table 5.1 summarizes the hierarchical arrangement of the ego functions corresponding to the personality disorders and neuroses.

In the following two chapters, cognitive organization is further developed within the framework of intelligence testing and intellectual functioning.

SUMMARY

In this chapter and the previous one, the nature of reality testing and ego functioning was considered in connection with Hartmann's concepts regarding cognitive organization. A hierarchical arrangement of five ego functions forms the basis for evaluating the patient's cognitive efficiency and for considering diagnostic implications in broad terms.

The most basic cognitive function is the *primary autonomous function of the ego,* which governs essential reality contact and alignment of perception, thinking, and feeling. If this function is impaired, a frank psychotic process is definitely present and perception, thinking, and feeling are fragmented. Only highly distorted, disintegrated ego functioning is possible in either a mood or thought disorder where florid psychotic material is evident.

The *secondary autonomous ego function* is the capacity for directed thought. When this function is impaired, directed thought can be

TABLE 5.1 Reality Testing and Cognitive Functioning: Character Disorders and Neuroses

---

Integrative Ego Function. Impairment in this function indicates the following:
- Nonpsychosis has been established.
- Reality contact is not in question.
- Pathological focus is on regulation of instinctual drives and management of anxiety.
- Lability and acting-out are still possible; therefore, the psychologist needs to assess defensive controls over impulses.
- Assess goal directedness and interpersonal relating, which may be impaired because of energy deflected in service of regulating impulses and anxiety. Such impulses and inner concerns can be expressed through sexual preoccupations, compulsions, dependency needs, and fantasies.
- Underachievement can be seen. Fantasies are characterized by grandiosity and are compensatory. An intuitive approach rather than the ability to accumulate information can be observed.
- A magical approach to problem solving is used, and reduced instrumental activity is seen. Thus, there is a significant distinction between aspiration and achievement.
- An action-orientation or a passive approach may be utilized. Diagnostic possibilities include hysteric, phobic, and narcissistic dispositions.

Synthetic Ego Function. Impairment in this function indicates the following:
- Ambiguity, passivity, and fantasy interfere with goal achievement.
- Frustration and aggressive functioning along with increasing discrepancy between aspiration and achievement are seen.
- Activity towards goals reflects interference.
- The capacity to deal with ambiguity and to utilize effort and energy in life is compromised.
Diagnostic possibilities include passive-aggressive and obsessional patterns.

Adaptive Ego Function. Achievement of this function indicates the following:
- Effective coping ability reflects adaptive behavior in school, at work, and in relationships.
- There is flexibility in problem solving, access to inner resources, and evenness in functioning.
- Sustained mastery can be seen.
- Anxiety is not translated into symptoms.

Basic Themes. The ego function system is organized with respect to:
- *Diagnosis:* psychoses and nonpsychoses
- *Intrapsychic phenomena:* regulation of impulses and management of anxiety
- *Interpersonal activity:* achievement of goals and management of relationships

---

discerned, but interference occurs from emerging primitive impulses. This signals the possible process of decompensation and is also a chief component in ambulatory and pseudoneurotic schizophrenia, as well as in severe borderline states.

At the level of the *integrative function of the ego* there is intactness and adequate reality contact. Regulation of energy, feelings, and anxiety, and the capacity to focus on the external demands of reality are central questions. When this function is impaired, interference with constructive interpersonal relating and inefficiency and inhibitions in goal direction are consequences, even though external goals and satisfying relationships are viewed as being important. Among patients with personality disorders and neurotic pathology, inner conflicts deflect energy from external ambitions to personal preoccupations, leading to underachievement in these diagnostic contexts.

In the *synthetic function of the ego,* reality contact also is unquestionably intact. When this function is impaired, however, the energy that can be used to deal with ambiguities, uncertainties, and inconsistencies in reality conditions is channeled into passive, compensatory fantasy rather than into active, assertive striving. In addition, activity that is instrumental toward goal achievement is significantly compromised when this function of the ego is impaired. Paralysis, dependency, rumination, passivity, irritability, and aggressive outbursts derive from impairment of this cognitive function, with detrimental consequences on planning, judgment, and commitment.

The final and most sophisticated cognitive function is the *adaptive function of the ego,* which achieves prominence when all other functions are operating with relative intactness. This ego function governs the capacity for flexible problem solving, creative and inventive resources, originality, stability, and adaptive assimilation of unconscious fantasies enabling full realization of external goals and gratifying relationships.

In communicating the findings relevant to these cognitive functions, emphasis was placed on describing the test subject in specific, nontechnical terms of intactness or impairment of reality contact, regulation of anxiety and impulses, assimilation of fantasy, and assertive goal direction.

6
Intellectual Functioning
The I.Q. Analysis

In this chapter, intellectual functioning as it is included in the test report is discussed in relation to cognitive organization. This section of the report includes far more than the simple reporting of I.Q. scores or even subtest scores. Reporting of I.Q. scores needs to be set in the context in which they are identified, that is, in terms of intellectual level and percentile level, and as part of an analysis that contrasts groupings of individual subtests and overall verbal versus performance results.

Following this clarification of I.Q. scores, the cognitive and emotional factors assessed from the results of intelligence testing also can be analyzed. Examples of the dimensions inherent in the tasks required on the individual subtests and selected groupings of them include memory, planning ability, judgment, frustration tolerance, the effects of anxiety on performance, capacity for synthesis, and abilities for abstraction and reasoning. Focusing on the analysis from this point of view enables the psychologist to develop a communication that assists the referral source in understanding the patient far better than would merely reporting an aggregate of numbers.

This elaborated approach can provide vital information for mental health professionals and other referral personnel who are concerned about practical intervention. Knowledge of the relative strengths and weaknesses of a subject in the area of cognitive functioning can contribute to the decision-making process in such an intervention. The report can effectively address these concerns by including elements such as subtest analyses as they relate to evaluation of the diagnostic and personality profiles. Such an approach can satisfy the great majority of referral sources who are more interested in the patient's functioning than in simply knowing scores. Furthermore, any contrast between the actual obtained scores and an estimate of potential functioning is a highly significant contribution to the report.

Finally, the results of intelligence testing are influenced by and reflect cultural and personality variables. Issues of acting-out, mental retardation, striving ambitiousness, or conspicuous passivity are examples of cultural and personality variants. Relative facility with verbal material, motor coordination, or complex, gamelike tasks may also be strongly influenced by cultural and diagnostic factors. A description and explanation of these influences are pertinent to include in the report of intellectual functioning.

DSM-III AND DSM-III-R AND TRADITIONAL I.Q. RANGE

In the past, I.Q labels of moron, imbecile, and idiot were utilized to describe subnormal functioning, but such terminology is no longer used. Psychologists today are more interested in reporting scores in terms of how they fall within well-defined ranges. The majority of contemporary psychologists rely on the ranges of I.Q. scores presented in Table 6.1 as a means of providing a meaningful descriptive context for reporting findings. Table 6.1 shows that pejorative implications have been eliminated from the description of I.Q. It is advantageous for psychologists to employ this current nomenclature, because it provides a readily understandable and meaningful way of communicating a subject's position in the spectrum of intellectual functioning.

Various factors make the I.Q. score discrepant from the patient's potential or maximal level of functioning. The obtained score shows only how the patient is functioning at the present time. To communicate what this level of performance means, it is extremely useful to include the percentile rank of the patient's I.Q. score in the test report. Thus, to state that the person's intellectual functioning is in a range that comprises the upper 2.2 percent of the population or that the patient's score is above 98 percent of the population readily describes the individual's standing in relation to the population on which the test was standardized. This communication is more meaningful and relevant than simply offering a specific I.Q. figure. The percentile is also more precise than merely stating the specific range that applies, such as "very superior." Table 6.2 relates

TABLE 6.1 Classification of I.Q. Scores on the Wechsler Scales

I.Q. Range	Description	Percent Included	
130 and above	Very superior	2.2	
120–129	Superior	6.7	
110–119	High average	16.1	
90–109	Average	50.0	
80–89	Low Average	16.1	
70–79	Borderline	6.7	
50–69	Mild retardation		
35–49	Moderate retardation	2.2	Mentally Retarded
20–34	Severe retardation		
19 and below	Profound retardation		

TABLE 6.2 Relation of I.Q. Scores to Percentile Rank on the Wechsler Scales

I.Q.	Percentile	I.Q.	Percentile
135	99	100	50
130	98	95	37
125	95	90	25
120	91	85	16
115	84	80	9
110	75	75	5
105	63	70	2
		65	1

Adapted from Wechsler, D. (1981). *Manual for the Wechsler Adult Intelligence Scale-Revised*. New York: The Psychological Corporation.

individual I.Q. scores to percentiles. The overall I.Q. obtained from the intelligence test is only a gross indicator of the patient's functioning. This overall I.Q. is refined and differentiated by considering its two major components: verbal and performance functioning.

VERBAL AND PERFORMANCE I.Q.

The intelligence tests used by most clinicians are the Wechsler scales.* The subtests of these scales are conveniently grouped into those relying primarily on verbal and language skills and those relying more strongly on performance and motor abilities. Consequently, a separate I.Q. can be derived to show the individual's functioning in each of these areas. Although the Stanford-Binet Intelligence Scale† is also frequently used, it does not yield separate verbal and performance scores.

Many important features regarding cognitive functioning, personality variables, and cultural influences can be understood and described in the test report on the basis of comparing and contrasting the two I.Q. scores. The verbal and performance I.Q.s have various implications in the analysis of overall test results.

Verbal Equals Performance.   When both verbal and performance I.Q.s are roughly equivalent, it can be said that the patient is comparably able in both of these general areas; the person's capacities for handling verbal and performance tasks also are broadly similar. The subject can be described in general terms as being equally capable in utilizing verbal material and in addressing verbal problems as well as at dealing with tasks that require visual analysis and motoric involvement for their solution. Such a person's cognitive capacities for reasoning, conceptualization, judgment, and planning are handled comparably through verbal or visual-motor expression and analysis.

Although some discrepancy typically occurs between the verbal and performance categories, a significant difference is required in order to present an analysis and discussion of meaningful personality and cognitive correlates. A significant difference can be defined as one in which a discrepancy of 15 or more I.Q. points is found, or one in which a discrepancy of 30 or more I.Q. points is found. The first discrepancy corresponds to one standard deviation; the second, to two standard deviations.

Verbal Greater than Performance.   When the verbal I.Q. is significantly greater than the performance I.Q., the first impression is of a person who is more facile and adept at verbal expression, analysis, and recall than at visual-motor functioning. A number of factors may relate

---

*Wechsler, D. (1981). *Wechsler Adult Intelligence Scale-Revised.* New York: The Psychological Corporation.

†Thorndike, R. L., Hagen, E. P., and Sattler, J. M. (1986). *Stanford-Binet Intelligence Scale* (4th ed.). Chicago: Riverside Publishing Co.

to this phenomenon. The subject may tend to rely on intellectual defenses, achievement strivings, and verbal interests. In addition, an emphasis on verbal over performance skills is often demonstrated by subjects who have absorbed mainstream educational and cultural experiences. By the same token, such persons may be described as having less of a capacity for action, performance skills, and mechanical applications.

As mentioned, the tendency toward developing verbal skills and interest at the expense of performance abilities can often be related to factors having to do with cultural conditions and emphases. In this connection, a higher verbal than performance I.Q. can be associated with achievement motivation and a great value placed on educational accomplishment. In terms of diagnostic and pathological implications, the configuration in which the verbal I.Q. is significantly greater than the performance I.Q. may reflect a conforming tendency, since broad cultural values that emphasize verbal skills have been so strongly complied with and adopted. Another contributing cultural as well as diagnostic factor may have to do with obsessional trends, in which a facility with words and verbally formed concepts are generally enriched with special meanings—either overdetermined or idiosyncratic—that contribute to easy productivity in verbal tasks.

In withdrawing from social interests, some persons with schizoid tendencies and schizophrenics with highly ideational approaches or with paranoid tendencies frequently come to rely on words and verbal symbols or expression in a manner that supports pathology. This overvaluing of verbal material may occur in order to avoid involvement in other areas. Because defensive needs are utilized by overdeveloping verbal facility and overrelying on verbal analysis, social interaction, for example, can be limited. The subtests based on verbal material in the intelligence test may fit in with a patient's proclivities to the extent that a relatively reduced capacity appears in most performance subtests, with the effect of a limited performance I.Q. in comparison with the verbal I.Q.

Other factors that may contribute to results in which the verbal I.Q. is greater than the performance I.Q. can be understood by considering the performance deficit in the configuration. Since all of the performance subtests are timed, the motoric slowness that frequently accompanies depression can cause impairment of the results contributing to the performance I.Q. In organic impairment, localization of the brain insult in an area specifically affecting visual or motor competence will depress the overall performance aspect of intellectual functioning and contribute to the appearance of a significantly higher verbal I.Q. Schizophrenic confusion may at times limit perceptual and visual-motor analysis more readily than verbal skills, especially if intellectual defenses are strong and an ideational character style is maintained. In such an instance, performance I.Q. can be substantially lower than verbal I.Q.

It is apparent that these verbal and performance I.Q. differences support the formation of diagnostic hypotheses. This point applies to many of the diagnostic inferences that are suggested throughout this chapter and the next one. Any diagnostic hypotheses that are formed must be checked against findings based both on other data from the test protocol and on content distortions obtained in response to the intelligence test questions. As a matter of fact, distinctly different configurations of scores may often imply similar pathological disturbances. The reasoning required to arrive at a diagnosis in each instance, however, is different. It is essential to determine the individual nature of the subject's pathology in order to appreciate how different findings can point to similar disturbances or, conversely, how similar findings can relate to different diagnostic implications in different individuals. The effort to establish and gradually refine hypotheses concerning pathology and diagnosis clarifies and resolves such seeming paradoxes.

Performance Greater than Verbal.   The person who scores significantly higher in performance I.Q. than in verbal I.Q. can be described as having a preference for action and activity over reflective inclinations. This preference may result from a variety of factors, including a well-developed interest in mechanical activities, strong capacities for visual analysis, or a well-coordinated motoric response. Another contributing factor may be the subject's background, if social and cultural conditioning have deemphasized verbal stimuli. In this situation, verbal skills that are needed to respond fully and skillfully are not well developed, resulting in lower scores on several verbal subtests. The final test results can easily indicate a lower verbal I.Q., with a correspondingly superior score on the performance I.Q.

Another reason for a performance I.Q. that is substantially greater than the verbal I.Q. stems from the subject's pathology, which may then be linked to diagnostic implications. Several diagnostic possibilities are suggested. The patient with a higher performance I.Q., for example, may be involved in an acting-out or psychopathic approach in which an impulsive, action-oriented style predominates. This tendency facilitates better response on performance subtests than on verbal subtests. In some schizophrenic patients, verbal material is drawn into symbolic usage or bizarre, tangential, echolalic, or clang associations are triggered as a result of the person's pathology, so that substantial impairment accrues to a number of verbal subtests. When this situation appears, the patient's pathology can contribute to a performance I.Q. that is higher than verbal I.Q. A final example of the contribution of pathology to the configuration under consideration involves the organically impaired patient. If the neurological problem involves parts of the brain that relate to verbal skills, the verbal I.Q. often will be quite substantially lower in comparison with the performance I.Q., which remains relatively intact.

Implications of Verbal-Performance Discrepancy

When the discrepancy between the verbal and performance I.Q. scores is unusually large, it can be a sign of substantial disturbance in the individual. For this reason, it is important for the psychologist to explore all of the test results in order to formulate a hypothesis that would account for such discrepancies when they are obtained. An especially important point is that a large discrepancy (of approximately two standard deviations, or 30 points on the Wechsler scales) is statistically unusual enough to oblige the psychologist to explain it in the report. This significant discrepancy may signal a psychotic process, organic impairment, or a significant developmental or maturational problem.

Since the results of intellectual testing largely reflect particular cognitive capacities, discrepancies between verbal and performance scores may mirror differences between intact and impaired aspects of the patient's cognitive functioning. Because of the sensitivity of the I.Q. instrument to cognitive processes, deterioration in psychotic patients may first be revealed as a loss of capacity in one of these two broad areas of intellectual functioning. In the organically impaired patient, deteriorated neurological functioning may also appear as a large discrepancy between verbal and performance abilities, especially if the impairment is localized so as to affect one area of functioning more than another.

In patients with developmental or maturational problems, it is often found that some areas of cognitive functioning are strongly developed and intact while other areas are markedly underdeveloped. Such a configuration can be reflected in an improbable difference between verbal and performance functioning. Learning disabilities may involve minimal organic problems in which disturbances of motor coordination or visual-motor coordination can be affected to such an extent that performance functioning is substantially impaired. In this instance, a contrast between verbal and performance capacities can readily be seen. The presence of a learning disability involving a developmental delay with minimal organic dysfunction may also impair verbal processing. Such pathology can also be reflected in discrepant functioning between verbal and performance skills on the intelligence test.

A PROPOSED DIVISION OF VERBAL AND PERFORMANCE SUBTESTS

It has been found to be clinically valuable to group certain subtests on the basis of cognitive and intellectual factors that they have in common. By analyzing and reporting the results of intelligence testing at this level of organization, the pooled information from more than one subtest can be summarized and conveyed. This grouped analysis further clarifies the cognitive strengths and weaknesses of the patient.

The advantage in forming groups of subtests for purposes of analysis involves several issues. Broadly speaking, the verbal and performance tasks may each be divided into groupings that differ in the extent to which active focusing is required of the subject. The verbal tests can be divided into an "A" grouping consisting of the subtests of Vocabulary, Information, Comprehension, and Similarities. These subtests require a problem-solving capacity that is reflective but highly automatic, since much of the material is overlearned, and may be simply called "verbal capacity." The second group, which may be called a verbal "B" grouping, consists of the Digit Span and Arithmetic subtests. In this group, a more focused effort is required in dealing with verbally presented material. Attention and concentration rather than automatic or inert problem solving is crucial, with little opportunity for reliance on overlearning.

In the same manner, the performance subtests can be grouped into two broad categories. This first may be called a performance "A" grouping and consists of the subtests of Picture Arrangement and Picture Completion. This group reflects a rather automatic cognitive capacity that may be indicative of visual organization, since it relies primarily on a thoughtful, visual analysis with minimal requirements for activity or motor ability. The second, performance "B" grouping consists of the subtests of Block Design, Object Assembly, and Digit Symbol. This category requires active and energetic application of both visual and motor skills, as well as their coordination.

The four-way division outlined here is particularly useful in view of the analysis of ego and reality functions developed in chapters 4 and 5 on cognitive functioning. Understanding the utilization of ego functions in the service of cognitive organization includes an evaluation of memory, planning ability, judgment, frustration tolerance, ability to abstract, control over anxiety, and so forth. Thus, this four-part analysis of verbal and performance subtests allows a parsimonious approach to cognitive analysis. For example, obtaining the average of the scaled scores on the attention and concentration tasks of Digit Span and Arithmetic can reveal the extent to which the subject tolerates frustration and is able to control anxiety. A detailed analysis of the subtest scores of the intelligence scale can go well beyond isolated numbers. Components of the I.Q. score are integrated parts of cognition and, consequently, are embedded in the structure of personality.

Use and Implications of "A" and "B" Groupings

The psychologist can utilize the four-fold analysis to describe important cognitive dimensions in the psychodiagnostic report. By gathering the actual scaled scores achieved by the subject on the particular subtests within each grouping and computing and comparing their means, the patient's relative strengths and weaknesses in these four areas become apparent. For example, comparing the means of group "A" and "B" in the verbal subtests offers insight into the patient's cognitive organization and personality orientation. Facility for automatic reflection or relatively effortless problem solving is revealed by higher scores in the "A" group. More active and focused concentration is reflected by higher scores in the "B" group. Similarly, the same relatively effortless problem solving capacity is revealed by higher scores in the performance "A" group, while more active and focused concentration is seen when higher scores appear in the "B" group of performance subscales. In addition, by comparing the means that have been computed for both the verbal and performance "A" group versus the verbal and performance "B" group, the patient's capacity for active focusing and implementation, as revealed by the mean of the scaled scores obtained in all of the verbal and performance "B" subtests, can be described in comparison with the capacity for more passive organization skills, as revealed by the mean of scaled scores in all of the "A" subtests.

Thus, an analysis of the comparisons and contrasts that emerge from all of the combinations of groupings can be undertaken: combined "A" versus combined "B", verbal "A" versus verbal "B", and so on. The psychologist is now in a position to communicate concretely about the cognitive skills and abilities that are relatively strongly or weakly developed in the patient's functioning.

The analyses discussed so far are based on and reflect the subject's current functioning in the present situation and circumstances. However, there is still to be considered the issue of the patient's potential or maximal level of functioning either at some past, premorbid time, or at a point in the future following a successful intervention strategy. Clearly, the actual performance of the individual is a matrix of premorbid skills, interfering pathological factors, historical development, cultural influences, and potential, maximal levels of functioning. The results of actual intellectual functioning must be discussed, but the potential level at which the patient may be able to function is also a significant sector to delineate and analyze. Yet, the patient's potential cannot be indicated either by the overall, full-scale I.Q. or by the verbal or performance I.Q. The potential level of intellectual functioning can be determined only by inference on the basis of an analysis of the patient's current performance and scores. Table 6.3 presents a summary of the I.Q. analysis.

TABLE 6.3   The I.Q. Analysis

- Subtest results can imply information regarding memory, planning ability, judgment, frustration tolerance, effects of anxiety on performance, capacity for synthesis, and ability for abstraction and reasoning.
- When verbal and performance I.Q.s are roughly equal, it implies that cognitive capacities for verbal processing and visual-motor activity are broadly balanced.
- A significant difference between subtests is defined as a spread of 15 or more I.Q. points. A profound difference is defined as a point spread of 30 or more and can signal a significant psychopathological process, organic impairment, maturational delay, or learning disability.
- A verbal I.Q. greater than a performance I.Q. is associated with achievement motivation, intellectual striving, and great value placed on education. Such a contrast can also imply an obsessional trend. Diagnostically, with respect to psychopathology, such trends can be seen in persons with overdeveloped ideational approaches, such as those with paranoid, schizoid, and schizophrenic, in addition to obsessive pathologies.
- Lower performance scores also may imply depression and, in severe cases, organic impairment.
- A performance I.Q. greater than a verbal I.Q. is associated with an acting-out, impulsive, or even psychopathic orientation.
- Lower verbal scores also may indicate receptive or expressive difficulties with language facility or language processing disturbances associated with a learning disability.
- Verbal subtests can be grouped as "A" subtests (Vocabulary, Information, Comprehension, and Similarities), with a high combined average indicating relatively automatic reflective capacity; and "B" subtests (Digit span and Arithmetic), where a high combined average indicates capacity for active, focused effort. The "A" group reveals facility for verbal processing, while the "B" group can indicate capacity to control anxiety and tolerate frustration.
- Performance subtests can also be grouped into "A" and "B" divisions. The "A" group consists of Picture Arrangement and Picture Completion and reflects facile cognitive capacity, while the "B" group comprises Block Design, Object Assembly, and Digit Symbol. A high average of the combined subtests in the "B" group reflects active, focused implementation of effort.

The following chapter considers several ways of analyzing subtest scores and estimating from them potential levels of intellectual functioning.

SUMMARY

An introduction to analyzing intellectual functioning was presented in which the use of descriptive categories of the various I.Q. ranges and percentiles was emphasized. Comparisons and contrasts between verbal and performance areas were also discussed. Various groupings of selected subtests comprising the Wechsler intelligence scales were presented; these groupings enable comparisons that clarify cognitive and personality dimensions. Finally, the importance of cultural factors as well as psychopathology were noted as affecting the results of intelligence testing.

7

Intellectual Functioning
Subtest and Scatter Analysis

This chapter presents a further development of the section of the report that corresponds to the analysis of intellectual functioning. Whereas the previous chapter involved an analysis of the significance of the overall I.Q., grouping analysis, and verbal and performance differences, this chapter focuses on the importance of estimating I.Q. potential as well as on the analysis of particular subtests. In totality, this chapter and the previous one offer a comprehensive means of organizing the section of the report that details cognitive structure and intellectual functioning and of integrating these domains with the subject's personality structure.

ESTIMATING POTENTIAL LEVELS OF INTELLECTUAL FUNCTIONING

A discussion of the results of intelligence testing can be considerably enhanced by including estimates of the subject's potential level of intellectual functioning. An analysis and discussion of the subject's potential broadens the usefulness of the report on several grounds. The reader of the report learns about an exceedingly important yet not readily visible dimension of the person's makeup. This information specifies the strength that is potentially attainable if impediments did not hamper a fuller expression of the patient's capacity. Thus, the subject's potential for growth is suggested by estimating optimal intellectual functioning. The information about this aspect of the person's potential for growth consequently enriches the perception of the individual in both present and future considerations.

An analysis and discussion of the patient's potential intellectual capacity necessarily focuses on the factors that interfere with the expression of this potential. An estimate of intellectual potential can be derived from analyzing the experiences that interfere with intellectual functioning. These impeding experiences may have several sources: for example, the effect of such variables as emotional conflict, disruptive anxiety, organic impairment, cultural conditioning, lack of conventional intellectual stimulation, and decreased opportunities for interplay with the environment that are ordinarily encouraged in economically advantaged settings. Any of these variables can affect the I.Q. score significantly. Whenever they are found to be relevant, it is appropriate to analyze their influence and to discuss these findings as part of the overall report of intellectual and cognitive functioning and I.Q. level. This analysis enables the reader of the report to understand the patient's potential and its inhibition, so that constructive decisions about goals and placement for the person can be made.

From the data collected in the administration of the intelligence test, including the I.Q. scores, subtest scores, and computations involving these scores, there are several ways to estimate the patient's potential. Three techniques for estimating potential or maximal levels of intellectual functioning are presented in the following sections.

Intrasubtest Scatter

An analysis of intrasubtest scatter involves the psychologist in a review of all the responses within a given subtest. The target of concern is the assessment of consistency, gaps in accuracy and judgment, and variation between responses. For example, gaps may appear as a result of failures on items followed by success on more difficult items within the same subtest. In effect, the patient is succeeding at difficult items after failing easier ones. This finding clearly demonstrates that the patient has the capacity to succeed at the failed items if it were not for some handicapping interference.

By analyzing all subtests with attention to gaps between failures and later successes, a clinical determination can be made of how much better the test scores could be if the subject's responses were more consistent. Essentially, this is an assessment of what the patient's level of functioning could be if intellectual ability were expressed and executed more evenly throughout the range in which it is found to apply. The value of the report is amplified if such an estimate of the patient's potential level of intellectual functioning is offered along with an indication of the nature of the interference that is handicapping the patient's expression of abilities.

Interference with intellectual functioning raises the question of determining the variables involved in reducing the patient's potential. Clarification of this point is especially helpful to the referral source. For example, if a subject scores poorly with easy arithmetic concepts and occasionally does better on harder items, one hypothesis would suggest the interfering effect of anxiety and tension on the patient's performance. Similar findings on related subtests, such as the Digit Span or Digit Symbol test, would help to confirm this tension hypothesis. Scrutiny of the projective material obtained in the test battery should also be undertaken to establish the likelihood of substantial anxiety that is interfering with maximal functioning.

Other sources of interference that produce a discrepancy between obtained scores and potential functioning on any given subtest can stem from processes associated with diagnostic conditions. For example, the state of confusion associated with schizophrenia can interfere with the logical presentation of responses. Premorbid strengths may allow occasional success with difficult subtest items following easier ones that are missed. Interference from organic impairment can affect scores in a similar manner. For instance, poor frustration tolerance may take the form of an impulsive rejection of a question, followed by a period of calm in which more difficult items on the same subtest are handled more effectively.

These examples show how an analysis of discrepancies between actual and potential levels of intellectual functioning can be clinically useful. Such analysis also helps in the formulation of diagnostic hypotheses.

Quality of Responses

A second approach to approximating an estimate of maximal intellectual potential is a content analysis of responses to subtest items. For example, although the overall score of a subtest may be low, reflecting poor achievement, responses to parts within the subtest may in contrast show a more sophisticated intelligence than the actual score of the subtest suggests, as revealed through the use of complex language, symbolization, or abstraction. Frequently, this picture of strength within failure may occur because of cultural conditioning or disadvantaged experiences. Such conditioning or experiences can interfere with the subject's expression or persistence so that the quality of response is not translated into scorable successes. In addition, there may be diagnostic reasons for such inconsistency. A subject with passive inclinations, for example, may frequently be unable to complete responses, resulting in a lowered score. Yet the quality of intelligence is readily revealed by analyzing the available partial answers. This analysis would show that if the gaps were to be filled in, potential functioning could be estimated at a higher level than was actually obtained.

The subject who has not been exposed to achievement orientation, but rather has been culturally conditioned to avoid verbal or ambitious striving, will particularly benefit by such an analysis. Thus, the referral source who is in a position to recommend treatment or placement will be able to understand that the nature of the patient's inadequate achievement lies ultimately in external cultural influences and does not reflect innate incapacity.

In consideration of the wide range of subcultures that exist in a pluralistic social framework, this point is especially important. The psychologist's role is not only to report scores, but also to illuminate strengths, potential, latent intelligence, and talent. This kind of analysis is essential if intelligence testing is to be undertaken in a comprehensive and informative manner.

Pro-rated I.Q.

A third, quantitative method of assessing the subject's potential level of intellectual functioning is based on an examination of the range of variability of intersubtest scores. An assumption can be made that the subtest with the highest scaled score indicates a standard level of functioning for all subtests. This is the level at which the individual would be expected to function on all subtests if it were not for the effects of interfering factors. Assigning the highest subtest score to all other subtests, then, shows the presumed highest level at which the patient could function if all interfering influences were removed. It also enables recomputation of the I.Q. score by multiplying this highest subtest score by the number of total subtests, thereby providing a hypothetical numerical estimate. This estimate permits inferences to be drawn about the person's potential in terms of maximal level of functioning.

The pro-rating technique can be utilized to note the difference in obtained subtest scores as they deviate from the hypothetical maximal estimate. This point is essential because it enables the psychologist to perform an analysis of the subject's relative weaknesses in various areas of cognitive functioning and intellectual capacity. These weaknesses can be related to the content of specific subtests on which the patient's functioning is significantly below the suggested optimal level relative to the highest subtest score.

The following section surveys discrepant subtest score analysis as it reflects cognitive and personality problems. Information about the cognitive dimensions tapped by the various subtests on the Wechsler intelligence scales are presented as well.

ANALYSIS OF SUBTEST SCATTER

In the analysis of subtest scatter, two approaches are helpful in uncovering, interpreting, and communicating clinically pertinent findings with respect to intellectual functioning and cognitive strengths and weaknesses. The first approach follows from noting subtests that are more than three scaled score points below the individual, hypothetical, maximal subtest score as revealed by the highest subtest. This approach has particular value in assessing the areas that are relatively underdeveloped in relation to the subject's maximum potential level of functioning. It reveals weaknesses derived from contrasting the patient's hypothetically highest level of functioning with the actual level of functioning.

A second approach is based on computing the mean for all subtest scaled scores and then noting which subtests lie more than three scaled score points above or below this mean. A variant of this method is to compute the mean for the verbal and performance subtests separately and then to assess subtests within each of these two categories as they differ from the respective means by more than three scaled score points. This approach is of particular value in analyzing and discussing the relative strengths and weaknesses in the subject's current intellectual functioning. By focusing on those subtests that fall above the computed mean (or means, if verbal and performance subtests are considered separately), an estimate of maximal functioning can be established.

Performing these kinds of analyses requires an understanding of the cognitive functions necessary for success on each subtest and the sorts of interfering phenomena to which some of the subtests are particularly sensitive.

Verbal Subtests (Wechsler Scales)

INFORMATION   This subtest involves the ability to store, recall, and utilize verbal facts formally learned as well as incidentally absorbed about the environment. The Information subtest also reflects the contributions of such qualities as alertness, remote memory, associative thinking, and range of interest. Success on this subtest often indicates a high achievement orientation and the benefits gained from early educational exposure and intellectual stimulation. A capacity for control of anxiety also is indicated by a high score, since the facts that are learned need to be integrated in an unencumbered fashion into the subject's personal frame of functioning. This integration enables the facts to be remembered and expressed effectively.

DIGIT SPAN.　This subtest is based on rote memory, involving the recall of elements in a current situation. Success in this area reflects a capacity for attention and the ability to control anxiety. Results are not dependent on achievement and overall success in educational training. The difference in performance between reciting digits forward and backward reflects the general success of the subject in controlling anxiety. This difference also reveals the subject's rigidity versus flexibility, because of the need to shift approaches.

When the Arithmetic subtest score is high and the Digit Span score is low, a depressive trend is suggested, since the element of attention associated with Digit Span can be impaired by preoccupations of mood. The focused concentration of Arithmetic may be retained. The past experience associated with the operations of the Arithmetic subtest facilitates this concentration. In contrast, when Digit Span is high and Arithmetic is low, diagnostic implications may involve schizoid or obsessive phenomena, because the suppression of anxiety in the schizoid or obsessive diagnoses aids in the ability to attend within the context of the rote memory task of the Digit Span subtest.

VOCABULARY.　This subtest is often highly correlated with overall intelligence, particularly when the subject has had ample exposure to verbal stimulation. Low scores on Vocabulary generally indicate deficiencies in educational exposure or in motivation to absorb material presented in an educational setting. Low scores may also reflect diagnoses in which repression is pervasive. Tendencies toward concrete functioning with poor abstracting ability may reduce performance on the Vocabulary subtest. Lowered Vocabulary scores may reflect a wide variety of particular cultural influences. The psychologist needs to analyze specific items to determine the level of conceptualization and quality of response. Lowered scores may diagnostically reveal the intrusion of anxiety because of its effects on memory and precision of definition. A high score on this subtest may reflect ambitiousness and educational striving and the existence of a broad range of ideas and conceptual skills, since the higher-level responses require greater facility for abstract thinking.

ARITHMETIC. This subtest reflects the ability to focus one's concentration, thus revealing mental alertness. Success on this task is also related to knowledge of the specific operations involved and the problem-solving orientation that is needed. Subjects who lack the culturally conditioned, problem-solving approach involved in this subtest may have difficulty with it. The Arithmetic subtest is especially sensitive to the intrusion of anxiety. High Arithmetic scores frequently contraindicate diagnoses involving hysterical or other problems with impulsiveness.

COMPREHENSION. This subtest reflects the ability to utilize practical judgment and common-sense reasoning. High scores imply that the subject manages comfortably in everyday circumstances even without formal academic exposure. Appreciation and recall of practical information that is utilized in connection with sound and intuitive judgment also is involved. In addition, the subtest requires sensitivity to a conventional moral understanding as well as awareness of social norms.

It is often helpful to evaluate the Information and Comprehension scores together. A significant difference in scaled scores, as defined by a discrepancy of three or more points, suggests certain diagnostic possibilities. A high Information and low Comprehension configuration suggests obsessional and achievement trends. The opposite configuration suggests the intrusion of anxiety or an action-orientation which curtails formal learning so that lowered information scores result. This intrusion of anxiety also implies that repression is high, so that retention and expression of facts are impeded. Thus, hysterical and psychopathic implications for diagnosis can be suggested by a low Information and a high Comprehension combination.

SIMILARITIES. This subtest involves the capacity for forming concepts, thinking in abstract terms, generalizing, and drawing relationships among different elements in the environment. The subject's level of concept formation — whether concrete, functional, or abstract — is important to note in evaluating intellectual functioning and potential. Whereas the Information and Vocabulary subtests involve specific facts that the subject knows and can express, the Similarities subtest involves relationships between facts, and consequently calls upon a different aspect of intelligence.

Patients with organic impairment frequently cannot produce the appropriate generalization or conceptualization needed for success on this task. The result of such a diagnosis is that the responses on the Similarities subtest occur at more concrete levels, reflecting a loss of conceptualization ability. At times, subjects offer differences instead of similarities between elements, and this may correspond with oppositional elements of the personality.

Thus, the verbal subtests of the intelligence test provide a sample of cognitive and personality variables, including channeling of anxiety, attention, concentration, abstraction, achievement, ability to learn in educational settings, exposure to stimulation, judgment, memory, flexibility, qualitative reasoning, conceptualization, and the inferring of relationships.

Performance Subtests (Wechsler Scales)

PICTURE COMPLETION.   This subtest involves the ability to concentrate and focus on details in order to differentiate between the essential and nonessential aspects of a situation. Conceptual and perceptual skills are required to enable the subject to organize the picture that is presented and to compare it with internal knowledge of the objects involved. Paranoid ideation can interfere with success on this task because of an overconcern with irrelevant details and a focus on the presumed personal motives of the people depicted. Interference also occurs with obsessional personalities because of the tendency to overfocus on numerous details instead of concentrating on the one that is central to the situation. A vigilant stance may also raise scores on this subtest.

PICTURE ARRANGEMENT.   This subtest requires knowledge of interpersonal relating, along with skills of planning, judgment, and perceptual organization. Capacity for insight into the interpersonal and conceptual nature of the situations involved also is necessary along with appreciation of appropriate sequencing. The results of this subtest can be compared to the Comprehension subtest in terms of diagnostic implications. A score configuration in which Picture Arrangement is high and Comprehension is low may indicate a psychopathic tendency. This would follow from the requirement in the Picture Arrangement subtest for rapid insight into interpersonal manipulation, followed by quick motor action. A corresponding lack of ability to discern more subtle moral and social judgments and a penalty for impulsivity can reduce scores on the Comprehension subtest.

BLOCK DESIGN.   This subtest requires the capacity for abstraction and concept formation along with planning, judgment, visual analysis, and visual-motor coordination skills. Patients with diagnoses of schizophrenia, organic impairment, or intense anxiety may have particular difficulty with this subtest because of the attenuation of the abstract attitude that is necessary for success on it. Patients with depression may also have difficulty succeeding on this subtest because of the complex analysis and synthesis required in a timed context.

OBJECT ASSEMBLY. This subtest involves capacities for visual-motor coordination following visual analysis, and the development of an overall conceptualization of familiar objects cued by their constituent parts. Facility with spatial relationships and the ability to quickly grasp a situation and to work effectively also are needed for success. If the results of this subtest are compared with those of Block Design, facility with a concrete approach in this subtest, as opposed to an abstract approach required in Block Design, may be a determining factor. The Object Assembly subtest is sensitive to persons who are highly anxious, depressed, or in the process of depersonalization or fragmentation, because it requires careful but speedy working habits, organization, and visual-motor coordination for success. Patients experiencing the confusion of schizophrenia or organic impairment are often handicapped in the tasks involved in this subtest because of difficulty in recognizing the object to be assembled or difficulty integrating the parts cohesively.

DIGIT SYMBOL. This subtest involves the ability to learn new material readily and efficiently. It requires attention and concentration in a context of speed with visual-motor coordination. Consequently, this subtest is valuable in assessing the ability for new, imitative learning where speed is appropriate. These requirements make the subtest especially useful in assessing organic impairment and clarifying learning disability problems. In evaluating such diagnostic problems, it is useful to note the accuracy with which the symbols are reproduced in order to determine signs of perceptual distortions. For the same reason, reversals should especially be noted. Since speed, accuracy, and the ability to learn new associations are needed for success on this subtest, it is sensitive to depressive phenomena as well as to the confusion associated with schizophrenia.

Thus, the performance subtests of the Wechsler intelligence scales sample a variety of cognitive and personality variables, including memory, planning, abstraction, conceptualization, the need for structure, the ability to learn new material, perception of details, perceptual analysis, visual-motor coordination, and sensitivity to social interactions. Since all of the performance subtests are timed, the subject's functioning in relation to speed can yield indications about a variety of diagnostic possibilities. For example, two broad diagnostic implications include depressive possibilities because of psychomotor slowness and impulsive conditions that cause a variety of errors.

CONCLUSION

This analysis has indicated the cognitive and intellectual skills that can be related to each of the subtests on the Wechsler intelligence scales. The particular capacities associated with each subtest can be utilized to compare and contrast the different subtests in order to indicate the relative strengths and weaknesses of the subject. In addition to the information provided by these comparisons, diagnostic hypotheses can be considered by contrasting subtest scores. Whenever possible, these hypotheses should be related to material derived from other instruments in the test battery, to ensure that they are relevant to and supported by the overall test data.

Underlying much of the person's style of responding to the demands of both verbal and performance items is the manner in which anxiety is mobilized and handled. Characteristic behaviors are utilized to manage the anxiety generated by the pointed nature of the questioning involved in the intelligence scales. Similarly, the quality and nature of the responses to test items are strongly influenced by the anxiety level and characteristic ways in which tensions are handled. As has been pointed out, the results of certain subtests are more readily influenced by anxiety than others.

Chapters 4 through 7 comprise an analytic framework in which to view a cohesive picture of cognitive organization and intellectual functioning. This picture enables the reporting of ego capacities such as integration, synthesis, and realistic, adaptive, creative functioning as well as a narrower determination of the nature of intelligence, I.Q., and analyses of specific cognitive strengths and weaknesses in the individual.

Throughout these chapters, the influence of anxiety and tensions on the functioning of the patient in the test situation, and on intelligence testing in particular, have been underscored. This important variable of anxiety — its presence, nature, and the ways in which it is channeled and managed — plays an essential role in understanding the infrastructure of the personality. Because the effect of anxiety on the personality is so important, an analysis of the nature of anxiety is the next discrete section in the test report. The framework for reporting this analysis is presented in

TABLE 7.1 Analysis of Scatter

- The potential level of intellectual functioning is important to indicate, as is whether obtained results are near or discrepant from potential levels. Interfering factors that may subtract from maximal functioning include emotional conflict, cultural factors, and general anxiety.
- Intratest scatter includes uneven responding *within* a given subtest, enabling assessment of consistency, gaps in accuracy and judgment, and variation of quality between responses within the particular subtest.
- Intertest scatter refers to uneven expression of intelligence *between* subtests, enabling comparisons of development of capacities reflected by differing subtests.
- The potential level of intellectual functioning can be estimated by use of scatter or pro-rating:
  - Crediting gaps where intratest scatter appears enables an estimate of functioning if intelligence were expressed evenly.
  - Pro-rating by using the highest scaled score as a standard for all subtests when intertest scatter is present allows recomputation of the I.Q. to indicate the potential if all areas were developed to the highest capacity.
  - Interpreting the quality of responses can yield an estimate of potential.
- The presence of tension that interferes with attention or concentration may be revealed by impaired performance on the Digit Span and Digit Symbol subtests.
- Confusion of schizophrenia may impair logic and abstraction; organicity may affect the capacity for abstraction; and passivity may cause incomplete responses.

the following chapter. Tables 7.1 and 7.2 present a summary of the main features of scatter and subtest analysis.

SUMMARY

In the previous two chapters, the analysis and reporting of intelligence testing in the psychodiagnostic report have been considered. The need to indicate the range in which the I.Q. falls, its percentile equivalent, and an estimate of the potential, optimal level of functioning in addition to the I.Q. score itself was discussed. In addition, methods for analyzing and reporting discrepancies between verbal and performance areas of intellectual functioning were presented. Clusters of subtests were organized in order to compare these groupings with each other. The intellectual and cognitive capacities of each subtest were identified and related to diagnostic hypotheses associated with particular findings.

TABLE 7.2   Clinical Implications of Subtests

VERBAL

Information. Reflects an achievement orientation, memory, and control of anxiety; educational exposure and/or cultural (home) emphasis on factual circumstances.

Digit Span. Involves the capacity for attention, ability to control anxiety, and short-term memory. High Arithmetic/low Digit Span suggests depressive trend; low Arithmetic/high Digit Span suggests a schizoid or obsessive tendency.

Vocabulary. Correlates well with overall I.Q.; reflects verbal processing, absorption, and/or reading habits at academic or cultural levels. Low scores may indicate repression.

Arithmetic. Relates to issues of focus, concentration, and memory. High Arithmetic may contraindicate hysteria or impulse problems.

Comprehension. Involves judgment, common sense, practical intelligence, and moral sensitivity. High Information/low Comprehension suggests obsessional trends; low Information/high Comprehension suggests the intrusion of anxiety and the presence of repression, or an action-orientation, and may suggest hysteric or psychopathic implications.

Similarities. Indicates conceptional ability, verbal abstraction, and the ability to draw relationships. May be impaired when organicity is present.

PERFORMANCE

Picture Completion. Highlights the ability to evaluate detail and to discriminate the essential from the inessential. Lower scores may result from paranoid ideation (overemphasis on minor detail; overfocus on inessentials that are missing) or obsessional trends (overfocus on numerous but irrelevant details, causing salient ones to be overlooked). Higher scores may reflect vigilance.

Picture Arrangement. Indicates the grasp of social nuances, sequencing, planning, judgment, and perceptual and conceptual integration.

Block Design. Reveals the capacity for abstraction, concept formation, spatial visualization, analysis and synthesis, planning, and judgment. Diagnoses of schizophrenia, organicity, anxiety states, or depression often correlate with lower scores.

Object Assembly. Reflects perceptual organization, part-whole integration, and visual-motor coordination. May be impaired by anxiety, depression, depersonalization, or the confusion of schizophrenia or organicity.

Digit Symbol. Involves visual-motor coordination, the ability for efficient new learning, attention, concentration, and short-term memory in a speed context. May be affected by organic impairment, depressive phenomena, and the confusion of schizophrenia.

8

The Nature of Anxiety

This section of the psychological report concerns the nature of anxiety, its quality and quantity in the personality, and how it is experienced and channeled. The logic of considering at this point the nature and role of anxiety follows from previous discussions of cognitive and intellectual functioning and the impairments in such functioning that can occur through the effects of anxiety. These impairments are significant ways in which the presence of anxiety becomes pathologically manifest in the individual's functioning. Exploring these phenomena leads to deeper levels of analysis related to the causes of the patient's anxiety and to the underlying conflicts that generate tension.

ANXIETY AS THE CENTRAL FOCUS IN THE REPORT

For several reasons, anxiety plays a central role in the functioning of the personality. It not only can cause cognitive and intellectual impairments, but it also exerts a major influence in the development of behavioral and somatic disturbances. Just as anxiety impedes smooth cognitive and intellectual functioning, it also interferes with efforts to utilize inner personality resources. The presence of anxiety and its effects reduce the patient's ability to constructively manage challenges, problems, and opportunities.

In addition, the manifestations of anxiety can signal the presence of underlying conflict and pathological processes. Consequently, a thorough analysis of anxiety leads to the uncovering of deeper conflicts and disturbances within the personality, the essential factors that are central in the development of the patient's symptoms and discomfort.

Pathological processes that are revealed by analyzing and reporting the details of anxiety comprise symptoms, their mechanisms, and the accompanying personal anguish of the patient. Psychiatrists, psychologists, therapists, teachers, and administrators who refer patients for psychological testing benefit from indications in the report that clarify the nature of the subject's discomforts. This is because the pain of the patient's anguish and suffering is often overlooked, but the distressing nature of this tension may be the patient's key motivational factor in seeking and sustaining treatment.

WHAT DOES THE TERM ANXIETY MEAN?

Anxiety derives from the Greek word *agon* from which such words as *anguish* and *agony* are clearly derived. The Greek term described a sport contest and, in particular, the struggle between antagonists in such contests. The Greek *agon* also relates to the German word *Angst,* used in modern times by Kierkegaard and Nietzche, for example, to describe a painful feeling of terror.

In Kierkegaard's existential focus, subjective feelings of anguish encapsulated by the word *Angst* are related to man's reaction to facing the unknown with regard to his purpose and future in the vast, mysterious universe. Freud, as well, utilized the word *Angst* in his effort to communicate the profoundly disturbing but unidentifiable suffering of the neurotic patients he treated.

Freud ascribed a central role to anxiety in the pathology he studied, and few subsequent personality theorists fail to do the same in their studies of the genesis and meaning of psychopathology. The meaningfulness of Freud's observations about the anguish of people in conflict also has had a striking effect at the popular level. For instance, the phrase *age of anxiety* as an accepted characterization of this turbulent century is an outgrowth of his impact.

To appreciate the place of anxiety in the psychodiagnostic report, this brief historical perspective suggests the central significance and seriousness connected to personal suffering in the subjective experience of the patient. Thus, one of the first issues of concern in reporting about the patient's anxiety is to assess and indicate the extent to which it disturbs the patient.

THE PATIENT'S EXPERIENCE OF ANXIETY

Whether or not the person is aware of experiencing anxiety, the effects of tension are always affecting the person's behavior. Anxiety's influences may first appear in the person's reactions to its disrupting and debilitating effects. In such instances, the experience of anxiety may interfere with the patient's efforts to marshal cognitive and intellectual strengths. Thus, it is important to report the disruptive, interfering effects of anxiety when they are present.

Failure to perform or reduced capacities for functioning in cognitive and intellectual areas that result from the interference of poorly managed anxiety also are significant to analyze and report, along with the impact of such a reduction in competence on the patient's tension and subjective distress. In this connection, the patient's ability to handle frustrating circumstances is of considerable interest.

Anxiety that impedes performance and the additional stress that failure brings about can evoke a variety of reactions. For example, the patient may withdraw from the task or become silent, uncooperative, or mute. Alternatively, the patient may persist at the task but become obviously discouraged or depressed. Another reaction to anxiety may be to focus on areas of competence that compensate for reduced functioning in other areas. The test, the purpose for testing, the tester, or even the referring individual or agency may be criticized by the patient in an attempt to restore a sense of personal value in the face of anxiety.

This partial survey of examples of maladaptive approaches to handling stress and failure reflects personality characteristics which are useful to report because they can be related to maladaptive approaches in the patient's overall functioning. These characteristic reactions reveal how the person is likely to behave when experiencing the distress and anxiety that accompanies loss of security. Indicating the individual's characteristic handling of anxiety-induced failure helps to explain personality functioning associated with self-defeating patterns and the inability to function at optimal levels.

Findings that are reported with regard to the interfering effects of anxiety suggest a problem area which is of concern to those utilizing the report. This problem area involves the patient's difficulty in handling, regulating, and managing anxiety that occurs in response to the challenges of living. Difficulty in managing anxiety can have much to do with the problem behavior or experience that brought the patient for evaluation. For example, a strain in the patient's capacity for constructively regulating and managing anxiety may involve pathological reactions that also contribute to problems of depression, withdrawal, inhibition of effort, school failure, job loss, the development of aggressive outbursts, dependent clinging behavior, or passivity.

There are several other aspects of the role and nature of anxiety that are necessary to analyze and report, such as the ways in which anxiety can be experienced and expressed. These significant aspects of personality functioning are necessary to include in a coherent study of the person being examined through psychological testing.

THE CENTRAL ROLE OF ANXIETY IN THE PSYCHODIAGNOSTIC EVALUATION

An extremely complex and shifting network of factors occurs in the process of experiencing the discomfort of anxiety. When the problem finally surfaces and begins to cause intense concern and confusion, those involved in the referral process, from the patient to the referring source and even the testing psychologist, invariably become enmeshed in a sense of urgency, desperation, and duress to produce the report. This flurry of expectation and activity will not solve the problem, but instead can become something of a problem in its own right.

The psychologist needs to realize that almost everyone connected with the patient is tense and unclear about the patient's difficulties. In order to bring clarity to the abundance of tension and confusion that accompanies the referral process, the psychologist must try to pinpoint the nature of the subject's anxiety without becoming caught up in it.

Anxiety is of central importance because it can impair work, relationships, and other vital pursuits. There are three general ways in which anxiety can be operative in bringing the conflicted or disturbed person to the attention of helping professionals. In order for an analysis of anxiety to take place, the following possibilities must be evaluated:

- Is the anxiety conciously experienced?
- Is the anxiety acted-out?
- Is the anxiety somatized?

Is the Anxiety Consciously Experienced?

The question of whether anxiety is consciously experienced concerns the patient's reaction to his or her own behavior, personality, and character traits. Is the patient's reaction one of acceptance, or are the traits viewed as being foreign? When the patient perceives such behavior or traits in an accepting or benign fashion, they are considered to be ego-syntonic, and no particular anxiety is experienced. On the other hand, when the person experiences internal qualities as foreign or unusual, they are considered to be ego-alien or ego-dystonic. The ego-alien nature of the behavior or functioning generates discomfort and leads to varying degrees of anxiety.

Within the report, it is helpful for the psychologist to communicate the extent to which the patient is experiencing anxiety, if at all. If the patient is indeed experiencing anxiety, it is extremely useful to specify the features in the person's functioning that are instrumental to the anxiety. This means that the patient experiences the symptoms as distressing and recognizes them to be problems.

A specific issue that becomes crystallized in focusing on anxiety involves relating the nature of the patient's anxiety to latent personality conflicts. Such latent personality issues include conflicts between control and impulse and how such conflict affects the intactness of the person's ego. Samples of responses reflecting personality elements of anxiety, impulse, and control appear throughout the test data. In this section of the report, the psychologist organizes these elements in the form of specific statements about the patient's state of anxiety. For example, if abundant anxiety indicators appear in the projective test data, the psychologist needs to indicate that the patient experiences anxiety.

Along with this analysis of the patient's experience of anxiety, the psychologist ties in information concerning the nature of the patient's response to such anxiety by indicating how it is handled. It is useful to discuss how the anxiety is managed in terms of whether it is experienced passively, stimulates fantasy, or leads to some sort of activity. On the other hand, some patients may be terrified about their needs and therefore become inhibited, socially inconspicuous, isolated, or withdrawn. Thus, the patient who consciously experiences anxiety may be driven toward aggressive activity, or a passive, paralyzed response may appear as another possible reaction.

Further possibilities regarding the handling of consciously experienced anxiety include a range of phobic responses which develop in an effort to avoid the distressing experience of the anxiety. If the anxiety cannot be channeled, a continuing, intense, but nonspecific sense of panic may develop. Periods of diffusely experienced anxiety may be interrupted by the utilization of obsessional ideation or ritual-like activities. The examples offered by the psychologist with respect to the patient's handling of anxiety suggest diagnostic possibilities.

Diagnostic Implications with Experienced Anxiety.   In writing this section in a way that presents diagnostic implications, the psychologist may be able to distinguish between characterological and neurotic problems. When the behavior is ego-syntonic, that is, when the patient's problematic behavior does not cause personal distress, the diagnostic impression of a character disorder can be entertained. On the other hand, when the problematic behavior is ego-alien, the resulting intense anxiety is consistent with a diagnosis within the neurotic range. When anxiety develops out of fears related to loss of ego-intactness, this ego-alien experience can suggest the possibility of an emerging psychotic fragmentation.

The nature of the patient's anxiety, the mechanisms used to handle it, and the alien or syntonic behaviors and traits linked to anxiety can all play a part in developing diagnostic impressions. As the vicissitudes of anxiety are detailed in the report, a certain diagnostic range is implied. Thus, the stage is set for the logical next step of pursuing a more extensive analysis of the patient's basic underlying conflicts.

Is the Anxiety Acted-Out?

The issue of acting-out is crucial to understanding any problem behavior because of the many subtle forms it may take, its relationship to underlying conflict, and its widely prevalent use as a mode of handling anxiety. The patient who acts-out usually does not consciously experience anxiety, primarily because the action is a substitute for the anxiety and accompanying frustration that cannot be tolerated.

Acting-out is usually defined as the behavioral substitute for a conflict; that is, a patient with problem behavior has not achieved insight with respect to the underlying conflict and therefore is unable to control, contain, or endure the frustration generated by it. Such a patient, then, is not likely to be in a position to begin to focus on or deal with the conflicts, since the emergence into conscious thought of any aspect of the conflict would evoke anxiety resulting in an immediate flight into action. Instead of *thinking* about the problem, the patient engages in *doing* or behaving in order to escape from anxiety.

The acting-out behavior may have qualities and characteristics that are important to assess and report. The acting-out may, for example, serve to eliminate or avoid anxiety, in which case the patient may characteristically be an acting-out type of person. Such a person is largely action-oriented, nonreflective, and unable to tolerate frustration in any form. On the other hand, acting-out behavior may only serve to reduce anxiety, never really eliminating it or allowing the patient to avoid it completely. In such an instance, additional means of handling the anxiety may be utilized, with acting-out playing a highly significant but not exclusive role.

When the anxiety is only partially reduced, what remains is a somewhat anesthetized form of the tension. The anxiety can lead, for example, to the appearance of obsessional thoughts or compulsive acts that share a good deal with acting-out. Under such circumstances, signal anxiety—the warning tinge of manifest anxiety that indicates a potential danger—can be tolerated, but it quickly evokes a sequence of thoughts or actions that restricts the spread and increase in intensity of the anxiety.

As is characteristic of acting-out, the sequence of thoughts and behaviors described in this example has continuity with the nature of the anxiety and underlying conflict being avoided. This continuity may be symbolically revealed by scrutinizing features of the acting-out sequence. Obsessional thoughts concerned with the prevention of danger may reflect the strenuous avoidance of anxiety associated with aggressive urges. Compulsive masturbation as a form of acting-out may address several issues, among them, sexual anxiety, the neutralization of anger, and the calming of feelings of rejection, as well as turning to the self for solace. Such compulsive behavior is also compensatory in nature and, as such, can eliminate the potential development of more intense anxiety regarding interpersonal relations.

Thus, the psychologist can report findings about the underlying nature of the patient's anxiety. Also important to report are the efforts undertaken to avoid experiencing the anxiety; the extent to which acting-out serves this purpose; the need, if any, for other methods to handle the anxiety; and the degree to which anxiety is experienced as distressing, as opposed to the extent to which the patient manages to avoid it.

Avoidance of Anxiety. The avoidance of anxiety, which can be accomplished by phobic symptoms, passivity, depression, and so forth, is also the hallmark of acting-out. Acting-out interferes with the patient's ability to learn and master intellectual and cognitive skills since the acting-out approach does not allow for reflection during periods when anxiety and frustration occur. Consequently, learning cannot take place in situations that trigger discomfort. The corresponding failure to benefit from experience and the difficulty with sustaining thought in tasks requiring reflection and organization are revealed by a variety of test indicators. For example, impairment may be seen in intelligence test items that require sustained reflective functioning and the application of past learning. Performance items are grasped more effectively because these tasks frequently benefit from such a patient's proclivity for action. Extremely impulsive, continuously quick, unreflective responses characterize the acting-out type of person. These characteristics may appear in the response approach as well as in the content of projective stories and graphic material. Throughout the projective material, indicators of action orientation, immaturity, limited frustration tolerance, and minimal capacity to contain or regulate anxiety suggest an acting-out profile.

In reporting findings of this sort, the psychologist can treat the issue of acting-out as the patient's means of avoiding discomfort from anxiety or frustration. The action orientation can be related to the patient's inappropriate handling of cognitive and intellectual problems. It is important to detail the extent to which acting-out exists for the patient. Accordingly, the extent of the acting-out style needs to be determined and explained. Attention should be drawn to the areas within the personality where anxiety can be tolerated. Clearly, therapeutic and educational efforts would be greatly enhanced by an analysis of areas in which the person is more likely to tolerate anxiety and how these differ from areas immediately connected to acting-out. The extent to which the patient displays an understanding of and appreciation for the consequences of behavior is also extremely helpful to evaluate and can be an important diagnostic indicator.

Diagnostic Implications with Anxiety Acted-Out. When an acting-out approach appears along with responses on the projective material that reflect limited considerations of conscience, underdeveloped superego features, opportunism, and magical wishing, a characterological disorder such as psychopathic personality may be considered. Responses that indicate externalization of responsibility for problematic behavior and a limited capacity to experience discomfort with one's behavior suggest a similar diagnostic implication. For example, stories in which destructive aggression is rationalized as being a fair response to provocation reflect externalization consistent with a characterological approach in which there is limited anxiety about the aggressive behavior or its effect on others.

Even when the patient's anxiety is not acted-out, but rather is bound within character traits, a diagnosis in the character disorder range is likely. For example, an aloof schizoid person who is forced to participate in a social situation may experience intense anxiety or even intense anger if it were not for the use of schizoid traits, such as remoteness and aloofness. When a schizoid person is forced to participate in the test situation, only minimal responses are offered. When passive-aggressive persons are required to perform, they avoid the experience of anxiety by the use of negativism, hostile withholding, and delayed responses to test requirements. Thus, the person with a character disorder may not be someone who acts-out, but nevertheless, the person's behavior is largely ego-syntonic and there is little ability to sustain the experience of anxiety or to maintain tolerance for frustration.

Diagnostically, the largely ego-syntonic acceptance of destructive or socially inappropriate behavior may sometimes serve as a facade for an underlying psychotic process. The anxiety that is warded off through acting-out prevents interpersonal involvement that could threaten an underlying psychotic vulnerability in the patient.

Another important diagnostic consideration concerns the patient who, although experiencing some anxiety, is inclined to view his or her own contributions to personal difficulties in largely ego-syntonic terms and is apparently in the character disorder range. The patient's typical characterological style may no longer enable anxiety to be warded off through the shifting of responsibility to others. As this characterological method of shifting responsibility fails, anxiety is experienced which may motivate the individual to seek treatment. The patient may then be referred for psychological testing to help evaluate the significance of the anxiety.

Is the Anxiety Somatized?

One of the most distressing ways in which patients attempt to manage anxiety without directly experiencing it involves channeling it to aspects of their own body. Parts of the body, internal organs, and psychological functioning become the transformation equivalents of this anxiety. Somatizers are variably referred to as persons with psychophysiological, psychosomatic, or conversion symptoms.

The somatizer attempts to manage anxiety by binding it or containing it with the aid of physical processes. This sort of person should be distinguished from the hypochondriacal patient who is preoccupied with thoughts about bodily functions, fantasied impairments, and overall ruminations frequently without actual organic involvement. Hypochondriacal patients actually experience substantial anxiety and do not bind it somatically. Instead, such patients refocus anxiety from psychological conflicts to bodily concerns. It is important for the psychologist to make clear which of these two possibilities is under consideration: physical complaints representing conversion of anxiety as opposed to displacement of anxiety to bodily preoccupations. The protocols of each have responses pertaining to illness, organs, and bodily phenomena, but with associations to different feelings and experiences.

In the protocol of hypochondriacal patients, manifestations of anxiety are consistent with the subject's continual tensions about possible bodily problems that relate to needs for attention, dependency, and passivity. On the other hand, the protocol of the somatizer is likely to contain indicators associated with underlying problems of aggression or sexuality, since anxiety about these feelings is largely somatized.

Acting-In. The somatizer is a person who, like the acting-out person, cannot easily tolerate frustrations and the direct experience of the distress of anxiety. Because of a difference in certain personality formations, the somatizer will "act-in" instead of acting-out in behavior. The person who acts-out engages in behavior to avoid experiencing anxiety; the person who acts-in binds the anxiety in bodily expression to avoid experiencing it directly. A patient who utilizes acting-in as a mode of handling anxiety often intensifies the discomfort it causes because of the amount of tension that becomes generated by the bodily impairment. Thus, the experience of anxiety may be intense, but it has shifted away from its troublesome source to a presumably more easily regulated target. The patient may, therefore, derive false comfort, subliminal though it may be, that the difficulties are under some personal control.

In the report it is beneficial to indicate when anxiety about the body is utilized in a way that shifts the target of disturbance. It is of particular benefit to be able to analyze and report the actual internal conflict or personality disturbance that the patient is seeking to manage through physical illness. The main point concerns the importance of relating the nature of the somatizing acting-in to the typical specific emotion such as anger or its derivative behavior of aggression and hostility or, in some cases, sexuality.

Diagnostic Implications with Anxiety Somatized.   The somatizer may reflect a wide variety of diagnostic possibilities. The acting-in characteristic of the somatizer may appear in the context of virtually any type of personality—neurotic, characterologically disordered, or psychotic. The first level of reporting is to discuss the finding of somatization as a means for handling anxiety.

At a deeper level of reporting, an indication of the specific diagnostic type of person with a somatizing problem may be attempted. It is also desirable to determine whether the diagnosis is in the neurotic, characterological, or psychotic range.

A difficult diagnostic problem that frequently requires the psychologist's expertise is to differentiate between hysterical conversion symptoms and somatization. A useful way to approach this problem is to bear in mind that conversion symptoms, which may appear similar to somatization symptoms, are more likely to be found in material reflecting a hysterical diagnosis. Material supporting the hysterical diagnosis may include, for example, an absence of inordinate detail responses on the inkblots, the "smile of denial" as well as an absence of pupils on the figure drawings, projective stories demonstrating magical thinking, and high Comprehension with low Information scores on the Wechsler scales.

Among some schizophrenic persons, hysterical conversion symptoms also appear and delusional qualities characterizing these symptoms help to establish the diagnosis. The somatic or conversion symptoms in psychotic or schizophrenic persons are generally associated with problems having to do with the vulnerability of the individual's intactness and possible fragmentation of the ego. In the case of a hysterical diagnosis, on the other hand, the conversion symptoms are quite likely to represent an effort to manage anxiety stemming from underlying, sexual pleasure conflicts. In this respect, the hysterical manifestations are also markedly different from the symptoms of somatizers, which are more likely to stem from underlying aggressive problems.

Thus, it is reasonably clear that the differential diagnoses that are considered in connection with the presence of bodily complaints can be analyzed effectively by focusing on the personality context in which the symptoms are embedded.

SOURCES OF ANXIETY IN THE PERSONALITY

As can be seen from the previous discussion, the mobilizing and management of anxiety can assume several forms. For example, individuals readily experience anxiety when challenged with novel circumstances such as the testing situation. The patient can be observed to handle this source of tension by any number of approaches, including dedicated efforts at problem solving, impulsive acting-out, nonreflective responding, avoidance and withdrawal, criticism of the test requirements, or complaints about feeling ill.

Thus, the anxiety typically mobilized in new situations can be analyzed in the context of the patient's handling of the demands of the testing situation. This handling of anxiety provides valuable information for the test report because it reflects the person's characteristic response and is a sample of the patient's typical reaction to stress outside of the testing situation.

At a deeper level, conflict between different aspects of personality, doubts about self-esteem, difficulties in dealing with sexual and aggressive impulses, and concern about the stability and integrity of the personality are underlying sources of anxiety that need further exploration.

It is apparent that the phenomenon of anxiety is central both in the individual's functioning and in the overall personality assessment. The person's management of anxiety relates to the operation of cognitive controls, the capacity for achieving potential levels of intellectual functioning, symptom formation, and subjective distress. For these reasons, a discussion of the manifestations of anxiety and anxiety-related behaviors in the psychodiagnostic report is important.

Throughout this chapter, numerous references have been made to the importance of ascertaining the source of the anxiety. It has also been noted that a careful analysis of anxiety in the functioning of the personality and as reflected in test responses will enable analysis of the person's problems at a deeper level. At this more basic level, there can be a focus on core conflicts and difficulties that generate tensions. This core level of disturbance will be discussed in the next two chapters and, in this regard, the interplay between impulses and controlling mechanisms will be analyzed. Table 8.1 presents some of the significant themes in the consideration of anxiety in the personality.

TABLE 8.1   Reporting of Anxiety in the Personality

Management of anxiety in personality functioning affects:
- operation of cognitive controls
- achievement of potential levels of intellectual functioning
- symptom formation
- subjective distress

A report should indicate how anxiety is manifested in the individual's functioning:
- does the anxiety disturb the patient?
- does the anxiety generate failure in performance?
- does the anxiety reduce capacity to deal with frustration?

If anxiety impedes performance, then the patient may show self-defeating behavior, such as:
- withdrawing from tasks
- becoming noncommunicative or uncooperative
- becoming discouraged or depressed
- engaging in impulsive behavior

If anxiety is not regulated or managed adaptively, then problems may emerge that include:
- depression, withdrawal, or inhibition of effort
- school failure or job loss
- irritability and aggression
- passivity or dependency

Is the anxiety consciously experienced, acted-out, or somatized?
- if consciously experienced, what is the subjective level of distress?
- does the anxiety generate fantasy, reinforce passivity, or stimulate activity?
- Are phobias or panic states developed?
- Are obsessions developed to generalized anxiety feelings?

A report should describe how anxiety affects the conflict between impulse and control. For example
- if anxiety is acted-out, the resulting behavior may be ego-syntonic
- the person may find it difficult to tolerate frustration even though the experience of anxiety is reduced
- acting-out also reduces attention span and, therefore, learning capacity

- when impulsivity increases, and overall action orientation in the subject is seen

A diagnosis of psychopathic personality can be made if qualities of immaturity, underdeveloped superego, and magical thinking are prominent. Other character diagnoses that avoid anxiety include schizoid and passive-aggressive types:

- schizoid individuals offer few responses
- passive-aggressive persons express negativism and withholding

When anxiety is somatized:

- actual conversion of psychosomatic symptoms may appear as acting-in
- acting-in frequently relates to anger, hostility, or sexuality
- conversion symptoms relate to a hysterical diagnosis

The prevalence of ego-syntonic (comfortable) traits suggests a characterological diagnosis (personality disorder). In contrast, the presence of ego-alien (uncomfortable) symptoms and anxiety experienced in relation to such symptoms suggests a diagnosis in the neurotic range.

SUMMARY

The role of anxiety in personality functioning was considered in this chapter from the point of view of the patient's experience of distress, interference with cognitive and intellectual abilities, and the ways in which anxiety is managed. Several characteristic methods of handling anxiety were discussed and related to diagnostic states. The conscious experience of anxiety, acting-out, and somatization were considered as major means of coping with anxiety.

9

Impulse Versus Control
The Vicissitudes of Impulse

Clarifying the source of anxiety in the patient's personality involves consideration of the patient's underlying conflicts. In order to illuminate the fundamental conflicts within the personality, it is necessary to examine the impulses that strive for expression along with the efforts toward control that both oppose and attempt to manage such expression. This dynamic opposition amounts to an ongoing but variable struggle that is reflected in the presence, manifestations, and nature of the patient's anxiety. Thus, in the psychodiagnostic report, it is logical to have a section dealing with impulses versus control follow the section that analyzes anxiety.

THE INTERPLAY BETWEEN IMPULSES AND CONTROLS

In individuals with adaptive personality functioning, a natural and relatively comfortable fluctuation occurs in the interplay between impulse and control factors. This interplay of impulse and control is generally flexible and smooth, so that a state of equilibrium is more or less maintained in spite of the shifts that occur either toward impulse or control. As positive functioning diminishes, the interplay between impulse and control becomes more erratic or more rigid and restricted. Either reduced stability or stereotyped patterns may emerge. Inflexible control or loss of control may occur, and an unsettled or distressed feeling may arise as a subjectively uncomfortable level of tension develops.

Inappropriate and maladaptive behavior may follow the experience of anxiety that is generated by awkward or uncontrollable shifts in the interaction of impulse and control. In a similar manner, inappropriate behavior may be immediately initiated and engaged in to prevent the development of tension that would occur were impulses not transformed into action. When a flexible balance between impulse and control cannot be maintained, rigid patterns of personality functioning develop that are poorly suited to circumstances. Such rigid and poorly adaptive modes of dealing with the conflict that is emerging between impulse and control may take two forms. There may be an overemphasis on controlling mechanisms of the personality, or there may be an overemphasis on the impulses. Thus, the departure from a flexible, adaptive interplay between impulses and controls can result in personality styles that are characteristically control or impulse dominated.

DIMENSIONS IN THE ANALYSIS OF IMPULSES AND CONTROLS

The analysis of impulse versus control may proceed on several levels or dimensions. One level focuses on the nature of the interplay between the two forces, such as its equilibrium, lability, variability, flexibility, rigidity, adaptiveness, and stability. Another level regards the maturity or immaturity inherent in the interplay of these impulse and control forces. The maturational level of the individual correlates with various adaptive behaviors. These behaviors can optimally include adaptive reliance on verbal expression or appropriate inhibition of impulses. Another level in the analysis of impulse versus control involves the delineation of the relative and persisting dominance of one aspect of the interplay over the other, as in the discussion of dominance of impulses over controlling mechanisms or of controls over impulses. The nature of personality functioning and pathology is clarified as being either impulse dominated or tending toward an overemphasis on control in the personality.

The psychologist can focus on the individual who is being tested in terms of impulse and control features in personality functioning. The presence of an impulse control imbalance and the anticipation of such an imbalance suggests anxiety and symptom formation related to imbalance. Analyzing the nature of the impulse control disequilibrium that is involved in the genesis of anxiety and corresponding symptom formation also reveals diagnostic implications inherent in the underlying conflict.

Just as the individual being evaluated can be considered from the point of view of the interplay between impulse and control features, much of the test data can be similarly analyzed. From a broad perspective, the test data can be grouped into the responses that correlate with impulse features of the personality and those associated with control features.

The balance that is strived for as well as the balance that is achieved by the patient in the struggle between impulses and controlling mechanisms define essential qualities of the patient's personality, social and behavioral functioning. Consequently, an important dimension of the person's basic psychological structure relates to this issue of impulse versus control and also reflects its vicissitudes. The individual's behavioral disposition is also based on the nature of the relationship between impulse and control. Behavioral disposition, or the operation of a person's typical behavioral pattern, is particularly significant because it is invariably linked to the patient's presenting problem or to the behaviors and events that necessitated the testing referral.

It will be helpful at this point to describe more specifically the impulse side of the personality and associated protocol findings. Control aspects of the personality are presented in the next chapter. In the following section, definitional properties of impulses are considered along with their influence on personality functioning. These issues bear directly on the psychologist's decision about how to analyze the nature of impulses.

THE NATURE OF IMPULSES

The psychologist's work is facilitated in the process of data analysis when the complex qualities of impulses are appreciated. This gives the psychologist a lead in evaluating the protocol for response samples that reveal the activity of impulses in the personality. Impulses are the internal inclinations or needs that the subject feels as urgent and striving for expression. In the most fundamental sense, impulses are energized emotions as well as amorphous arousal phenomena of the need system. In the psychodynamic framework, more specifically, the energized emotions usually considered in the impulse category are anger, aggression, hostility, and pleasure responses, such as sexuality. In psychoanalytic theory, these impulses are considered to be derivative id expressions.

There are generally two conditions that create pathological manifestations with respect to the expression of impulses. The first condition of a maladaptive expression of impulse exists when acting-out occurs. In this condition there is a spilling over of impulse. The second condition of the maladaptive management of impulse exists when overcontrol distorts or impairs expression of these impulses. Thus, in order to clarify the contribution of impulses to psychopathology, problems related to the acting-out as well as to the overcontrol of impulses must be considered.

IMPULSE AND ACTION ORIENTATION

It is instructive to analyze the action-oriented person from the impulse perspective because this dyscontrolled disposition involves a range of psychological dimensions that are adversely affected. For example, persons who are clearly or characteristically impulse-laden are likely to reveal impairment in judgment and questionable frustration tolerance. In addition, the thinking and reality testing of impulse-laden persons are likely to be infiltrated with labile fantasy material. These kinds of findings reflect the urgency in the personality of a particular impulse in question, especially with respect to its effect on the subject's functioning. The propensity toward impulse expression over control becomes significant only when the impulse in question is consistently translated by the subject into action orientation.

A substantially different circumstance occurs when impulses are reflected throughout the protocol but the action orientation is not represented. In such an instance, a conflict between impulse and control is apparent, but because of the presence of significant control mechanisms in personality functioning, the impairments associated with an acting-out proclivity do not obtain. The psychologist must report the conflict between impulse and control as well as the presence of controls that contraindicate acting-out despite the presence of strong impulse.

When substantial signs of impulses are seen in the test data but action orientation is not indicated, the psychologist needs to evaluate the presumed internal struggle that exists between these rather strong impulses and controls. By clarifying the pressure of the conflict, the psychologist's discussion reveals important sources of anxiety. Another source of anxiety is generated from the nature of the impulses and controls that are in conflict. For example, hostility, confused psychosexual identity, or a problematic fragility of control may emerge as specific sources of anxiety following analysis of the impulses and controls in conflict.

When the indicators of impulse in the test protocol are abundant and signs of an action orientation are also present, an acting-out probability is high. In such cases, the presence and experience of anxiety is likely to be diminished although such reduced anxiety occurs as a result of a pathological process. As discussed in the previous chapter, acting-out the impulse is a substitute for tolerating the anxiety that would be stimulated by not acting-out. A major problem for the psychologist in the acting-out circumstance is to define the anxiety that is avoided through the acting-out condition.

There are frequent occasions when the referral source, whether a school counselor, psychiatrist, or therapist, is perplexed because of the striking absence of anxiety in the presence of acting-out problem behavior. The psychologist therefore performs a valuable function in analyzing and communicating to the referral source the nature and meaning of both the patient's acting-out and the anxiety that is being avoided.

IMPULSE AND COGNITION

Unlike the acting-out patient, other implications exist with the individual whose controls, although still not sufficient, are greater than those of the acting-out person. In such cases, acting-out is reduced, but important personality functions nevertheless are adversely affected. Thus, urgent impulses appear and features of control are present but not secure enough to handle and regulate these impulses adequately. In such instances of urgency, the impulses may intrude into and affect the individual's cognitive and intellectual functioning. This impulse intrusion can disturb and interfere with thinking, judgment, and perception. Thus, the nature of the impulse in question can color the thinking process, reduce the efficiency of judgment, and impair effective intellectual operation. The impulse involved can frequently be determined by analyzing manifestations of its intrusions into these functions as they are reflected in the test protocol. For example, if responses to the projective material reveal fighting, belligerence, or arguing, it is likely that distortions of thinking, judgment, or perception reflect the operation of the impulse of anger.

In addition, anxiety, tension, and agitation usually accompany the state in which there are urgent impulses that are not acted-out and in which comfortable, smoothly working controls are not reliably available. These tension reactions, developing out of a threat that a frightening and therefore unwanted impulse will overtly emerge, can produce additional impediments to the use of efficient thinking and judgment. In such instances, capacities for memory and perceptual functioning also can lose precision.

When controls are not secure, the expression of impulses can frequently influence the behavior of the individual and disrupt cognitive and intellectual functioning. Therefore, a valuable interpretive aid for the psychologist is to determine the specific vicissitudes of the various sorts of impulses, which now can be delineated and defined.

TYPES OF IMPULSES

Anger

Anger is part of a sequence of events including feeling, thoughts, fantasies, and behavior. It may be helpful to define *anger* as the emotion, *hostility* as the main ingredient of fantasy and rumination, and *aggression* as the behavior. When the psychologist is analyzing the anger impulse, it is important to indicate the emotion of anger as an impulse vying for expression. An analysis of the nature of the anger will include whether it appears as an emotion; whether it is translated into hostility toward an object which is more or less displaced in fantasy, rumination, or indirect behavior; or whether the sequence forgoes, to a large extent, this rumination, and instead leaps directly into aggressive, impulsive behavior.

Thus, in connection with anger a continuum between feeling the emotion and overt behavioral action can be envisioned, with a range of events along the continuum which represents how anger may be expressed. First, the emotion of anger can be experienced by the person. This experience may be followed by rumination and fantasy. The sequence can build to covert hostile verbal expressions such as sarcasm and insults. This sequence of the vicissitudes of anger may finally end with overtly destructive behavior.

Some individuals characteristically handle anger around only one end of this continuum. Where anger is experienced in the absence of action, for example, it is important to specify this tendency and also to determine the control mechanisms that are utilized. Similarly, if the person tends to be at the other end of the continuum where the anger is readily translated into aggressive destructive behavior, then this tendency must be reported. In the latter case, implications about the likelihood of acting-out and the conditions under which its occurrence is probable also need to be specified.

Hostility is an intermediate phenomenon between the experience of anger as an emotion and the overt expression of anger in terms of aggressive behavior. The clinical variations of hostility are broad, making precise reporting of the findings in this area particularly valuable. A first formation of hostility, for example, may be limited to the appearance of the impulse of anger in fantasy and rumination.

Hostility may also appear somewhat farther along on the continuum in behavioral manifestations which fall short of overt acting-out of anger. A second form of hostility, designed to minimize anxiety in the subject, can include the use of sarcasm and cynicism as guarded, disguised verbal expressions of anger. Another form of the expression of hostility is passive-aggressive behavior, in which frustration is induced in someone else by utilization of such behaviors as delay, withholding, and incompleteness. A polemical, quarrelsome interpersonal manner also expresses the impulse of anger more directly.

A final stage in the sequence is reached when anger is directly acted-out, and destructive behavior takes place.

Reporting the Anger Impulse. This sequence of anger-hostility-aggression enables the psychologist to offer the reader of the report a map of the vicissitudes of the impulse of anger. The discussion in the report should include the ways in which the impulse affects, infiltrates, or impairs perception, judgment, fantasy, and behavior. In contrast, the extent to which the anger can be constructively integrated with these varied functions also requires assessment. It is pertinent to clarify the form in which the impulse appears — as an angry feeling, a hostile fantasy, rumination with or without an inclination toward covertly hostile behavior, or acted-out directly in aggressive behavior.

This kind of analysis should include a discussion of the anger impulse in the context of anxiety in the personality. When the overt aggressive expression of anger elicits anxiety in the individual, then the individual is likely to express anger in more indirect terms. For example, hostile verbalizations, fantasy, or rumination may reduce anxiety as a result of the diminished potential for overtly destructive behavior that is established.

Thus, the portion of the response sequence characteristic of the subject reflects the nature of the anxiety that is evoked by the potential expression of anger. Consequently, to say only that anger is present is insufficient in reporting on the role of anger in the personality. An analysis must be presented of the patient's typical handling of the impulse, the propensity to move to other response patterns involving the impulse, and the conditions under which this shift in the sequence might occur. Analyzing the role of anxiety in the expression and inhibition of anger is another component of the report. A third component is the effect of the anger impulse on perception, cognition, and intellectual functioning and the extent to which the impulse can be adaptively integrated. Together, these findings contribute to a thorough understanding of the complex role of the impulse of anger in the personality of the patient.

Once the various aspects of anger, hostility, and aggression in the functioning of the subject are delineated in the report, the role played by each of these anger manifestations in the patient's behavioral disposition and regulation of anxiety needs to be analyzed. For example, if the indications of anger on the drawings, responses to inkblots, and projective stories suggest generally intense feelings of anger that strive for expression, this should be noted. If these strivings activate hostile behavior, the extent to which such behavior discharges occur can be suggested. The analysis may also require an additional indication that anxiety stemming from possibilities of more direct expression of aggressiveness limits the subject's behavioral disposition to a covert handling of hostility. Personality characteristics such as depreciation of others, oppositionalism, stubbornness, and hostile withholding may be manifestations of covert hostility. Characterology associated with the covert management of hostility is discussed in depth in chapters 10 and 11 on the defensive and characterological elements of the personality.

Also pertinent to report after discussing the individual's experience of anger and likelihood for expressing hostility is the individual's propensity to engage in overt aggressive behavior. This would include consideration of the anxiety that the propensity toward overt aggression generates, the controls that can be imposed to regulate it, the sufficiency and reliability of such controls, and the likelihood of acting-out. Whether direct acting-out of the anger impulse is probable and continuous, or sporadic, unusual, but nevertheless possible, also can be clarified.

Anger and the Special Problem of Rage.   An important feature with respect to anger as a major impulse in the personality is rage. The feeling of rage can occur quite unexpectedly and can be intense enough to threaten the integrity of the ego. Such a threat to the ego can evoke extreme tension in the personality and place intense pressure on reality testing, causing interference in judgment and planning. Such a finding must be included in the report so that the referral source can deal with this potential, if not actual, ego impairment.

In addition, rage may create a circumstance in which internal controls are inadequate. Absence of control over intense emotionality increases the likelihood of overt acting-out in destructive behavior. Again, the psychologist needs to alert the referral source by reporting the patient's potential for destructive acting-out. When the emotion of rage is present and controls are insufficient, a possibility also develops for self-destructive acting-out. Suicidal acting-out would be an extreme possibility and is an urgent and crucial finding to report. Such findings reveal again the special care that needs to be devoted to communicating the probability of acting-out whenever samples of rage are seen in the test data.

The elements involved in a comprehensive view of the impulse of anger, therefore, include anger, hostility, aggression, and rage.

Sexuality

The concept of a sequence of events that characterizes anger also applies to sexuality. On the emotional, experiential level, this impulse can be defined as libidinous or as an instinctual wish for gratification. Sexuality can be mediated by fantasy and rumination consisting of overall pleasure wishes, erotic fantasies, and power themes that are expressed in sexual terms. These mediations are designed to create relief from anxiety associated with more direct, active expression of sexually related behavior. In terms of overt acting-out, sexual impulses can be expressed by a range of actions from benign behavior to that which is extremely complex and sometimes involves serious consequences. For example, acting-out of the sexual impulse can include compulsive masturbation, forms of perversion, homosexual or heterosexual promiscuity, and other forms of excessive sexual activity.

Comparable to the impulse of anger, a continuum can demonstrate the sequence of potential responses deriving from the sexual impulse. At one end of the continuum, sexual feelings are experienced and strive for expression, and at the other end, they are acted-out in any number of ways. Between these possibilities is the infiltration of sexual preoccupations in fantasy, rumination, and other covert expressions. The portion of this sequence that reflects the patient's management of sexual impulses needs to be delineated in the report. When the protocol contains signs of intense sexual impulse, a determination is made of the likelihood of acting-out that impulse. The sexual impulse may be inhibited and not acted-out, or if controls are inadequate acting-out can readily occur. Fantasy and rumination are intermediate means of managing tension associated with direct behavioral expression of the sexual impulse.

When control functions in the personality are insufficiently integrated to regulate intense sexual impulses, cognitive functioning—including judgment, planning ability, concentration, and memory, as well as abstract reasoning and comprehension—can become impaired. Interference in cognitive functioning can be precipitated by anxiety stemming from the inability to integrate and sublimate sexual strivings. Thus, any reflective activities can be adversely affected.

The aspects of the sexual impulse that need to be considered in the report are the ways in which it is experienced, if it is channeled in a manner that leads to resolution, and if it can be integrated successfully in the general functioning of the individual.

This discussion of the manifestations and effects of anger and sexuality underscores the extent to which the impulses permeate the individual's personality. In a similar manner, the controls utilized in managing and regulating these impulses have far-reaching implications in personality structure and functioning. In the following chapter, an analysis of the nature of controls as they relate to feelings, fantasies, and action emanating from impulses is presented. In addition, consideration is given to an analysis of the level of maturation that derives from the vicissitudes of the impulse-control interaction. Table 9.1 presents the major considerations of the impulse-control balance with a focus on impulse.

TABLE 9.1 Impulse Versus Control: Emphasis on Impulse

- Impulses are implied by urgent needs of the personality that strive for expression. They are energized emotions or amorphous arousal phenomena of the need system.
- Impulses in the form of energized emotions include anger, aggression, hostility, and sexuality.
- When indicators of impulse are high within a context of high action orientation, then the probability of acting-out increases.
- Impulse types are prone to action orientation and reveal a probable impairment in judgment and questionable frustration tolerance.
- Acting-out of impulses is the pathological method of reducing anxiety.
- Types of impulses are

  Anger
  - The anger dimension includes hostility, fantasy, rumination, and aggression.
  - It is important to describe whether anger is translated into hostility and fantasy, or is transformed into direct aggressive behavior.
  - Other forms of anger include sarcasm, quarrelsomeness, and passive-aggressive behavior.
  - The anger impulse should be discussed with reference to anxiety, perception, and judgment.
  - The level of anxiety can be viewed as a result of how the angry impulse is expressed: as a feeling, as a fantasy, or in acting-out.

  Sexuality
  - Sexuality is defined as libidinous impulses and wishes for gratification.
  - It is important to note pleasure fantasies, power themes, and sexual fantasies. These associated sexual variations also are designed to mediate anxiety regarding direct sexuality.
  - Acting-out of sexual impulses includes compulsive masturbation, perversions, and promiscuity. Sexual acting-out can impede judgment, planning, concentration, and memory.
  - The inability to sublimate sexual strivings can impede several cognitive functions, especially reflective activity.

SUMMARY

This chapter considered the interplay between the impulses that strive for expression in the personality and the resources for control and regulation that are available. This interplay of forces was analyzed and related to the question of whether impulse or control dominates functioning; the emphasis was on domination by impulse. The nature of the impulses as related to aggression and sexuality was described and a continuum was discussed, from feeling the impulse, through disguised or covert expression of it, to overt behavioral action. The issue of anxiety in relation to impulse was presented along with the acting-out propensities that occur with an impulse-dominant mode of personality functioning.

10

Impulse Versus Control
The Nature of Control Mechanisms

There are several distinct kinds of controls in the personality structure. These controls are employed in the individual's effort to regulate impulses and the corresponding anxiety associated with such impulses, as discussed in the previous chapters. For example, cognitive controls, including intellectual approaches, are quite different in their operation and consequences from the integrating effects of ego controls, which in turn are different in their quality and influence from individual defense mechanisms. Defense mechanisms also differ significantly from character traits, in that defense mechanisms largely manage the transitory nature of emotions while character traits persist in a stable and enduring form in the personality.

Another control function in the personality structure is the use of fantasy; that is, control over impulses and anxiety becomes possible through the imagined enactment of behavioral sequences. Finally, a special form of control in the personality results from reactions to the emotions of fear or terror. Phobic paralysis and somatization are the forms of control employed to contain and manage panic. Counterphobic reactions are secondary attempts to control potential paralysis and feelings of terror.

From the psychoanalytic point of view, the function and nature of this amalgam of controls are considered to be derivatives of both ego and superego control functions in the personality. This applies also to the cognitive controls which, like the individual defense mechanisms, are mobilized under both ego and superego influence in response to impulse. As pointed out in the previous chapter, from the psychoanalytic viewpoint the impulses represent derivative id expressions in the personality. The manner in which controls are available to regulate and manage the impulses then completes the description of essential conflict in the personality.

Since impulse features derive from id sources and control aspects relate to ego and superego features of the personality, one essential area of tension involves id and superego conflict within personality organization. The struggle between id and superego weakens the individual's resourcefulness and generates disorganizing anxiety.

In all instances of personality conflict, a central issue is the type of control utilized to oppose, manage, regulate, and integrate the impulses in order to contain anxiety and tension. Each of the various forms of control and the manner in which they operate to manage impulses and control anxiety are described next.

Cognitive Controls

When intellectual functioning is flexibly responsive to and aligned with the strivings, goals, and interests of the person, cognitive controls are represented. The presence of these controls in the personality is indicated when the responses in the protocol demonstrate evenness of functioning and relative freedom from the interfering effects of anxiety, as well as intactness of attention, concentration, and a well-represented fund of information. Consequently, when cognitive controls are intact, a capacity for abstraction is evident and inappropriate tendencies toward concretization are absent.

Controls involving cognitive functions also are reflected when achievement strivings are realistic and generally consistent with the subject's intellectual capacities and ability to implement goal-oriented behavior. For example, rather than acting-out anger or the distress that may accompany it, a good measure of cognitive control exists when the subject relies upon goal-directed, focused activity. Furthermore, cognitive control elements of planning, judgment, thinking, and reasoning will be free from idiosyncratic and ruminative fantasies when these controls are intact.

The presence of cognitive controls reflects strength, resourcefulness, and flexibility in the personality. Whenever applicable, these areas of strength should be cited by the psychologist in terms of estimating the resilience in personality functioning. Positive cognitive controls further imply that ego elements and their organization in the personality are correspondingly strong and well integrated.

Ego Controls

In chapter 5, on cognitive functioning, a hierarchical structure of ego functions was proposed. Impairment of the ego was generally associated with impairment of particular dimensions of control, ranging from conditions of poor control corresponding to more primitive ego impairment, to good control reflecting comprehensive ego integration. This hierarchy of ego functions may be conceived as ranging from controls that reflect ego fragmentation to those that indicate the presence of a viable aggregate of ego controls.

In terms of impulse versus control, the functions of the ego, described as integrative and synthetic when operating efficiently, reflect goal orientation, a capacity to tolerate frustration, and the ability to synchronize wishes and action in the form of instrumental behavior toward the attainment of goals. Most important, the efficient operation of the integrative and synthetic functions of the ego reflects the constructive and productive channeling of impulses in the personality, thereby demonstrating a cohesive integration of perception, thinking, feeling, and behavior.

When indicators of strong ego integration appear in the test protocol, the psychologist can report that control mechanisms in the form of ego-mediating functions are available and utilized, and impulses can be managed constructively. This means that ego-control mediators can help the individual in working toward goals, ambitions, and external achievements. Thus, cognitive controls are reflected in the protocol on the basis of their relevance to specific intellectual functions and capacities. In contrast, ego controls are reflected in the protocol on the basis of their relevance to specific process behaviors, such as the instrumental activity required to achieve and work toward goals. Sufficient ego controls enable the avoidance of significant detours such as idiosyncratic fantasies or acting-out.

Defense Mechanisms as Controls

A third element of the aggregate of control features on the protocol are the individual defensive operations that are designed to manage and direct specific emotions. If it were not for the various individual defenses, such as repression, denial, regression, reaction formation, rationalization, undoing, compensation, projection, and displacement, emotions would be experienced as urges requiring immediate expression. This relation of the individual defenses to emotion reveals the management functions of defenses.

When individual defenses do not sufficiently fulfill their function of management and control, the subject will experience anxiety associated with expression of the emotion. One of the psychologist's tasks is to attempt to define the original emotion that has become associated with the patient's anxiety. This basic principle suggests that when the control function of individual defenses does not adequately operate, anxiety occurs because expression of the emotion is anticipated as being threatening. Consequently, where there is anxiety, there will also be a specific underlying emotion. The issues that are addressed in the report are, first, what is the emotion that evokes anxiety, and second, what about the emotion is so threatening that anxiety is generated.

In order to analyze the emotion that is involved in the development of anxiety, the psychologist must first realize that impulses and anxiety are frequently experienced in the context of interpersonal or object relations. Consequently, the emotions in question and the anxiety associated with them usually refer to sexuality, affectional needs, dependency, loss, anger, or fear. These emotions are usually involved with the vicissitudes of object relations. The specific emotions can be assessed both by analyzing protocol data and by observing the patient's behavior during the testing session. In addition to assessing the nature of the emotions involved, the psychologist can discuss the intensity of any anxiety that surfaces and the functioning of the defenses enlisted to manage the emotions and to regulate the anxiety.

In the analysis of defensive operations with respect to the control of impulses and the regulation of anxiety, it is useful to identify the particular defenses being utilized. This analysis is presented in the next chapter.

Character Traits as Controls

In terms of their function and operation, character traits in the personality are distinctly different from individual defense mechanisms. Character traits reflect an aspect of the control system that can be referred to as the pattern of control; that is, a person displays a configuration of behavior which becomes the person's behavioral signature. In this respect, the pattern of traits displayed during the testing situation presumably reflects in microcosm the same pattern of behavior that operates in the patient's life.

By observing patterns of behavior during the testing session, the psychologist can establish the particular kind of character configuration being displayed. This organization of traits or character patterns frequently may be broadly separated into an active as opposed to passive pattern. The pattern of character traits associated with the compulsive characterology is active, for example, because the need for control is extensive and necessitates a broad range of idiosyncratic activities such as rituals, efforts toward closure and completion, manifestations of orderliness, and a careful organization of schedules and activities. Such a weave of highly active character traits is all-encompassing, binding substantial anxiety so that little tension or emotion is able to surface. In contrast, in a passive-aggressive characterology there is a studied neglect with respect to the completion of tasks, exasperating delay, lack of closure, and inconsistent attention to detail. Since "not doing" maintains the suppression of anxiety, passivity and reduced activity are the key elements in this character pattern.

The organization of character traits may be described as effective or ineffective in terms of anxiety that is successfully bound. It should be noted that the more efficiently the character pattern controls anxiety, the more deeply entrenched the characterology is. Conversely, the less effective the character pattern is, the greater the anxiety that is experienced.

The pattern of character controls may range from traits that are described as arising from sublimating mechanisms to those governed by impulse urges. For example, the sublimating traits usually are generated by superego concerns and include behaviors relating to conscientiousness, studiousness, industriousness, and responsibility. This cluster of traits corresponds to levels of functioning that reflect greater maturity in the personality. In contrast, traits dominated by impulse forces involve aggression, impetuousness, and efforts to achieve immediate gratification. This cluster of traits reflects id strivings and corresponds to less mature functioning. Analysis of the character trait profile also provides an opportunity to determine whether the patient's behavior is dominated by id-derivative impulse traits or by superego-derivative control traits. Therefore, an analysis of the person's pattern of character traits contributes to understanding the aggregate of impulse and control features in the total personality. This character configuration concerns the specific formation of behaviors that endure and persist in a stable way and appear in a predictable manner in response to varied and repeated stimuli.

In analyzing the character control aspect of personality, it is helpful for the psychologist to describe the cluster of traits as comprising a character syndrome. By discussing these behavioral characteristics and dispositions in terms of a character syndrome, meaningless and random adjective stringing can be avoided. The psychologist generally needs to be concerned with only a few basic character clusters of syndromes. These patterns correspond to pleasure-dominated traits, anger-dominated traits, fear-dominated traits, and traits dominated by a need for affection and dependency.

Examples of the pleasure-dominated traits are the forms of hedonistic inclination represented by magical wishing and a need for immediate gratification. Also included are behavioral characteristics such as sociability, gregariousness, cordiality, seductiveness, and optimism.

With respect to anger-dominated traits, aggressive and passive behavior in the service of hostility, such as oppositionalism, defiance, and stubbornness, form a configuration. Quarrelsomeness, sullenness, and belligerence are also involved in this cluster. Examples of behavior in a fear-dominated trait configuration include inhibitory responses such as caution, phobic reactions, and behavior reflecting shame and self-consciousness. Traits such as timidity, pessimism, reticence, and obedience are also included in this cluster. Of the traits formed out of the need for affection and dependency, examples are passivity, deference, and obedience. These clusters of character traits suggest definite personality styles and behavioral approaches that can characterize the person being evaluated. Additional analysis of specific character structures are presented in the next two chapters.

Fantasy as Control

The nature and makeup of fantasies are another type of control mechanism of personality. Fantasy may be considered a mechanism of control in the personality insofar as it represents a mediating phenomenon between feelings and behavior. Fantasies can be a harmless staging area for experiencing a host of emotions. The control feature inherent in the mechanism of fantasy is the imagining of a specific behavior without actually engaging in it. Thus, acting-out behavior might occur more frequently if it were not for the dilution and discharge of intense emotion played out in imagination.

Fantasy can control impulses and anxiety through a variety of compensatory mechanisms that are designed to assuage tensions associated with a sense of inferiority, interpersonal confrontation, and rage. Fantasies of grandiose accomplishments can compensate for feelings of inadequacy. Because fantasy affords some gratification, more constructive efforts toward behavioral resolution of the sense of inadequacy are avoided. Fantasy can also be employed to contain aggressive or sexual impulses when their overt expression would be threatening.

On the test protocol, excessive human movement determinants with limited responses to color on the inkblots suggest that solutions to conflicts are sought through the use of fantasy rather than through behavioral activity. The production of grandiose images or references in response to the inkblots, or themes of superior accomplishment or the achievement of extensive personal recognition on the projective stories, also indicate fantasies of grandiosity as a means of managing a sense of inadequacy. Projective drawings that depict enlarged or overelaborated features may support this kind of interpretation.

The construction of fantasies containing bold interpersonal confrontations and the successful expression of direct aggression or sexuality, which are often revealed in projective stories and even in inkblot responses, are frequently attempts to fulfill through imagination what the individual feels unable to perform in reality. In the construction of such fantasies, the impulses involved in direct assertion and overt expression of anger are controlled. The use of fantasy to control and manage urgent impulses such as rage can be an important safeguard in curtailing highly destructive behavior. On the other hand, the appearance of such fantasies in the protocol also raises the possibility that the patient may ultimately act-out. The intensity of the impulse and the nature of the patient's controls will determine whether behavioral expression is likely.

When there is no sharp demarcation between what occurs in fantasy and what occurs in reality, the value of fantasy as a means of control is lost. This point indicates that the essential value of fantasy as a control mechanism is limited in more pathological instances. Furthermore, when the utilization of fantasy as a controlling device becomes predominant, another danger appears. The patient who excessively fantasizes may behave extremely passively, seeking to resolve conflicts exclusively in fantasy as a substitute for relying on more appropriate problem-solving behavior. A reliance on fantasy also may be associated with an isolated or schizoid withdrawn style that implies distinct pathological qualities.

The value of fantasy as a means of control may be compromised when rumination is excessive or emotion is intense. Thus, the fantasy is insufficient to dilute tensions and other controls may be necessary. If the excess tension is neither managed by fantasy nor acted-out, then acting-in as a control may occur, and anxiety is managed through somatization.

Fear as Control

Fear and terror are rather special correlates of control mechanisms of the personality, insofar as they generate excessive behavioral maladjustments. These control mechanisms are quite complex, but they can be evaluated by the psychologist on the basis of the projective material whenever phobic contents appear. Phobic paralysis is an attempt to control panic associated with an impulse urgently striving for expression. In order to control panic, the phobia temporarily provides relief from the individual's anxiety, albeit an agonizing one, and represents and ingenious method of establishing strong controls. In phobic reactions, the true source of the individual's fear (most likely another person or some kind of commitment) is displaced to a relatively harmless context.

The task for the psychologist is to analyze the meaning of the phobic symptom in terms of its displacement significance. The fear and terror involved in the phobic reaction are generally displaced responses to unacceptable impulses (probably regarding a primary figure). These impulses include anger or pleasure, for example, and the anticipation of danger or injury that would be a consequence of experiencing or acting upon such an impulse.

The various control mechanisms utilized in handling impulses create a complex network. In order to clarify further the vicissitudes of control and impulse in the personality, their relation to the subject's maturational level is important to analyze.

MATURATION: AN INDEX OF
IMPULSE VERSUS CONTROL

Broadly speaking, findings reflecting an impulsive tendency in the personality indicate a relatively immature level of development. As the level of maturation increases, the balance between impulse and control stabilizes toward the successful operation of controls. When controls over-dominate the expression of impulses, an immature level of functioning also is represented

Immature: Impulse Dominated

In virtually all of the projective tests, features of impulse can readily be determined. For example, in the human figure drawings and other projective drawings, slapdash gestalts, disorganized line quality, and productions indicative of a striking lack of reflection or consideration are obvious features of a specific syndrome consisting of impulse elements, an action orientation, probability of low frustration tolerance, and a poorly organized control system representative of a low level of maturity. The Rorschach may provide additional samples of such features; for example, the presence of a high animal movement content would support a fundamentally immature action orientation. A color-dominated protocol in which form controls are arbitrary at best can reveal the profound impact and preeminence of impulses in the life of the patient.

An impulse-dominated subject reflects in perception, thinking, and feeling the preoccupations that characterize immature stages of development. For example, children characteristically respond to projective material with a high percentage of animal contents and animal movement determinants. These responses are associated with and reflect the child's need for motoric expression and immediate gratifications. It is expected that adults, on the other hand, have replaced immediate needs for gratification with the ability to delay such gratifications in the interest of long-range goals. When this has not occurred, the adult subject responds in ways comparable to the child subject — immaturely.

The entire protocol can be divided broadly between impulse and control responses, the balance between the features of impulse and control corresponding to levels of maturation. At a primitive level of personality organization, impulse far outweighs the subject's controlling resources. This immature level of development renders a high probability of action orientation. A basic test profile can be hypothesized; for example, in a low-maturational more primitive adult subject, the profile might consist of a high animal movement and color-dominated Rorschach with a reduced reliance on form and human movement. On the graphic material, poor use of line quality and impaired line control especially can occur along with impaired line control on the Bender Gestalt. Magical and action-oriented solutions to conflict on the Thematic Apperception Test can appear along with an absence of implementation of activity toward goals. Finally, the intelligence scale can reveal significantly lowered reflective and verbal skills in comparison with good performance strengths, emphasizing concrete rather than conceptual skills. In addition, a trial-and-error approach can be seen as opposed to one reflecting learning through persistence.

This test profile is representative of an immature individual with a relatively poorly developed capacity for delay. Consequently, such an individual's approach would be marked by haste and lack of reflection that lead to a rather inappropriate and inadequate channeling of effort. The psychologist determines whether this immaturity will promote acting-out or if other data suggest that the subject's impulses are contained to some extent in fantasies. These fantasies may involve themes of power, adequacy, or overall identity, and they imply less likelihood that the subject will act-out.

Another element that must be evaluated in determining maturational level is the fragility or strength of the patient's ego resources. These resources serve to contain any sudden or unexpected increase in impulse experience. For example, the immaturity and underdevelopment of a patient's controls require the psychologist to decide whether an increase in impulse pressure may lead to acting-out or overwhelm the patient's immature controls. Where immature controls can be overwhelmed, the emergence of a psychotic process becomes a possibility. In either case, sufficient danger to the patient or other people because of ego fragmentation or destructive acting-out can be linked in the report to a lack of development of the patient's controls.

Immature: Control Dominated

The basic syndrome corresponding to the immature maturation level that was just presented consists of an action-oriented, impulse-dominated level of development. A second kind of immature maturation syndrome associated with excessive controls can also be described. In this profile, the subject consistently adheres to behavioral inhibition. For example, in a decision to commit oneself to action or remain inert, the decision will virtually always be to remain passive. Such a person is guided by caution and frequently by a fierce desire to maintain strict controls over either impulse or action.

The psychological test results of an inhibited person can include an absence of impulse-dominated responses on the Rorschach, a restricted and narrow range of determinants, and a substantial concern with and focus on form. A predominance of restricted responses reflects protection against expressive behavior. Maturational level is accordingly underdeveloped, even though controls may be excessively developed. The protocol profile includes extremely well-defined line quality in all of the graphic material, reflecting excessive concern with the management of anxiety. On the Thematic Apperception Test, stories frequently appear to be rather descriptive but lacking in affect and action. On the intelligence test, the subject's performance on subtests emphasizing a fund of accumulated knowledge, such as Information and Vocabulary, may yield unusually high scores.

From a diagnostic point of view, subjects in whom control and a need for caution are apparent reveal compulsive, obsessive, or passive elements in their profile. When controls are brittle and psychotic potential is increased, states of agitation can be seen. This agitation reflects an underdeveloped adaptive control system. Such subjects have not yet achieved a capacity to channel impulses into behavior in a way that leads to gratification; rather, a rigid, constricted control system is employed in order to reduce any sense of threat associated with impulse activity. Consequently, overcontrol actually represents an underdevelopment of constructive controls, leaving the individual ungratified and immature, with a lack of balance between impulse and control.

An understanding of the subject's maturational level can be derived from an analysis of the types of immature development that may exist with respect to impulse and controls. It is helpful to view maturation in terms of a balanced organization of impulse and control features. Immaturity is related to either an excessive acting-out of impulses or overly rigid, constricted controls. In both instances there is a failure to strike a healthy balance between impulse and control.

Mature Balance of Impulse and Controls

In the psychodiagnostic report, the psychologist frequently neglects to indicate the strengths of the patient. This may occur because of the fact that the referral was determined by the patient's aberrant or problematic behavior. Nevertheless, the reader of the report will appreciate indications of personality resilience, and restitutional or recuperative powers whenever possible. Therapists, teachers, counselors, and other referral sources need this information so that particular areas of strength can be reinforced and utilized in the overall intervention, of which the report is but one aspect.

The psychologist has a unique opportunity to discuss the patient's strengths in the report, especially when the balance between impulse and control is adaptive and mature. This complementary relationship between impulse and control signifies that the patient can utilize inner resources involving the adaptive integration of perception, thinking, feeling, and behavior. This balance contributes to constructive coping, since delays in acting upon impulses can be sustained while appropriate activities are resourcefully considered. A healthy balance between impulse and control provides an immediate index of the personality's overall resilience, maturity, and flexibility and also reflects a well-organized defensive structure with flexible character patterns. The extent to which an imbalance is present reveals a corresponding impairment in the overall organization of the subjects defense system and characterology.

In the next chapter, the various levels of defenses and types of character patterns are discussed. This presentation corresponds to the sequence of sections in the report that lead from an analysis of the phenomenon of anxiety to consideration of impulses and controls as a deeper configuration of the expression of anxiety. An analysis of the various types of defenses and defensive syndromes is an inextricable part of this sequence of sections in the report. Table 10.1 presents the main features of the vicissitudes of controls in the personality.

TABLE 10.1   Nature of Control Mechanisms

- Control mechanisms are derived from ego and superego functions.

- Controls include cognitive, intellectual, ego, superego, individual defense mechanisms, character traits, fantasy, and phobic reactions. The types of controls are:

    Cognitive Controls. Concentration, attention, and consistent functioning are seen. Intellectual functioning is aligned with strivings and goals. Anxiety is well-managed. The achievement drive is also consistent with the ability to implement goal-directed behavior. Cognitive control is usually seen in terms of specific intellectual functions and capacities.

    Ego Controls. Integrative and control functions of the ego reflect goal orientation, a capacity to tolerate frustration, and an ability to implement activity toward goals.

    Defense Mechanisms. Defense mechanisms are designed to manage, regulate, or control specific transitory emotions including anxiety. Anxiety can signal the poor or insecure control of a specific emotion. Knowledge of the specific emotion associated with the anxiety clarifies the use of defenses as an aspect of control. The emotion in question usually relates to another person and to sexuality, affectional needs, dependency, loss, anger, or fear.

    Character Traits. These are enduring patterns of control or patterns of behavior. These characteristics may be separated into configurations of active traits versus those that can be considered passive traits. In compulsive characterology, active patterns are seen, while in passive characterology, passive patterns appear. Both types serve to control anxiety. Successful control would consist of character patterns that bind anxiety in a sustained, sufficient way. Such character patterns can be construed according to the following trait clusters:

    - *Sublimating traits* involving the superego dimension include conscientiousness, studiousness, industriousness, and responsibility. Sublimating traits reflect greater maturation.

    - *Impulse traits* involving the id dimension include aggression, impetuousness, and need for immediate gratification. Impulse traits reflect inadequate maturation.

    - *Pleasure-dominated traits* include hedonism, magical thinking, need for immediate gratification, sociability, gregariousness, cordiality, seductiveness, and optimism.

- *Anger-dominated traits* include aggressive and passive behavior, hostility, oppositionalism, defiance, stubbornness, quarrelsomeness, sullenness, and belligerance.

- *Fear-dominated traits* include caution, phobic reactions, shame, self-consciousness, timidity, pessimism, and obedience.

- *Dependency-dominated traits* include deference, dependency, and need for affection.

Fantasy as Control. Mediates between feelings and behavior and involves thinking instead of behaving. Control occurs through compensatory and grandiose feelings generated by fantasy. Success in fantasy neutralizes anxiety related to doubts regarding actually performing. Overuse of fantasy implies a passive or schizoid orientation.

Fear as Control. Appearance of phobias to control panic. A phobia is presumably a displacement of anxiety related to expression of anger or sexuality that is actually targeted toward another person.

- An impulse-dominated personality relates to immature development:

  Impulse-dominated protocol may contain high animal movement and color-dominated Rorschach determinants with a lower form percentage and fewer human movement responses. Graphic material may show poor line quality. Fantasy in TAT stories can include magical wishes for attainment of goals in the absence of instrumental activity toward such goals. The intelligence test may show lowered verbal skills and higher performance scores. A trial-and-error approach is likely while delay is poor.

- A control-dominated personality reflects more mature development as well as pathology of inhibition:

  Control-dominated protocol emphasizing inhibition reflects signs of great inertia. There is an absence of impulse signs on projective material, a restricted range of determinants, and a focus on form. Good line quality is seen on graphic material. TAT stories may lack affect and activity. Verbal scores on the intelligence test are often higher than performance scores. Compulsive, obsessive, and passive dispositions can be included here.

SUMMARY

In the previous two chapters, aspects of the conflicting elements of impulse and control and their dynamic interplay in the personality were presented. The specific impulses of anger and sexuality were discussed. Consideration was given to characteristic expressions of these impulses, as well as to the range of impulse expression that is possible. The discussion centered around the experience of the impulse, its expression in fantasy or rumination, its appearance as indirect covert behavior, and finally, its overt acting-out. In addition, the influence of impulses on cognition, perception, judgment, and learning was explored. Control features of the personality that were emphasized included cognitive and ego controls, defense mechanisms and character traits, fantasy, somatization, and fear. The nature of maturation was considered with respect to acting-out, constricted, or adaptive functioning.

11
Defensive Structure

A good deal will have been presented in the report with regard to defensive operations even before the formulation of this section. In the section on impulse versus control for example, exposition of the control aspects of the personality revealed the use of defense mechanisms as well as the associated character style of the patient. Character and defensive structures have been referred to and described in the sections on cognitive functioning and anxiety. It also has been pointed out that defenses mobilized in response to anticipatory anxiety can significantly impair cognitive and intellectual functioning.

The purpose of this section of the report is to present an organized and integrated analysis of the individual's entire defensive structure. The psychologist therefore reports in this section the particular defense mechanisms typically utilized by the patient, the extent to which anxiety and emotions are controlled by these defenses, and the bearing they have on the patient's strengths, pathology, flexibility, and intactness. The specific defense mechanisms that are employed in the patient's characteristic handling of interpersonal events can be related to aspects of emotionality. For example, an individual who is anxious about direct assertion may defensively avoid assertive behaviors by utilizing the defense of displacement so that the forceful behavior may then be expressed toward a less threatening person. In addition, the patient's defensive responses to signals of anxiety that are triggered by the anticipation of threat or danger can be elaborated. Proclivities toward acting-out can then be clarified in terms of the lack of more adaptive defensive resources. Thus, the patient's development of characteristic defensive syndromes and all the specific elements comprising them are described in this section of the report. In addition, the implications for diagnostic conditions that can be derived from all these aspects of defensive operations as well as from the patient's characteristic defensive arrangements can receive attention in this section as well. This analysis of defense operations helps sharpen the diagnostic focus that has been proceeding throughout the construction of the report.

In general, a major assumption of psychodynamic psychology concerns the central role played by the defensive structure in the way this defensive structure affects the regulation of behavior, behavioral responses to signals of anxiety, and the relation of behavior to emotion. Thus, to understand defenses and defense syndromes, the same dichotomy of impulse versus control that was applied in understanding maturation can be utilized to advantage here. In such an analysis it is helpful to introduce diagnostic formulations that clarify the connection between defenses, emotions, anxiety, and behavior. Individual defenses can be delineated in terms of their function as emotion-coping devices; however, their typical use, as well as the various forms in which they combine, often reflect diagnostic states that provide information about the way in which the personality is organized.

In the following sections, analysis of defense mechanisms and defensive syndromes clarifies how defenses are utilized individually and in combination. First, specific information about individual defense mechanisms and their role in the person's functioning will be discussed.

INDIVIDUAL DEFENSE MECHANISMS

An important aspect of the operation of defenses in the personality can be appreciated by considering the experience of impulse, emotion, or anxiety that occurs within the person as a response to either an internal or external stimulus. Such a stimulus phenomenon can trigger tension, especially when a negative emotion is experienced. Tension may be perceived only dimly or not at all; nevertheless, the presence of such tension provides a strong and reliable signal that elicits defenses in an automatic manner. The automatic evoking of defenses in response to signal anxiety has far-reaching consequences for the individual.

These consequences regarding the operation of defenses in response to signal anxiety follow from the repeated utilization of characteristic behavior patterns when a threat to the individual's well-being, integrity, or security is experienced or anticipated. This threat to well-being can stem from internal sources in the emotional life, such as fantasies or impulses, or from external situations. The operation of each defense has implications for the individual's behavior in terms of orientation toward goals, achievement of satisfactions, reality testing, and interaction with other people.

Because specific defenses and combinations of defenses become regularly and automatically employed in an unreflective manner, they often contribute to the repeated occurrence of problem situations. For example, an individual faced with examinations in academic work may repeatedly experience signal anxiety in anticipation of potential failure or competition. If the need to study is defensively denied and avoided in order to assuage the anxiety, a continuing struggle with procrastination or a poor academic performance can be the result.

A qualifying analysis of individual defenses is necessary at this point. A frequently held assumption about defenses is that they protect the individual from danger and therefore are considered to be almost axiomatic with negative emotions as well as with popularly considered "undesirable" diagnoses. For example, the emotion of terror and the defense of repression are frequently correlated. The emotions of anger and hostility frequently are related to the defenses of repression and displacement. The diagnosis of paranoid thinking is associated with the defense of projection. Thus, it is usually assumed that defenses are only associated with negative states. This assumption severely limits the psychologist's analytic perspective and potential contribution to the overall understanding of defense and diagnosis.

Individual defense mechanisms are not utilized exclusively in the service of negative emotions. In fact, defenses relate to all emotions, positive as well as negative. Subjects whose test results reveal avoidance of depressive feelings, for example, frequently seek continual external stimulation and engage in compensatory fantasy and behavior. The purpose of this defensive operation which specifically utilizes the mechanism of compensation is to secure sustained feelings of pleasure. This positive feeling would be diminished if the defense did not operate and in such a case the depression would surface.

A complexity arises in understanding the utilization of defenses. A particular defense such as repression or denial may be used to ward off depression; however, to be successful it needs to be combined with the mechanism of compensation, which insures that a generalized pleasure emotion continues to be available in the experience of the person.

Another variation on this theme of the implementation and purpose of specific defenses concerns the utilization of individual defense mechanisms to manage, transform, and even diminish the feeling of sexuality. For example, it is usually the case that the defense mechanism of reaction formation disguises and ultimately transforms the person's pleasurable sexual responses into opposite states or moods, namely revulsion or disgust. Examples of this transformation occur in test productions when subjects offer idiosyncratic responses to inkblots involving protestations of ugliness and disgust, or when responses emerge such as "take it away, I can't look at it," "this makes me sick," and so on. What is presumably involved in such instances is an underlying pleasure attraction that cannot be faced and accepted. This pleasure attraction is expelled from consciousness in an automatic, characteristic fashion through instituting the reaction formation defense. In this way, the reaction formation serves the specific purpose of attenuating pleasure emotions.

Corresponding support for the hypothesis that defense mechanisms address positive as well as negative emotions is suggested by psychoanalysts, who understand dreams in which the subject feels nauseous, disgusted, or revolted as sometimes reflecting opposite inclinations of sexuality or pleasure. Thus, appreciating the full nature of defense mechanisms can enrich the psychologist's understanding of the protocol. For example, responses of disgust or revulsion provide immediate access to information regarding emotion and specific defenses as well as to possible diagnostic implications.

The varied roles played by defensive operations in the personality require the psychologist to understand and clarify defense syndromes and their diagnostic implications as well as the nature of individual defense mechanisms. In order to further this analysis, a consideration of individual defenses is presented in the following section. This exposition is divided into two categories. The first delineates individual defense mechanisms designed to manage individual emotions. The second category presents individual defense mechanisms that become instrumental in the process of character trait formation.

Defenses Used to Manage Individual Emotions

COMPARTMENTALIZATION.   This defense reduces anxiety by keeping aspects of personality apart so that contradictions do not register. The usual integration of personality functioning is disrupted by these dissociations so that parts of the personality can become unaware of each other in dramatic ways. Hysterical disorders often reflect use of compartmentalization and this defense is especially utilized in multiple personality disorders.

COMPENSATION.   This defense mechanism is frequently utilized to counteract both depressive and inferiority feelings by means of fantasies of aggrandizement, quests for recognition, and overall positive feedback. Disturbances involving narcissistic deficiencies also involve the use of this mechanism.

DENIAL.   This defense wards off the perception of any negative or critical component associated with the external object. Thus, denial aids the person's effort to receive only positive information. It is frequently seen in hysterical personality types. Because of its use in limiting absorption of information to only the positive, people utilizing this defense frequently make poor judgments.

DISPLACEMENT.   This frequently used mechanism is designed primarily to manage the emotion of anger. The subject places blame, anger, and aggression on less threatening substitute figures so that these emotions, associated judgments, and behaviors are not focused on the real, more threatening target. A frequent manifestation of displacement is a recurrent belligerence toward authorities representing a displacement of resentment toward parental figures to whom an expression of anger would have been highly threatening. Passive-aggressive and dependent subjects, in their reluctance to express hostility directly, typically utilize displacement.

INTELLECTUALIZATION.   An objective and dispassionate view of relationships and events conceals the individual's inability or great reluctance to be decisive or to make a commitment. Thus, emotion is avoided by means of a focus on intellectual concerns. This defense is associated with the diagnosis of obsessional or compulsive disorders. Intellectualization is also part of an obsessional syndrome that consists of the mechanisms of isolation, rationalization, sublimation, and undoing. This syndrome frequently operates to manage the emotion of anticipation by controlling the environment and thereby minimizing any elements of surprise that could cause confusion or generate anxiety.

ISOLATION.   Ideas are kept separate from the feelings appropriate to them. Thus, action and guilt are avoided because the importance of an idea that lacks corresponding affect is more easily minimized. This defense is frequently observed in obsessional and compulsive disorders.

PROJECTION.   Faults, feelings, and impulses that cannot be faced or tolerated in oneself are attributed to others. Projection can occur in virtually any diagnosis, but is the major defense utilized by persons with paranoid inclinations. In paranoid functioning, projection is employed to manage critical feelings toward the self by directing them to the outside world. In this way, the individual is spared the stress of critical self-evaluation, but becomes ritualistically committed to maintaining a critical stance toward the world and finding fault with others.

RATIONALIZATION.   A justification process occurs in which unacceptable motivations, feelings, or behaviors are made acceptable and tolerable through explanations that have the appearance of logic. This defense is often seen in obsessional and compulsive disorders as part of the ideational and intellectual emphasis in these disturbances.

REACTION FORMATION. Emotions of pleasure or attraction that are intolerable are transformed into their opposites which can be accepted, experienced, and expressed. Even hostility, for example, can be converted to overconcern or solicitousness, provided that the hostility was experienced as threatening because it was pleasurable. Thus, an emotion is turned into its opposite only if the original emotion contains a threatening component of pleasure. This defense is specifically used to manage the experience of sexuality which is perceived as dangerous or undesirable by transforming it into an opposite feeling of revulsion. Reaction formation is frequently utilized in the manic condition, especially when combined with sublimation. In this way, in the manic state, the impulse of pleasure is diminished and blocked by the operation of reaction formation and becomes transformed into work energy by the effect of sublimation. Hence, manic patients frequently engage in a host of projects. The translation of pleasure urges into work energy is further accomplished when reaction formation and sublimation are combined with the defense of compensation. The defense syndrome of compensation, reaction formation, and sublimation enables the manic-depressive patient to counteract depression. The point at which depression does emerge signals an impairment in the compensation defense, and a weakening of sublimation. The remaining emphasis on reaction formation indicates that the patient will not experience pleasure. Rather, the patient, because of the operation of reaction formation, will experience the opposite of the pleasure — agitation, dissatisfaction, or depression.

REGRESSION. This mechanism involves the use of an immature level of functioning. In the psychopathic and impulse disorders, it is chiefly responsible for the maintenance of motoric behavior. Regression functions as a motoric coping device, because in the absence of this mechanism the person feels inhibited, immobile, and even paralyzed. Nightmares in which a person becomes immobilized by threatening figures or dream contents of being buried alive or drowning are examples of an impaired mechanism of regression. In such cases movement or motor behavior is not possible and some form of inhibition or paralysis is exhibited in a nightmare.

REPRESSION. This is a common underlying element in all defense mechanisms because it involves the expelling and withholding of intolerable ideas and feelings from consciousness. Consequently, since all defense mechanisms prevent the conscious experiencing of such material they all contain some element of repression. Repression is particularly utilized to manage intense, threatening feelings of fear and terror. The more pervasive this mechanism is in the personality, the greater the likelihood of passive, schizoid, or hysteric personality features.

SUBLIMATION.   This mechanism is generally utilized in the personality to attenuate impulses, sexual urges, and other drives by channeling such impulses into productive, goal-oriented activity. Such productivity is frequently also considered to be socially valuable.

UNDOING.   This mechanism is designed to maintain a balance or symmetry of response and is typical of obsessional and compulsive states. Prior acts or thoughts are always counterbalanced by their opposite or symmetrical form. In compulsions, an example of this theme is handwashing that is utilized to erase the presence and possible effects of undesirable urges. Other forms of ritualistic behavior, as well as counting and repetitious thoughts, also constitute attempts to counterbalance and eradicate the effects of impulses.

DEFENSES AND CHARACTER TRAIT FORMATION

In the previous section, individual defenses were defined with respect to their function as emotion-coping devices and, where appropriate, in terms of diagnostic implications. This section defines defenses that correspond to and are instrumental in the formation of enduring trait patterns of the personality. Consequently, these defenses are associated with more stable and enduring aspects of the personality.

Defenses Forming Character Trait Patterns

IDENTIFICATION.   This mechanism may be considered in terms of its importance to the development of enduring trait patterns in the same way that repression is a common underlying element of individual defense mechanisms. Through identification, the developing individual aims to form him or herself isomorphically in relation to an important person in terms of overt mannerisms as well as internal dispositions. This identification process enables the individual to regulate and control emotion and tension by internal means rather than by relying exclusively on external constraints. The identification thereby permits the person to institute controls in a reflexive or internal manner. The adaptive value of such controls depends on the features that have been copied. The profound importance of identification lies in the fact that it is an axiomatic part of development and cannot be prevented. As far as parent-child and family relations are concerned, the development of identification occurs by example, not by instruction. Consequently, identification becomes isomorphic and replicative. Apparently, cultural admonitions and folklore that advise "like father like son," "like mother like daughter," and "the apple doesn't fall far from the tree," are based on psychologically valid principles of identification.

INTERNALIZATION.   This mechanism is built upon the foundation of identification and adds to it an imprinting of values. Imprinting takes place through the individual's unconscious adoption of the standards and attributes of another significant figure. Regardless of intentions, the subject comes to feel controlled by emotions as a result of internalizing values, even though the intellect may dictate different conclusions as a result of rational thought. Thus, even inappropriate standards from childhood are internalized, though questioned intellectually.

SPLITTING.   Elements of denial and displacement are utilized in this mechanism. Identification occurs even though disparate values exist in the object of identification. Splitting is accomplished with the aid of self-contained compartmentalizations: one individual can be viewed as being all good and another as all bad. In addition, the same individual can be seen at one time as all good and at another time as all bad without any accompanying experience of contradiction. Because the nature of splitting is unconscious and the compartmentalizations are self-contained, perceptions of good and bad are reversed without feelings of tension or a recognition of conflict. Consequently, splitting prevents the feelings of ambiguity and distress that would ordinarily be associated with an experience of conflict.

SYMBOLIZATION.   Internal, covert ideas and fantasies become disguised through specific external representations. Thus, ideas or fantasies support characteristic behavior without any accompanying distress. For example, submissive, deferential or even competitive or dominating behavior may be set off in persons who experience problems with authority, whenever they interact with others who symbolize greater authority through external features such as physical appearance or advanced age.

TURNING AGAINST THE SELF. Hostility is made more tolerable by shifting its target from another person to the self. The person utilizing this defense develops traits of blaming, denigrating, and attacking the self instead of directing these feelings to the appropriate target person. Central to the process is an underlying identification with the person to whom the anger is unexpressed. This important identification is protected and hidden by turning the anger against oneself. This process operates frequently in diagnoses involving depression and in the persistence of masochistic traits and self-mutilation, in which typical self-defeating and self-attacking behavior is maintained.

The idea of typical behavior is important because it explains the use of defense mechanisms in the formation and perpetuation of enduring character behavior. In analyzing and discussing the patient's system of defense, the psychologist considers both categories — defenses designed to cope with transitory emotion, and those that facilitate and reinforce trait behavior.

DEFENSES AND THE REPORT

In discussing the operation of defense mechanisms in the report, the first effort the psychologist can make is to identify the defenses that play a prominent role in the individual's functioning and to indicate how they are employed in managing tension and emotions. The use of defenses is reasonable and appropriate and does not necessarily imply the presence of pathological conditions. For example, in a protocol in which intellectualization appears without emphasis on rationalization and undoing, a severe obsessional state would not necessarily be signaled. On the other hand, in a protocol in which excessive intellectualization, rationalization, overconcern with symmetry, and undoing appears, the psychologist can look for additional samples of obsessional rumination that interfere with the integration of perception, thinking, and feeling.

In identifying the particular defenses that are involved in the patient's functioning, it is important to maintain consistency between the defenses cited and the ultimate diagnosis that is formulated. Hypothetically, a person in any diagnostic category can utilize any of the defense mechanisms, but the use of some defenses in certain diagnoses would be extremely unusual and would require additional explanation. Usually, certain specific defenses are typical of persons within a given diagnostic group.

Several diagnostic implications involving the use of particular defense mechanisms were pointed out in the definitions of defense mechanisms. For example, the use of denial is typical of hysterics. The constellation of defenses consisting of intellectualization, isolation, and undoing, often in conjunction with rationalization and sublimation, is characteristic of obsessives and compulsives. The use of displacement is typical of passive-aggressive persons. Compensation in patients with depression and narcissistic disturbances also is frequently found, since bolstering or maintenance of self-esteem is a major need for them. Utilization of projection is typical of persons with paranoid inclinations. Splitting in the borderline diagnosis and regression among psychopathic types are other examples of defense mechanisms that typically are seen in specific diagnoses.

Thus, because of the association between certain diagnostic categories and typical defensive operations, the reporting of specific defenses must be consistent with the diagnostic conclusions that are presented. In the unusual circumstance in which a final diagnosis is reported with the use of a highly atypical defensive operation, an explanatory discussion of this somewhat contradictory finding would be essential.

Another finding that the psychologist can report when discussing the operation of defenses is the occurrence of a weakened defensive system. This sort of impairment of defenses that are typically used by the subject can occur when crisis conditions evoke unusual emotional agitation. Therefore, during times of external crises along with a corresponding upsurge of internal impulses, a weakened defensive condition is seen within this turbulent context. In such a case, problems with identification and internalization can lead the subject to feel influenced by forces beyond personal control. These problems can in turn lead to agitated conditions and crises in personality functioning. By providing information about any weakened defenses, the reader of the report can be helped to understand the essence of a subject's difficulty. In addition, the report can clarify that impulses can become unmanageable during both psychotic and nonpsychotic crises. In such episodes, the inexorable explosion and flow of emotion injure the integrity of the personality. Trait patterns and behavior, rather than being regular and predictable, can be erratic and irrational.

When crisis situations exist and individual defenses as well as character patterns are overwhelmed, the subject can become increasingly flooded with highly idiosyncratic primary process impulses, images, and ruminations. This personality disorganization and its expression in primary process responses can be seen throughout the protocol. Extremely scattered subtest scores on the intelligence test are an effect of this sort of disorganization. Certain subtests, such as information and vocabulary, utilize intellectual defenses that may aid the subject in attempting to be more organized; thus, scores on those subtests may tend to be higher. Other subtests require intact organization of the personality and consequently, the demands of such subtests tend to exacerbate the subject's disorganization, producing lowered scores.

In response to inkblots, the patient in crisis may reveal idiosyncratic contents, such as animals "digesting" each other, or other responses which reflect direct intrusions of primary process ideation. On the Thematic Apperception Test, indications of poor frustration tolerance may appear, and the stories may be characterized by primitive needs for protection along with fears of annihilation. With figure drawings and other graphic material, bodily integrity may be severely compromised, and bizarre transparencies or inappropriate juxtapositions of body parts may be apparent.

In examining this data, the psychologist can be guided by the recognition that a flow of emotion unencumbered by controls reflects impairment of a number of specific defense mechanisms. Projections, displacements, and regressions are more likely to be relied upon in such cases. When ideation is bizarre or idiosyncratic it is likely that primary process material has intruded on functioning. At this point, identification as a major character defense is interfered with and can no longer help to regulate behavior. As a result of this defense disorganization, the patient may experience a loss of the sense of self. Consequently, trait behavior that was formerly enduring, reliable, and predictable is now fragmented. The psychologist can help the referral source to understand the importance of supporting particular individual defenses that have weakened, as well as the corresponding opportunity to provide the patient with more adaptive models and identifications.

When data in the protocol suggest impairments of defense structures leading to disorganization and fragmentation, the psychologist can contribute to the intervention process by pointing out the disintegrating state of the defensive structure and clarifying the nature of defense trait patterns as they relate to identifications.

The concept of identification as a primary character defense that contains powerful integrative properties needs to be emphasized fully in the report. Identification is the major ingredient of the personality that helps to establish characteristic or typical behavior patterns. These patterns become each person's behavioral signature, enabling the individual to respond to others in a consistent way. The psychological and emotional health of any individual and especially of the subject under consideration must be ascertained in large measure through the assessment of personal identity and interpersonal behavior. Thus, analysis of personal identity and interpersonal behavior is derived from individual defense functioning and personality trait formation requiring the intactness of identification and internalization.

In the following chapter, a discussion of the important features of personality is presented. What has been described as intrapersonal phenomena in the last few chapters can now be viewed in terms of interpersonal expression, based on identity and characterology. Table 11.1 presents definitions of the defense system, and Table 11.2, connections between diagnoses and defenses.

TABLE 11.1   Defensive Structure

- Signal anxiety or inner tension evokes the operation of a defense.
- Signal anxiety occurs in response to an internal threat (fantasies or impulses), or an external threat (other people or demands of life).
- Individual defenses include:

    Compartmentalization. Different aspects of the personality are kept apart and dissociated instead of remaining integrated. Often seen in hysteric reactions and especially prominent in multiple personality disorder.

    Compensation. A focus on positive fantasy used in the management of depression and narcissistic interests to alleviate depression and inflate self-esteem.

    Denial. Distortion of aspects of reality used in the management of hysteric and otherwise expressive personalities by screening out negative information.

    Displacement. Shifting reactions from appropriate targets to less threatening figures. Utilized by passive-aggressive and dependent personalities to manage anger and hostility by expressing such feelings indirectly.

    Intellectualization. Emphasis and exaggeration of thoughts over feelings to achieve a dispassionate, objective stance. Obsessional or compulsive types also utilize isolation, rationalization, sublimation, and undoing in addition to intellectualization in order to fortify a sense of control over the environment.

    Isolation. Ideas are kept separate from any connecting feelings. This defense is seen in obsessional and compulsive disorders.

    Projection. Issues of the personality that cannot be faced are attributed to others. The main defense in paranoid functioning.

    Rationalization. A justification process in which flaws sensed as threatening are excused. Ubiquitous, although prominent in obsessional disorders.

    Reaction Formation. The emotions of attraction and pleasure are reversed. For example, sexual feelings are turned into revulsion, or hostility into solicitousness because of the threatening nature of the pleasure that would otherwise be experienced; one of the defenses utilized in manic states.

Sublimation. Pleasure is transformed into work energy, as frequently seen in obsessional and manic states.

Regression. Reliance on behaviors mastered earlier in development. Observed in the psychopathic motoric style.

Repression. Expulsion of threatening material from consciousness. Germane to all defenses, repression sustains the unconscious amalgam of memories and feelings, and is used extensively by passive, schizoid, and hysteric personalities.

Undoing. Designed to sustain a position of balance by canceling threatening material, undoing is seen in obsessive and compulsive states.

- Defenses that form character trait patterns include:

Identification. Replicating the persona of an important figure as a way of controlling tension.

Internalization. Introjecting values, standards, or traits of significant others that neutralize conflict with such important figures. The internalized values and attitudes tend to control the individual and powerfully contribute to the shaping of behavior.

Splitting. Contains elements of denial and displacement so that other figures can be seen as purely good or purely bad without a sense of contradictions; or a single figure can be seen at different times in ideal or devalued terms without an awareness of contradiction.

Symbolization. Ideas and fantasies are disguised through external representations.

Turning Against the Self. Hostility is more tolerable toward the self than toward another person, as seen in depression.

TABLE 11.2 Typical Diagnosis-Defense Correspondence

Diagnosis	Defense
Hysteric	Denial, repression
Obsessive-Compulsive	Intellectualization, isolation, undoing, rationalization, sublimation
Passive-Aggressive	Displacement
Depression	Compensation, turning against the self
Narcissistic disturbance	Compensation
Paranoid	Projection
Borderline	Splitting
Psychopathic	Regression
Manic	Reaction formation, compensation, sublimation

SUMMARY

The role of the defensive structure in the management of emotion in the personality was discussed. Individual defense mechanisms were defined and related to diagnostic syndromes. In addition, defenses were differentiated on the basis of whether they managed individual transitory emotion or involved character trait formation. The central roles of repression in the formation of individual defense mechanisms, and identification in the formation of character traits, were emphasized. The need to report defenses in a manner consistent with the patient's final diagnosis was indicated. Findings related to the weakening of defenses in psychosis and crises were cited.

─────────────────────────────12

Interpersonal Behavior
Identity

It is useful for the reader of a psychological report to have information about a patient's intrapersonal or intrapsychic personality structure in order to appreciate how the patient's interpersonal behavior is affected by such inner structure and dynamics. At this point in the report, the theoretical bridge between the intrapersonal and the interpersonal becomes a salient communication. It is the point at which the patient's interpersonal behavior with respect to the presenting problem can be viewed in a broader manner. This wider perspective embeds the presenting problem in a total framework involving the subject's inner life and its effects on the subject's interpersonal behavior.

THE BRIDGE BETWEEN INTRAPERSONAL AND INTERPERSONAL FUNCTIONING

The connection between the intrapersonal and the interpersonal involves a theoretical view about the existence of derivatives. This means that basic personality conflicts which correspond to particular early developmental difficulties ultimately lead to current interpersonal behaviors. Thus, current behaviors are linked to the specific developmental stages from which they derive. Relating intrapersonal conflicts to interpersonal behavior involves the important task of recognizing derivative connections. In the process of determining derivatives, the psychologist interprets the protocol data in order to locate and identify basic conflict stages. In the psychoanalytic framework, these are the oral, anal, phallic, and oedipal psychosexual stages. Each of these stages is characterized by particular behaviors arising from specific conflicts and unresolved developmental issues.

The psychologist can draw inferences between early developmental phase difficulties and the expected interpersonal ramifications that are extrapolated from these difficulties. A comparison of the presenting problem and the patient's trait profile can be included, with implications derived from the particular developmental conflicts. This introduction of an organizing framework that relates intrapersonal conflict with derivative interpersonal functioning, including presenting problem behavior, is a key contribution that the psychologist can offer. This framework also enables the psychologist to consider the patient's functioning with respect to self-esteem and personal identity concerns. Stage-specific conflicts contribute directly to the formation of self-esteem and personal identity concerns.

CONFLICT STAGES AND DERIVATIVE BEHAVIORS

According to most psychodynamically oriented theories, early character formations—that is, early trait behaviors—become organized with reference to certain developmental themes of dependency, control, assertion, and competition. These themes roughly reflect derivative concerns associated with the Freudian psychosexual stages of oral, anal, phallic, and oedipal development, respectively. Although each developmental stage generates major derivative personality trait themes, nevertheless, derivatives from more than one such stage appear in the fully formed personality and reflect a range of variability. In the following sections the organization of derivatives is described in ideal form. In practice, the psychologist seeks to determine the specific derivative mixtures that occur.

Oral-Dependent Conflict

Disturbances in the early oral-dependent phase of development can generate enduring trait behaviors that include excessive dependency-related needs. A constellation of needs and their corresponding traits may include strong urges for immediate gratification, hostile-dependent frustration reactions, petulance, urgent demand, deference, and similar behaviors that comprise a particularly immature reaction to interpersonal requirements. Core oral-dependent features of interpersonal behaviors reflect a frantic search to have needs met, depressive reactions, or typical rage reactions toward the object of dependency.

In the test protocol, responses that reflect this conflict stage can include the presence of magical solutions to problems in projective stories, images of food or nurturant needs or emphasis on nurturant figures, an emphasis on animals rather than humans, an excessive focus on affectional needs through the appearance of shading determinants, and undifferentiated and perhaps primitive graphic representations lacking significant detail, as in drawings of stick figures or roly-poly figures or in relatively empty productions. There may be depressive implications in productions having a constriction of response, a miniaturization of graphic production, and a lack of attention to the chromatic aspects of inkblots as well as a focus on the dark elements of the inkblots.

Certain inferences can be drawn about the patient's identity, with particular reference to self-esteem, by examining the underlying intrapersonal conflict. As can be expected, persons whose interpersonal behavior is largely determined by dependency problems will be likely to suffer from impairments and fragility in the development and maintenance of self-esteem. However, the psychologist should be aware that patients with such early conflicts who can be described with the familiar term "inferiority complex" will often mask such concerns with compensatory grandiosity, magical strivings, and a show of self-sufficiency. All of these coping behaviors can also be part of the subject's interpersonal syndrome and become understandable when viewed from the perspective of derivative functions. This framework organizes intrapersonal conflict and interpersonal behavior and makes clear to the reader of the report the inextricable connections between psychosexual identity concerns, self-esteem issues, and interpersonal behavior.

Anal-Control Conflict

A second developmental theme that is central in the formation of early character and derivative trait behavior involves the challenges offered by developmental tasks during the period called either the anal or control phase. During the earlier dependency period, a successful nurturance experience and resolution of excessive dependency needs generate a more independent response in the developing child. The child is able to come to grips with issues such as the experience of separation, increased locomotion, more reliable muscular control, and other physical and emotional achievements that are consistent with greater maturity and age-appropriate independence.

During the phase of development concerned with control versus dyscontrol, the child is confronted with demands to perform, control, and master. Thus, the chief developmental concern of this anal-control phase is mastery. Such a concern is reflected in interpersonal behavior relating to the accommodation of demands that are inherent in any relationship, as well as in the resolution of conflicts over control and dyscontrol. The nature of the child's interpersonal experiences with respect to these demands determines subsequent character formations and derivative behaviors. For example, if encouraged to accomplish what is consistent with its abilities and motivations at this stage, the probability that the child will develop a sense of personal mastery is enhanced. This potential or actual achievement is similar to the achievement the child gains at the earlier, dependent level, when the problem of separation is successfully met. The combination of coming to grips with experiences of both separation and mastery contribute to a developing sense of independence. Success in the development of the child's autonomy contributes to the fiber of ego development. Difficulties in development therefore arise early in the child's experience, when developmental requirements involving themes of dependency and control are significantly contaminated with conflict. Under these circumstances, early character formations ensure subsequent problematic interpersonal behavior.

At the anal-control level, some of these developmental conflicts and impairments include conflicts of overcontrol that generate subsequent behavior consisting of a cluster of such traits as rigidity, orderliness, cleanliness, righteousness, objectification, and reduced empathic capacity. Another conflict during this period is the presence of undercontrol or dyscontrol. The cluster of traits that can be generated from this sort of difficulty includes acting-out, impulsivity, and argumentative, impetuous, impatient, and generally unrestrained behavior.

Diagnostically, conflicts of overcontrol frequently are indicative of an obsessional or compulsive character type. In contrast, the dyscontrolled person displays derivative behavior that, as an aggregate or pattern of response, resembles the psychopathic or acting-out diagnostic type.

On the protocol, the overcontrolled person may produce a preponderance of details. On the graphic material, productions may be constricted, symmetrical, and mechanical rather than inventive. A need for symmetry may also be noted as a typical response on the projective material.

In contrast, the undercontrolled or dyscontrolled person primarily shows a lack of consideration for boundaries and limits, especially on the graphic material where body integrity is minimized and one figure may collide with another. Furthermore, this personality type may reveal lability in the integration of color on the Rorschach by using a predominance of color determinants and under-utilizing form determinants which would reflect control. The reliance on color determinants is consistent with the emotionally impulsive style that may also be represented by extremely short reaction times and little reflection in forming productions.

In interpersonal relationships, the overcontrolled patient tends to strive for an element of control and correspondingly monitors relationships to secure this control. Inferences that can be drawn from this derivative interpersonal behavior involve difficulty with closeness, the quality of unempathic objectivity, and an emotionally stingy manner of relating. Thus, a trait cluster encompassing domination, rigid expectations, and emotional coolness tends to characterize relationships.

The undercontrolled or dyscontrolled subject is always moving away from relationships so that commitment and deeper involvement can be avoided. This behavior leads to an interpersonal style that is largely superficial as a coping strategy. It is based on the presupposition made by the dyscontrolled type of suffocating demands that are anticipated in any commitment or relationship. Here again, the bridge between intrapsychic conflict and problematic interpersonal relating can be discerned.

Strains in interpersonal commitment can be related to problems of identity and self-esteem. Among the debilitating emotional effects that accumulate from poorly resolved conflicts during the oral-dependent and anal-control phases are increasing frustration, anger, and resentment. The accumulation of anger resulting from an impoverished oral phase and exacerbated in a poorly managed anal phase is a precursor of a syndrome consisting of anger-related traits. These traits emerge as a permanent part of character formation and underlie the patient's interpersonal behavior as well as sense of identity. They include manipulative and exploitative approaches to people and a characteristic way of disappointing others because of difficulty in keeping promises, largely due to the need to avoid the commitment implied in such promises. An inauthentic sense of self is conveyed and, consequently, only relatively superficial involvements can be maintained.

Impairment in self-esteem during this stage can generate derivative behavior in which the person becomes entrapped by angry feelings that cannot be directly communicated, adopts an attitude of righteous indignation and criticality toward others, and pursues a never-ending quest to rationalize dissatisfactions. Thus, self-esteem is intensely and negatively colored when the anal-control phase is not reasonably mastered. It becomes apparent that anger and anger-related behavior play an important role in psychosexual identity, in self-esteem, and in the interpersonal behavior of the subject.

Phallic-Assertion Conflict

A third developmental theme in the formation of early character and derivative interpersonal behavior is the phase of development that requires a person to become assertive in the pursuit of needs and goals. The focus on assertion presupposes a foundation based on the relatively successful resolution of dependency and control needs derived from earlier stages. Then, when there are disturbances in the phallic-assertion period, certain specific problematic character formations are likely to develop around the theme of assertion. For example, difficulties in meeting the demands of this phase can produce passivity as well as the limitation of becoming assertive only through anger. There also are various forms of passive and aggressive behavior, including passive-dependent approaches. Therefore, the key compromise during this stage is the formation of a passive-aggressive pattern.

In the test protocol, samples of derivative responses representing phallic-assertion problems along the passive and passive-aggressive dimensions include delays in response or excessive reaction times consistent with hesitancy in the expression of assertion needs. Hostility features may appear on the graphic material, suggested by details on the figures such as the presence of teeth, fists, or clawlike fingers. At the same time, the gestalt can tend to appear infantile, weak, small, and seemingly unthreatening. In projective stories, responses reflecting these problems include themes revealing the subject's indirect expression of needs or readiness to express anger, rather than the direct expression of needs in a nonangry, self-confident, and assertive manner.

The characteristic inhibition about expressing and asserting needs directly and straightforwardly also implies reduced self-esteem associated with the phallic-assertive conflict. Since goals are usually viewed as inaccessible, it becomes apparent that the perceived inability to achieve one's goals further diminishes the sense of self-esteem.

In particular, it becomes less likely for goals to be viewed as legitimate when assertive behavior and self-esteem are underdeveloped. Consequently, it is only when the person's frustration leads to overt anger that assertive behavior can be risked. However, this risk can only be undertaken in the context of provocation, anger, or protest. This provocative interpersonal behavior has a damaging and limiting effect on the quality of relating that can be developed.

The limiting effects on interpersonal relationships that derive from impairments of assertion and self-esteem become manifest when intimate interpersonal relationships are attempted. For example, a person may be alternately passive and inappropriately explosive in a relationship because of anger that has accumulated during the apparently passive period. This kind of pattern underlies many marital relationships and presumably resembles the early pattern of relating that was present when the conflict was established; that is, passive-aggressive behavior generally evokes an angry response from those related to in the present just as it did in the earlier, formative stage.

Another interactional pattern that may characterize passive-aggressive involvement includes the symptomatic expression of impotence either in broad areas of occupation and nurturance roles, or in the narrower sexual context. An example is the husband who is sexually impotent with his spouse as a means of expressing self-assertion and power in a retaliatory way. This pattern of passive-aggressive, provocative withholding symbolically expresses anger in a passive but nevertheless frustrating form. Thus, the predominating conflict of the phallic stage contains passive-dependent and passive-aggressive qualities.

Oedipal-Competitive Conflict

A final developmental theme to be considered is the oedipal-derivative theme of maladaptive competitive strivings as a response to the unresolved early competition and rivalry with the parent of the same sex. The early unsuccessful management of this problem generates power solutions to conflict in interpersonal relationships. Such solutions can assume several forms. One derivative behavior, for example, may be frequent conflicts about feelings of loyalty and disloyalty. A typical acting-out solution can include repetitive sexual conquests. Guilt reactions following presumed disloyal behavior is another example of the form in which oedipal derivatives may appear.

When the conflict between loyalty and disloyalty becomes excessive, a person may experience ambivalence in interpersonal involvements. This ambivalence derives from the overly strict sense of loyalty to past nuclear involvements which inhibits full commitment in sexual as well as platonic terms. This particular dynamic reveals that in addition to issues of competition and rivalry, conflict associated with commitment is another derivative of the oedipal stage.

Data reflecting oedipal conflict can appear in the protocol, for example, in the appearance of frequent struggles for primacy among figures in the projective material. Concern with the symmetry of the inkblot may reflect basic competition themes as well as indicate the presence of ambivalence. In the projective stories, oedipal problems in interpersonal relationships may be characterized by themes of doubt, guilt, and impediments to overall commitment in long-term relationships. The theme of compulsive sexuality in the absence of a permanent, enduring relationship may also be representative of the difficulties of this psychosexual period.

Mastery of oedipal-competition conflicts can generate conditions in which cooperation, companionship, and commitment become valued achievements. When impairments occur in character formation during this stage, however, later derivative interpersonal behavior is influenced by reduced self-esteem. Consequently, the ability to assume an adult stance is diminished. A person whose identity is thus compromised can develop stage-specific derivative attitudes in order to reduce the anxiety associated with lowered self-esteem. One means of avoiding the threat of reduced self-esteem is to assume an agreeable stance. Persons who adopt this dispositional attitude have a tendency to be easily influenced and highly suggestible. Another stage-specific derivative trait in a person whose self-esteem is reduced is the development of a critical stance toward the world. This critical stance is designed to focus criticism at the world instead of toward oneself.

Impairments to psychosexual phase development contain diagnostic implications. Hysteric dispositional attitudes are reflected by childlike suggestibility, and paranoid characterological inclinations are reflected by criticality and suspiciousness. Thus, diagnostic implications are inherent in considerations of identity and interpersonal behavior and contain characterological elements.

As a prelude and framework for the analysis of diagnosis and prognosis, in the next chapter the organization of character and its diagnosis are discussed. Character configuration constitutes the mortar for the entire range of diagnostic possibilities and represents an intersection between the intrapsychic and interpersonal aspects of personality. Table 12.1 presents the chief psychosexual variables with respect to identity and interpersonal behavior.

SUMMARY

The bridge between intrapsychic conflicts in the early development of identity and the resulting needs and traits that govern interpersonal behavior was presented. The early, formative stages of development from which are derived needs and traits typical of the person were considered. Accordingly, issues of dependency and independence, control and dyscontrol, assertion and passivity, competitiveness and rivalry were discussed. The central characteristics deriving from such conflicts in each of

TABLE 12.1   Interpersonal Behavior: Identity

Current behavior is linked historically to psychosexual stage derivatives:

Psychosexual Stage	Developmental Theme
Oral	Dependency
Anal	Control
Phallic	Assertion
Oedipal	Competition

Derivative oral traits:
- The need for immediate gratification
- Hostile-dependent behavior: petulance, deference, depression, and rage reactions
- Lowered self-esteem
- Magical strivings, grandiosity, and compensatory behavior
- Diagnostic syndromes include attitudes of the depressive type or the mood of the grandiose manic type

Derivative anal traits:
- Demands to perform, control, and master
- The need for autonomy
- Behaviors and attitudes appear related either to cleanliness, rigidity, rightousness, and reduced empathy or to acting-out, impulsivity, argumentativeness, and impatience
- An objective, controlling approach, or an impulsive, manipulative approach contribute to interpersonal strains
- Self-esteem is lowered by an accumulation of anger and resentments
- Diagnostic syndromes include the overcontrol of the obsessive-compulsive or the dyscontrol of the acting-out or psychopathic type

Derivative phallic traits:
- Needs for assertion are denied, yielding passivity, or are expressed only through inappropriate overt anger
- Goals are sensed as inaccessible, contributing to lowered self-esteem and feelings of impotence
- Diagnostic syndromes include a passive-aggressive approach, and narcissistic exhibitionism

Derivative oedipal traits:
- Conflicts regarding loyalty and sexual acting-out with an experience of guilt in relation to disloyalty
- Ambivalence protects against involvement and commitment
- Competitive strivings and a sense of rivalry are overdeveloped or denied
- Diagnostic syndromes include a paranoid critical stance in which competitive strivings are overdeveloped or a hysteric mode in which an agreeable, suggestible stance denies competitiveness

these stages were related to a variety of emerging interpersonal tendencies and diagnostic dispositions with a focus on derivative interpersonal functioning.

The interpersonal section of the psychodiagnostic report ties in all previous sections concerning the organization and structure of dynamics, character, and personality trait formation. This sequence analysis then presents the information in a form that reflects the way the patient actually behaves.

This section of the report also enables the psychologist to draw final hypotheses regarding the patient's functioning. These hypotheses are offered and refined throughout earlier sections of the report. The final statement about the patient's functioning and prognosis puts a sharper focus on these carefully refined hypotheses.

13

Interpersonal Behavior
Character Diagnosis

The essence of character structure concerns the organization of enduring personality traits or dispositions within the individual. Character structure is reflected clearly in the person's behavior. Therefore, it is possible to describe a person in terms of his or her typical character structure or behavior.

Character formation develops from birth onward as the accumulation and consolidation of typical or characteristic reactions to the social and psychosexual stresses and demands that are made upon the growing individual from both external and internal sources. The compromises that the individual makes in meeting these demands are the determinants of character. Thus, no individual can totally satisfy the consistent and persisting stream of demands and requirements that continually impinge upon one's repertoire of needs. Each person inherently and naturally meets the demands emanating from parents, peers, outside authorities, or internal pressures with a necessary sense of compromise. Some demands are met more fully than others. The main point is that the psychologist should be clear that the way in which any developing individual meets consistent demands and expectations is through the imprinted and consistent expression of the individual's traits.

Various patterns of traits can be developed and expressed in the personality. In diagnostic terms, these patterns can be considered character diagnoses or personality disorders. The following sections present the most frequently discussed clinical syndromes that relate to character diagnoses. These character states also comprise the basic complement of *DSM-III* and *DSM-III-R* Axis II personality diagnoses as well as clinical diagnoses of characterologies not included in *DSM* nosology, yet frequently encountered in clinical experience.*

The fundamental character types can be organized into general categories based upon various criteria or underlying commonalities. In the following presentation, twelve basic character diagnoses will be organized in terms of the management of emotion and anxiety so that four major diagnostic clusters are formed.

Diagnostic Cluster 1: The first of these character categories or clusters is composed of the obsessive-compulsive, paranoid, and schizoid types. These personality types manage affect, tension, and anxiety through various mechanisms emphasizing control. In this way, patterns of defense are also utilized for purposes of control. Thus, the obsessive-compulsive, paranoid, and schizoid personalities can be considered *emotion-controlled types* and constitute the first characterological cluster.

Diagnostic Cluster 2: The second of these character clusters is composed of the hysterical (referred to in *DSM-III-R* as histrionic personality disorder), narcissistic, and psychopathic types. These personality types manage affect, tension, and anxiety through various mechanisms that can ensure the dyscontrol of emotion. In this dyscontrolled orientation, patterns of defense are also utilized for purposes of facilitating emotional expression and avoiding excessive control. Thus, the hysterical, narcissistic, and psychopathic personalities can be considered *emotion-dyscontrolled types* and constitute the second characterological structure.

The emotion-controlled category, emphasizing control over tension and feelings, and the emotion-dyscontrolled category, emphasizing expression of emotion and attenuated control, can be considered to be opposite personality dispositions. In this sense, the emotion-controlled character diagnoses of obsessive-compulsive, paranoid, and schizoid are quite disparate from the emotion-dyscontrolled character diagnoses of hysteric, narcissistic, and psychopathic.

Diagnostic Cluster 3: The third of these character clusters is composed of the dependent, passive-aggressive and inadequate personality types. These types manage affect, tension, and anxiety through various mechanisms emphasizing attachment to the nurturing object. In this way, patterns of defense are also utilized for purposes of nurturance, attachment, and acceptance. Thus, the dependent, passive-aggressive, and in-

*American Psychiatric Association (1980). *Diagnostic and Statistical Manual of Mental Disorders* (3rd ed.). Washington, D.C. Author; and (1987) *Diagnostic and Statistical Manual of Mental Disorders* (3rd rev. ed.). Washington, D.C.

adequate personalities can be considered *emotion-dependent* or *emotion-attached types* and constitute the third characterological cluster.

Diagnostic Cluster 4: The fourth character cluster is composed of the borderline, schizotypal and avoidant types. These personality types manage affect, tension, and anxiety through various mechanisms that promote insularity, isolation, and detachment with respect to the nurturant object. Thus, particular patterns of defense are also utilized for purposes of protective isolation. The borderline, schizotypal, and avoidant personalities can be considered *emotion-avoidant* or *emotion-detached types* and constitute the fourth characterological cluster.

The emotion-attached category, emphasizing dependency, needs for nurturance and attachment, and the emotion-detached category, emphasizing isolation and detachment from the nurturant object can also be considered opposite personality dispositions. In this sense, the emotion-attached character diagnoses of dependent, passive-aggressive, and inadequate personality are quite disparate from the emotion-detached character diagnoses of borderline, schizotypal, and avoidant personality.

In the following presentation, each of the four basic character clusters is presented with respect to essential clinical and theoretical features. It should be noted that character is understood to be formed on compromises based on the person's response to internal and external demands. Such compromises crystallize the individual's characteristic responses. A characterological aspect develops and becomes part of the person's stable, enduring, and narrow approach to a wide range of circumstances. If the pressures that go into the formation of such characterology are great, nearly all of the person's functioning is involved and a character or personality disorder, as it is referred to in *DSM-III* and *DSM-III-R*, is the result. The term character or personality disorder is utilized to indicate that most of the individual's personality is involved and the broad range of circumstances in which these characteristic traits appear is maladaptive enough to be considered a disorder.

EMOTION-CONTROLLED TYPES

Obsessive-Compulsive Personality

Persons with obsessive and compulsive character traits show an inordinate response to detail that reflects a perfectionistic approach. In addition, there exists a strong need for closure and an extremely controlling sense of the world. Pleasure is frequently only associated with the completion of projects or with a sense of effort directed toward organizing in an elaborate manner. Such persons are consumed with needs for controlling tension and anxiety, and consequently only minimal energies are available to devote to sharing and giving in interpersonal relations. Compulsive individuals are also overly concerned with rules and regulations, and their behavior is characterized by a focus on form rather than content. For example, the student who underlines textbooks in multicolored inks, always careful to use a rule so that each page becomes a colorful, well-organized object of perfection, frequently cannot absorb the content of the material. The issue that assumes importance is the orderly completion of a task designed to control anxiety, rather than learning the work. In addition, projects frequently are not completed because of concerns and ruminations having to do with accomplishing the tasks only through proper procedures. A moralistic preoccupation and excessively intense self-judgment also can be seen. Whenever such persons cannot gain control over their surroundings or over other persons, depression may be experienced.

On the test protocol, compulsive features are usually pervasive in every test. The graphic material is neat and orderly, measured and even, and replete with numerous details. The focus on detail, which is easily apparent in the responses to inkblots and in the projective stories, may also show a loss of perspective of the larger view.

Responses reflecting indecisiveness may be characterized by rumination about priorities or the need for reassurance from the examiner so that the task becomes more protracted. In *DSM-III-R*, this compulsive character diagnosis is referred to as obsessive-compulsive personality disorder. From the cluster of specific traits and dispositions that become evident in this compulsive type, the need for control of emotion and tension constitutes the fundamental criterion for inclusion of the compulsive type within the emotion-controlled cluster.

Paranoid Personality

The usual conception of paranoid suspiciousness and mistrust also applies to this character disorder. Persons with this characterology are hypersensitive and, most important, are highly critical of the external world. The character trait of criticality serves the purpose of deflecting criticism of oneself onto others. Associated character traits include hostility, stubbornness, argumentativeness, and jealousy of the progress of others. In addition, affect is generally cold, unemotional, and restricted. Further, the paranoid characterological configuration includes typical attitudes in which exploitation by others is expected, loyalties of friends are questioned, and insults are deeply experienced so that grudges become entrenched. Associated with this sort of sensitivity to real or imagined insults, such persons may respond with visible expressions of anger, sarcasm, or cynicism. Consequently, an overall attitude of caution is expressed in interpersonal relationships.

The test protocol contents may reflect rigid and oppositional tendencies and interpersonal relations characterized by hostility and power themes. In addition, the figure drawings may display a rigid line quality, a suspicious expression in the eyes, and the frequent occurrence of drawings in profile. An abundance of space responses on the inkblots, as in the reversal of figure and ground, frequently points to an oppositional attitude. A focus on inanimate movement responses reflects a paranoid sense of power in the external environment and may also characterize responses to the inkblots. Finally, a lack of use of varied determinants and a corresponding excessive focus on the use of form as the major and perhaps only determinant may be characteristic. All of these findings can occur in a context that is devoid of psychotic indicators.

Schizoid Personality

The traditional view of schizoid personality concerns the person's characteristic style of aloofness, coldness, and remoteness. Complaints frequently are made of such persons that they are unable to express or perhaps even feel warm emotions toward others. Schizoid persons rarely develop close friendships, including any meaningful family relationships. They are indifferent to feelings, praise, or criticism expressed by others. An absence of interpersonal contact also indicates the trait of withdrawal. Because withdrawal and remoteness are central in the personality structure of the schizoid character, such a person's ability to establish close and enduring relationships is effectively minimized and social skills are limited. Correspondingly, fantasy life takes on a compelling, motivating feature for the person and gratifications are accomplished largely through this fantasy activity. The fantasies of such persons frequently have a hostile quality that rarely is expressed directly in behavior. In many cases, work performance is not unduly affected and accomplishments may be achieved.

On the test protocol, the psychologist will frequently discover responses characterizing the schizoid disorder that involve minimal interpersonal or human contents. An absence of color responses and limited use of a range of determinants, along with an emphasis on form as the major determinant employed, are found on the inkblots. On the figure drawings, stick figures are not uncommon. An absence of shaded line quality reflects attenuated tensions, although instruments of aggression also may appear.

EMOTION-DYSCONTROLLED TYPES

Hysterical Personality

Individuals with this disorder—referred to in the *DSM-III-R* as histrionic personality disorder—are frequently absorbed by exaggerated needs for gratification and attention. They are overreactive, emotionally labile, impetuous, and frequently petulant. Most important, they show high suggestibility and an absence of useful evaluative sensibility. Such persons tend to become bored easily and therefore require excessive external stimulation. They also appear to be shallow and may behave in a helpless and dependent fashion or in a coy, seductive, and dramatic manner, spending inordinate time involved in romantic fantasies. In addition, hysterical attitudes include excessive needs for reassurance along with a corresponding need for self-centeredness. A particular diagnostic indicator here concerns poor ability to delay gratification.

On the test protocol, the psychologist may note that stories typically are construed with magical solutions to problems involving interpersonal activities. On the figure drawings, cosmetic features will reveal a narcissistic orientation. The absence of eye detail along with the presence of a smile may appear, reflecting denial as a major defense mechanism. Denial nourishes the hysteric's minimal use of evaluative capacities. In addition, the psychologist can detect the person's inability to complete a task. On the inkblots, there may be excessive or arbitrary use of color. Quick reaction times and an absence of concern with the logic of detail may be seen.

Narcissistic Personality

Persons of this type are frequently difficult to differentiate from those with a hysterical personality. Whereas the hysteric is focused largely on romantic fantasies, the narcissistic person also is concerned with achievement; that is, any and all achievement is over-valued. The major problem for the narcissistic person, however, revolves around concerns with self-esteem. An exaggerated sense of self is reinforced by any meager evidence as well as diminished by minor slights. Consequently, there are moments of profound self-doubt in which the self is correspondingly undervalued. Fantasies are concerned largely with endless conquests characterized by themes of power, admiration, and exceptional success, along with anything else that may be perceived as exceptional about the self. In addition, such persons expect special entitlements and cannot understand why their needs cannot be gratified. Their interpersonal relationships tend to focus on what people can offer them rather than on deeper or more substantial aspects of involvement.

In addition, narcissistic attitudes are reflected in the general absence of empathy and in excessive feelings of shame or rage in response to critical comments from others. Feelings of envy fuel a need for adoration and the narcissistic personality type is on a constant search for compliments in order to satisfy the adoration need.

On the test protocol, the psychologist may find that a cogent data profile revolves around exhibitionism. Responses reflecting compensatory needs such as grandiosity may appear. These attitudes can be observed in the content analysis of the inkblots and projective stories. Similarly, the figure drawings may be expansive, and they most likely involve some display of grandiosity and aggrandizement.

Psychopathic or Antisocial Personality

Persons with this character disorder show significant and impelling needs to act-out unresolved internal conflicts in their behavior. Acting-out may or may not be antisocial. The psychopathic trait syndrome is associated with aggressiveness, truancy, inability to maintain employment, short attention span, and the need to justify behavior by lying or other manipulative strategies. Mood problems such as depression frequently underlie this acting-out disorder.

It is necessary to differentiate the antisocial acting-out person from the general dyscontrolled psychopathic one. The general dyscontrolled psychopathic person can occasionally come to grips with internal conflicts and gradually minimize the acting-out. Children who were once diagnosed as having behavior problems and as being underachievers by teachers and social officials may later prove to be able to deal more flexibly with challenges and demands. This is less possible for the antisocial acting-out person, who can become trapped, for example, in a prison setting which limits the likelihood of rehabilitation or growth.

In addition, the acting-out type can be involved in physical confrontations, cruelty, and overall delinquent behavior. Irritability and impatience are typical aspects of the acting-out process. Planning ability and judgment are adversely affected by the pressure to act and expedience and lying are often utilized. This overall immaturity along with the absence of guilt or remorse make it very difficult for such a person to establish a meaningful monogamous relationship. Correspondingly, the deemphasis of conscience results in adoption of manipulative behaviors as a major characteristic. The severe aspect of this dyscontrolled acting-out type in its most pathological form is consistent with criminal behavior and not simply petit delinquency.

The protocol findings for this personality disorder are amply presented in chapter 9 on impulse versus control. It suffices to say that the protocol in virtually all aspects — responses to inkblots, graphic material, projective stories, and the results of intelligence testing — will be permeated with impulse features.

EMOTION-DEPENDENT TYPES

Dependent Personality

This disorder was formerly viewed as one version of the passive-aggressive personality disorder. The dependent feature of this character disorder contains an essential ingredient of passivity, so that autonomous or independent decision making and functioning is avoided and an effort is made instead to develop parent-child replications in all interpersonal engagements. Such persons tend to avoid demands and responsibilities, and they can also reveal an underlying propensity for depression and covert anger. Depressive feelings may be experienced during periods of separation; therefore, separation issues are a major concern. Derivative dependent behavior in adulthood is frequently expressed in submissive attitudes. Within such submissive and dependent patterns, the person continues to need excessive reassurance in a number of conventional activities. In addition, decision making becomes problematic and the person may find it difficult to initiate customary social interactions. The person may also behave in an unusually deferential manner in order to gain acceptance. Such a person can also feel deeply diminished by disapproval and can be profoundly hurt by any threat of separation or abandonment.

In the test protocol, projective stories may be characterized by excessive dependency features, magical solutions to problems, and the reliance on others for implementation of activities leading to the accomplishment of goals. The figure drawings may be characterized by childlike representations. Although the inkblots may generate an average number of responses, they may frequently lack an appreciable focus on detail. Rather, percepts will center on simple, whole, and easily formed conventional responses. The frequency of animal contents may be high and regressive circles may appear in graphic material.

Passive-Aggressive Personality

A passive-aggressive trait organization essentially is designed to gratify authority and avoid punishment simultaneously. This is accomplished in a way that frustrates the person who is perceived as the authority, so that the individual is able to salvage some sense of autonomy along with the expression of defiance.

For example, the child of an overdemanding parent extracting full obedience and absolute deference frequently responds with a passive-aggressive obedience that is invariably qualified with traits such as tardiness, stubbornness, procrastination, forgetfulness, and incompleteness. In this way, the individual's character partially forms along the line of passive-aggressive traits, which begin to occupy a specific place in the personality structure. In addition, as described in chapter 11 on defensive structure, the development of characterology is also reinforced through identification and internalization mechanisms. In the example just cited, not only does the developing person begin to evolve character traits as a result of compromise in relation to demands and expectations, but the person also identifies with and internalizes such demands and expectations. The identification process shows that the child or adult who operates with such passive-aggressive compromise formations on a deeper, motive level experiences an autocratic or tyrannical impulse which mirrors the parental style as well as reinforces the automatic passive-aggressive reaction.

In terms of behavior and emotion, the passive-aggressive person can also become strident with qualities of sulkiness, quarrelsomeness and inordinate protest. Such a person also frequently exhibits a grandiose sense of accomplishment while others generally do not share this assessment. As a result of this inflated sense of self, the passive-aggressive person resists suggestions for improvement and frequently becomes obstinate and self-defeating.

On the test protocol, passive-aggressive responses can be detected immediately by an unnecessary delay of responses, which reflects a withholding trait. The use of obsessional ambivalence also frequently reflects passive-aggressive manipulation. The figure drawings may be replete with overtly or subtly hostile features in the treatment of fingers and teeth. However, spontaneous remarks by the subject paradoxically can indicate a benign motivation. Projective stories show power imbalance and yet create solutions that thwart authority. The cardinal finding in this disorder is the quality of intentional inefficiency that covertly conveys hostility.

Inadequate Personality

Closely allied to both the dependent and passive-aggressive personalities is the inadequate personality disorder. Although no longer recognized as a specific entity in *DSM-III* or *DSM-III-R,* it is nevertheless included here because its frequent occurrence gives it more than historical interest. The major feature of this diagnosis involves a profound underresponse in virtually every aspect of the person's functioning. This includes underresponses in relationships, school, jobs, and sexual functioning. Associated with underresponse are traits such as strong feelings of inadequacy and inferiority, a weepy sentimentalism which often emerges in the context of melodramatic events, and an inappropriate sobriety with respect to authority relationships. Although such persons may demonstrate high intelligence, high reading skills, and high levels of conceptualization, performance skills and self-assurance are extremely poor.

On the test protocol, percepts may be interesting and varied but all performance tests will be impaired. Although few responses may be offered on the Rorschach, for example, some of them may reflect originality, high intelligence, and creativity. In contrast, on the figure drawings stick figures may be produced, and on the intelligence test performance scores can be significantly constricted.

EMOTION-AVOIDANT TYPES

Borderline Personality

Three major factors describe this character disposition. First is the superficiality and lack of depth of any existing relationship. Second, there is an intense reservoir of anger just beneath the surface of ordinary interaction. Finally, instability characterizes self-image, self-esteem, and personal and sexual identity. Along with the store of anger, a complement of tenuous, shifting controls exists. The borderline personality, unlike the schizoid type, may report discomfort with periods of isolation and loneliness. Additional traits include pessimism and impulsivity. Addictive problems or traits reflecting compulsive, obsessional, paranoid, schizoid, and narcissistic tendencies frequently may exist. Additional formulations, with respect to the need system of the borderline, concern fears of abandonment that are anticipated by the subject. Instability of mood also corresponds to protracted feelings of an absence of a sufficiently developed inner life manifested in the experience of boredom.

On the test protocol, the psychologist may have the impression that the subject is easily annoyed, and a brittle quality becomes apparent. A host of inconsistent and aberrant responses also can be seen. Thus, a mixed symptom picture suggests the borderline diagnosis. In the protocol, for example, responses containing primary process elements similar to the responses of psychotic patients can occur, especially on the most ambiguous tasks, such as the inkblots. In contrast, on more structured tests, responses can reveal sustained logical integrity. Thus, the protocol as a whole is largely inconsistent and erratic and reflects an unpredictability. In addition to having a mixed diagnostic impression, the psychologist should be able to detect a palpable store of anger in the subject, as well as to gather samples of responses from the projective stories that show identity confusion and an essential superficiality in relationships.

An inconsistency may be noted between the coherent stories of the TAT, which reveal adequate reality testing, and the poor form quality and primary process material that may emerge on the Rorschach. The tendency for obsessional, schizoid, narcissistic, and paranoid features to appear in the protocol is also typical. Concerns with personal and sexual identity may appear in the protocol in a wide range of forms. Finally, idiosyncratic responses on both the Rorschach and projective stories tend to show considerable concern with themes of loneliness, merging, and separation.

Schizotypal Personality

This character disposition, which is newly designated in *DSM-III* and *DSM-III-R,* encompasses various eccentricities and unusual personality qualities although it is not equivalent with typical schizophrenic or psychotic processes. Typical behavior in the schizotypal character type involves social isolation, constricted affect expression, and a variety of idiosyncratic behavioral peculiarities that together constrict usual interpersonal experiences. Thus, the amalgam of these schizotypal symptoms associated with limited social interactions contributes to the definition of the schizotypal personality as an emotion-avoidant type. Additional traits encompassed by this characterology include the suspiciousness and even ideas of reference of the paranoid and a strong attraction to magical beliefs and special sensitivities which, at times, dissolve into manneristic rituals. Ideas of reference do not reach the proportion of full-fledged delusions, nor does magical wishing regress to the syncretistic or correlational level of thinking. Thus, the schizotypal personality is distinguishable from the schizophrenic.

In addition, circumstantial thinking and discursive or digressive speech is also seen in the schizotypal person, but it appears in the absence of a breakdown or loosening of associations and incoherence that would be typical of a schizophrenic pattern. Yet, the schizotypal person may be unkempt and affect can even be inappropriate. The *DSM-III-R* characterization of the schizotypal personality also indicates first and foremost that this type will show a pervasive pattern of deficits in the social sphere.

On the test protocol, the basic differential diagnostic problem for the psychologist involves a distinction between schizoid configurations, schizophrenia itself, and a schizotypal pattern. The main distinguishing features of the schizotypal pattern concern the plethora of magical and wishful thinking, the appearance of some confusion with peculiar ideas regarding causation, and the appearance of a combination of a mixed defensive picture that includes obsessive, paranoid, and hysterical defenses. Thus, the schizotypal personality tends to produce more ideational content than the schizoid and, for the most part, content that is more coherent and not as fragmented as in the schizophrenic.

Avoidant Personality

In contrast to the schizotypal character who seeks protection and isolation, and in contrast to the schizoid character who in withdrawal radiates a distinctly remote quality, the avoidant character seeks primarily to ensure protection of self-esteem as a prerequisite to any attempt to attain social gratification. Thus, the avoidant personality shows a primary concern with social discomfort and rejection. Such a person is easily deflated by the slightest hint of criticism, and a great amount of energy is devoted to the anticipation of negative evaluations. Because of this degree of sensitivity, the avoidant character tries to protect self-esteem by avoiding social engagements unless acceptance is seen as highly probable. In a corollary sense, the avoidant personality can be expected to be socially at ease with very few individuals, limited to those who are certain to be approving of the subject. In protection of relatively continuously low self-esteem, symptoms will appear when self-esteem is further threatened. These symptoms can involve any number of anxiety signs, including blushing or crying.

In the test protocol, the anticipation of and sensitivity to criticism can be expected to produce a constriction of responses as well as some paranoid expectations regarding negative judgment toward the self. In addition, thematic material may reveal the subject's fear of rejection, especially seen in projective stories. A characteristic sense of low self-esteem may be seen in some of the responses to inkblots. Themes of a desire for acceptance in the absence of any hostility differentiate this character type from the schizoid character.

In this review of basic character diagnoses consisting of the most recent *DSM* nonsological considerations along with character disorders outside of *DSM* nosology, the complement of the twelve diagnoses may be better understood when they are grouped in this four-fold schema labeled emotion-controlled and emotion-dyscontrolled along one dimension and emotion-attached (dependent) and emotion-avoidant (detached) along the second dimension. Within this organization of personality types a multitude of behavioral manifestations, appearing throughout the twelve basic character types, can be better understood with respect to how each type manages emotion and relationships — whether the character structure is based upon a need to control emotion or a need to prevent control of emotion, or whether the character type is based upon the need to adhere to and depend upon a primary relationship or the need to prevent or avoid such attachment.

This discussion of basic character styles acts as a bridge between the previous chapter on interpersonal functioning and the following chapter on diagnosis. The vast majority of interpersonal styles and needs can be construed within a framework consisting of the basic personality types or of combinations of traits drawn from more than one type.

The psychologist will find it useful to gather the various samples of responses on the protocol as well as to utilize the hypotheses developed throughout the report in order to distill the patient's essential personality prior to discussing diagnosis.

In the following chapters the issues of diagnosis and prognosis are discussed, with an emphasis on the complexity of factors that comprise the diagnostic formulation. Table 13.1 presents the basic character types arranged according to the four diagnostic clusters.

SUMMARY

This chapter and the previous one considered intrapsychic functioning and interpersonal behavior. The specific tasks and conflicts pertaining to the various psychosexual stages of development were discussed, their derivative ramifications in character structure and interpersonal behavior were explored, and the effect of characterology on interpersonal relating was considered in terms of typical trait patterns. Self-esteem and personal identity were also discussed as being derived from conflict in specific developmental stages. Finally, the main personality disorders and

TABLE 13.1   Organization of Basic Character Types

Emotion-Controlled Types manage tension and character formation through the control of emotion.

- Obsessive-compulsive personality: Emphasis on intellectualized defenses to secure feelings of control and avoid threat from the unexpected
- Paranoid personality: Emphasis on projection of criticality in order to sharply distinguish the object from the subject and to avoid experiencing personal inadequacy
- Schizoid personality: Emphasis on self-containment, with aloofness and hostile fantasy

Emotional-Dyscontrolled Types manage tension in character formation through the dyscontrol of emotion.

- Hysterical personality: Emphasis on self-dramatization and denial of negative information
- Narcissistic personality: Emphasis on demand for admiration with exhibitionism and expectation of special entitlement
- Psychopathic personality: Emphasis on acting-out to avoid a sense of emotional paralysis ensuring diminished reflectiveness and reduced ability to learn from consequences

Emotion-Dependent (Attached) Types manage tension in character formation through excessive reliance on parental-type authority.

- Passive-aggressive personality: Emphasis on retaining dependency, attachment, and sense of individuality by covert power struggles with authority
- Dependent personality: Emphasis on magical wishes for gratification in the absence of instrumental activity toward goals
- Inadequate personality: Emphasis on broad-scale underresponsiveness to demands of the environment, requiring consistent input and support from authority

Emotion-Avoidant (Detached) Types manage tension in character formation through withdrawal and protection from authority structures.

- Borderline personality: Emphasis on limited relationships, a reflex toward anger, and unstable elements of identity
- Schizotypal personality: Emphasis on protection of self-esteem resulting in paucity of relationships
- Avoidant personality: Emphasis on needing excessive assurance of acceptance because of intense fear of rejection

representative protocol findings were described in terms of an organizational schema of basic character types. These character types represent the consistent and integrative aspects of personality functioning based on stable and enduring traits, dispositions, and emotional reactions. Since further diagnostic refinement would invariably encompass characterological dispositions as the unifying aspect of personality, it is important to clarify the individual's particular characteristic personality inclination prior to delineating diagnosis further.

$$\text{14}$$

Diagnosis and Prognosis
Diagnostic Principles

The principles that enable the psychologist to formulate a condensed and meaningfully presented diagnostic summary are discussed in this chapter. The value of a distilled, diagnostic statement is that it encapsulates the patient's functioning and the role that the presenting symptom complaint plays in the patient's overall personality structure. Clarification of the role of the symptom complaint relates the diagnostic assessment to the presenting problem that gave impetus to the referral for psychological testing in the first place.

A well-formulated, meaningful diagnostic statement summarizes the patient's functioning, problems, and strengths in a manner that indicates the nature of the disorder and potentials for change that exist. The identification of such possibilities for change can lead to the purposeful design of intervention strategies that sensibly and systematically relate to diagnostic findings.

In addition, a carefully formed diagnostic analysis, along with its implications for appropriate intervention, present the opportunity to evaluate the patient's prognosis. Thus, the diagnosis leads to a prognostic assessment. Just as the diagnosis presents the patient's total functioning in an encapsulated framework, the prognostic statement indicates what sort of change, growth, repair, or even deterioration may be possible or likely.

Since the prognosis for the patient and the choice of intervention are so dependent on implications contained in the diagnostic assessment, a careful analysis of the structure of diagnosis is of primary importance.

ELEMENTS OF DIAGNOSIS

The formulation of a diagnosis for the patient who has been tested brings together a complex array of several thematic and structural elements that the psychological analysis has served to clarify throughout the report. In addition, these features of the patient's personality have to be considered along with factors that are implied by the diagnosis itself. For example, some diagnostic conditions are chronic, and others tend to be more transient in their effects. Some diagnostic states involve deeper, more serious pathology; others reflect superficial disturbances.

A number of diagnostic categories are inherently fluid and changeable while others tend to be crystallized and rigid. The former are more amenable to modification and the latter tend to be recalcitrant to efforts toward change. Similarly, the presenting problem may be superficial within the personality or it may represent more profound, long-term ramifications. An additional feature about the phenomenon of diagnosis is that the reporting of different levels of pathology may be the most effective way to compose a diagnosis.

As can be seen, diagnosis involves several interconnected features, including:

- The potential for shift within any diagnostic formulation;
- The relationship between the presenting problem and the overall diagnosis of the personality;
- The presenting problem as an onset phenomenon which bears on the acute versus chronic dimension of pathology;
- The presence of various levels of pathology and their interconnections;
- The impact of these diagnostic features on the development of intervention strategies and prognostic formulations.

Diagnosis as a Shifting Phenomenon

It should be noted that the diagnosis is formulated at a specific point in the patient's life. This raises the implication that in certain cases the diagnosis may represent only a temporary or time-limited statement about the patient, and so can be a shifting phenomenon. Examples of diagnostic shift are the incipient, emerging psychosis or, conversely, the psychosis proceeding toward remission in which a relatively stable characterology emerges. An additional example is the change in character type that follows psychotherapeutic treatment. This example also reflects the fact that diagnosis may be an evolving phenomenon.

There are also instances in which fluidity and shifts in diagnosis are less likely to occur or may not occur at all. The most striking example of this diagnostic inflexibility may be the profoundly organically impaired patient. Even in this case, however, psychological elements related to the patient's comfort and maximal functioning can be enhanced within the limits of obvious pathology and, thus, be part of interventions involving change. The persisting acting-out of some psychopathic individuals may also be relatively unchanging; yet a deeper analysis of overall personality functioning may provide opportunities for change.

Therefore, reporting the potential for change with respect to the formulation of any diagnosis is an important contribution that the psychologist can make.

Connections Between Diagnosis and the Presenting Problem

One consideration the psychologist can make in a diagnostic formulation concerns the manner in which the presenting complaint is embedded in the context of the patient's overall functioning. The importance of this portion of the diagnostic process results from the fact that the presenting disturbance is a sample of the underlying personality problem and both the symptom and underlying problem have contributed to the test referral. The presenting symptom represents an outgrowth of psychological pressure in the subject and may also reflect the difficulty imposed on the subject's social network. Inherent vulnerabilities within the individual's overall personality structure or a shift in an internal aspect of personality functioning provide the occasion of symptom development. Thus, the relationship between the presenting complaint and the diagnosis may be clarified by demonstrating certain linkages. The presenting symptom, the prognosis, and the choice of intervention may depend on the nature of the linkage between the structure and functioning of the overall personality and the outgrowth of the singular or apparently more limited presenting symptom.

For example, the complaint of sudden hyperactivity in a school-age child requires diagnostic delineation of the symptom based on its nature, consistency, context in which it appears, duration, and corresponding signs of disturbance. Clarity about the nature of the presenting problem

is not fully useful, however, unless the nature of the personality disturbance that generates it is also understood. Consequently, the diagnosis
must be connected to the context of the presenting complaint. In the instance of a hyperactive student, the intervention and prognosis will
mainly depend upon the underlying personality problem to which the
original symptom is tied and which it reflects in microcosm.

As one possibility, the hyperactivity may develop from a recent organic trauma, such as one emanating from a head injury; it may stem
from the crystallization of symptomatology deriving from underlying
minimal brain damage which suddenly surfaces in response to increased
demands for concentration and learning in school; it may be generated
by upset in a neurotic child silently furious and fearful in reaction to a
recent parental separation; or it may be a sign of an emerging psychosis
in a child whose vulnerabilities have been stimulated by an increase in
social pressure.

These examples are presented to alert the psychologist to the complexity and intricacy of any approach to diagnosis. The link between the
original, overt symptom at the behavioral or experiential level and the
current diagnosis needs to be clear in order to bring effective focus to the
meaning of the symptoms, their purpose, the person's potential for
change, and an appropriate intervention. In a similar way, the choice of
intervention strategy and consequent prognosis, which can include or
combine medication, psychotherapy, or special educational placement,
closely depends on clarification of the symptom's connection to its underlying source.

Acute Versus Chronic Pathology

Another element that contributes to the formulation of the diagnosis is the duration of the symptom complaint. A determination needs to
be made with respect to onset of the disturbing behavior, which then enables an assessment of the length of the individual's difficulty and
whether any precursors to this particular disturbance have previously
appeared.

The importance of the duration of patterns of pathology is often
tied to the seriousness of the diagnosis as well as to the prognostic optimism or guardedness. Generally speaking, the estimate of prognosis and
depth of pathology in clinical disorders follows the same rule as in general medicine: acute disorders have better prognoses, and chronic disorders are more problematic and therefore more resistant to change.

For example, endogenous depression, in which a historically long-
standing depressive mood exists without an obvious external precipitant,

can suggest a poor prognosis. In contrast, the diagnosis of reactive depression—incorporated in *DSM-III-R* as dysthymia—indicates a depressive mood of recent onset in which the symptom is directly tied to a specific traumatic event such as loss or injury. In such cases of recent onset, the depression is a reaction within the personality which is designed to allay panic and anxiety and allow the individual to gain time to cope with the problem. Under these circumstances of acute onset, prognosis is generally positive. When the traumatic event is not dealt with adaptively, however, the acute reaction can potentially develop into a more protracted depressive state. Since in the majority of instances acute onset cases have a positive prognosis, the psychologist should be aware that when reactive depressions become chronic, a character structure that fosters crystallization of depressive features is sure to have existed beneath the surface. The underlying characterology may, for example, relate to needs for affection and dependency. The psychologist is, therefore, in a unique position to evaluate an acute symptom as well as long-term character trends that may complicate diagnosis of the acute problem. The coexistence of acute or reactive disturbances along with more enduring, underlying disorders reveals that there are various levels of functioning within the personality, and the diagnostic formulation needs to reflect them.

Levels of Diagnosis

In earlier parts of this book, references to preliminary diagnosis were defined in broad terms as a four-fold system consisting of neurosis or anxiety disorder, character or personality disorder, psychosis, and organicity. This classification system should be considered a heuristic device that is empirically based; it permits conceptualizations appropriate to the formation of preliminary diagnostic hypotheses. As additional findings are further analyzed, refinements in the diagnostic hypotheses are possible, since more complex possibilities and combinations become apparent.

Once finer diagnostic considerations are reached, the four-fold classification model becomes a basis for a more complex diagnostic statement. This classification model is founded upon clinical distinctions between the four major diagnostic categories. The neurotic diagnoses are determined by the predominance of anxiety and symptoms related to anxiety. The character or personality disorder diagnoses are based upon the relative absence of anxiety and the prominent role of enduring maladaptive trait patterns. The diagnoses involving psychoses are based upon profound thinking or mood aberrations that interfere with fundamental reality testing. Finally, the organic disorders are based upon physical or neurophysiological traumas that underlie disturbances in personality functioning.

In addition to sorting diagnoses into categories, the psychologist can establish a theoretical and integrative network on the basis of the conventional and pragmatic catalogue of discrete diagnostic entities. One way to provide an integrative approach to diagnostic formulation is to consider pathology or aberration as a reflection of three levels of diagnosis. The first of these diagnostic levels may take relatively external forms, such as behavioral manifestations. The second level of diagnosis involves internal phenomena such as deficits, anxiety, and idiosyncratic ideation or mood. A third diagnostic level includes character structure, which is intermediate between the internal and external dimensions.

Integrating Diagnostic Levels. One constant in the personality and in the corresponding diagnostic component linked to it is the character structure. This is the relatively stable, enduring network of traits and dispositions that expresses the typical personality style or approach of any particular individual. Since the presence of characterology is universal, it is appropriate to present whenever possible a diagnostic assessment that includes this level. If the psychologist consolidates the overall test results and summarizes the analyses throughout all the preceding sections of the report, the patient's character formation can usually be specified.

The patient's typical character formation exists regardless of the superficiality or depth of pathology. Consequently, an individual functioning at a neurotic level, a patient in a psychotic state, or an organically impaired person all possess, at a basic level of their personality, the quality of character structure. The importance of the characterological aspect of functioning makes it essential to specify its nature, even if it is damaged or fragmented. On the basis of the analysis of character functioning throughout the report, and in connection with material relevant to character traits presented in chapters 12 and 13 on interpersonal behavior, the diagnostic impression most consistent with test results regarding the patient's character style should be specified. For example, a diagnosis of obsessive-compulsive personality disorder would reflect this level.

If the findings additionally indicate the presence of neurotic phenomena, these can be considered to be components of the diagnostic formulation at a separate level. Such neurotic features can be specified in the diagnostic assessment that summarizes the totality of the patient's pathological functioning. In keeping with the previous illustration of the obsessive-compulsive personality disorder, if phobic disturbances also are reflected in test results, the neurotic level of diagnosis can become a diagnostic qualifier: the diagnosis becomes obsessive-compulsive personality disorder with phobic features. If, in addition, the test findings that have been reported indicate the presence of a psychotic process or organic impairment, these levels of personality disturbance would also be encapsulated in the diagnostic assessment to elaborate further the summary of pathological functioning.

An integrative diagnostic formulation will also indicate qualitative features that add clarity and refinement to the summary description of the patient. In this way, the relative contribution made by each level toward personality functioning can be delineated. The reader of the report can be informed in the diagnostic formulation if, for example, a psychotic process is chronic or acute, incipient and emerging, or progressing toward remission or residual status. The psychosis may be an underlying process in relation to the patient's character structure, or it may be overt.

In addition, even if the character structure is not fully intact, the specific nature of the characterological context that is impaired by a psychotic or organic process can be specified. If an organic impairment is found, it is useful to clarify whether it is mild or profound, acute, or chronic. The characterological context in which the organic impairment occurs is essential to report, as is the presence of any neurotic symptoms that have appeared. This kind of specificity can have a significant bearing on prognosis and intervention. For example, if a phobia or sexual impotence is linked to a neurotic level of functioning in an organically impaired patient, quite different implications would be drawn than if these phenomena appeared to derive from the organicity itself.

Any outstanding features that distinguish the diagnostic status of the patient can be added to the diagnostic statement. This addition enables the diagnostic summary to reflect more accurately the major factors of personality functioning; for example, the addition of an indication of depressive features to any diagnostic formulation where this is appropriate. Information concerning a subject's alcohol abuse or drug addiction might also be appended in cases in which these involvements are known and have influenced the test results sufficiently to warrant reporting of associated findings.

The various kinds of added features that are linked to the diagnostic formulation may or may not be related to the original presenting complaint or symptom. Nevertheless, the summary of diagnostic levels and their integration affords a context in which the presenting problem that brought the patient into the referral sequence can be considered in depth.

THE PATHOLOGICAL CONTEXT AND DIAGNOSIS

Since the patient was referred for testing and evaluation because of presenting complaints and the confusion surrounding them, it is logical to address the context of the presenting complaint in developing and formalizing the diagnostic summary. Simply restating the problem in diagnostic terms is not sufficient, because it fails to enhance the explanatory power of the assessment and does not summarize the test findings. For example, simply reporting alcohol abuse lacks clarification of any processes involved. Consequently, a diagnosis of the pathological context in which the presenting problem is embedded is a crucial part of the diagnostic effort. Thus, relating the presenting complaint to its pathological context is the logical conclusion to the entire report. This means that the essential diagnostic effort and conclusion by the psychologist will involve detailing the aspects of personality disturbance that relate to and clarify the presenting problem.

Alcoholism can serve as an example to indicate that a presenting problem needs to be embedded in a careful diagnostic formulation, since it illustrates the way in which a symptom gains meaning through more careful assessment of the accompanying personality problems. The patient's presenting drinking complaint may relate to underlying psychotic vulnerabilities, together with a pathological character structure. For instance, a characterological disturbance involving phenomena of dependency and passivity may lead to excessive reliance on drinking in order to reduce anxiety and attempt to retain integrity in personality functioning.

Diagnosing the pathological character structure of the patient clarifies the role of the presenting complaint as a reflection of specific personality conflict. Similarly, if there is an underlying psychotic process to which the dependent and passive characterology is affixed, this can also be useful in understanding the phenomenon of the presenting drinking problem. Thus, the personality context in which the presenting problem occurs is an important focus of diagnostic effort.

In relation to this example of a drinking problem as a presenting symptom, additional diagnostic factors may need to be considered. If the drinking is maintained for a period of years, an organic brain syndrome may result. The diagnosis of this syndrome and its effects on the patient's current functioning and prognosis would be crucial in the diagnostic assessment that summarizes the findings of the psychological testing. This example has been elaborated to illustrate the complexity of the context of disturbance that needs to be diagnosed in order to assess the patient's pathology meaningfully and in such a way as to clarify the prognostic considerations.

Another example of a presenting problem that illuminates the complex relationships among levels of pathology that need to be diagnostically clarified is sexual impotence. As a conversion symptom, the problem of impotence in the male may simply be associated with the diagnosis of a conversion type of hysterical neurosis. However, the context of character formation that exists in the individual is also important in understanding the nature and role of this symptom. Therefore, an assessment of the character structure would be essential to include in the diagnostic summary. For instance, this characterology may reveal the individual's readiness to rely on withholding, passive-aggressive interpersonal traits, which is not only a compatible context for the conversion symptom of impotence, but also helpful in revealing additional problems derived from character structure. These problems may in turn reflect a

TABLE 14.1 Diagnostic Principles

The elements of diagnosis include:
- *Diagnosis can shift.* Character change can occur as a result of therapy intervention; symptoms can be alleviated; states of remission can be achieved; or pathology can intensify.
- *A relationship obtains between the presenting problem and the diagnosis.* The presenting disturbance is usually an example in microcosm of the underlying personality problem.
- *Pathology may be acute or chronic.* The duration of the symptom complaint is the key question. Generally, an acute diagnosis suggests a better prognosis.
- *There are levels of diagnosis.* Diagnosis can refer to characterology, anxiety or neurotic symptoms, psychotic, and organic phenomena, as well as to any incipient pathological process. The prominence of any of these four levels also corresponds to the principle of the diagnostic shift.

The levels of diagnosis should be integrated. This integration is made with reference to character structure, neurosis, or even underlying incipient psychotic states. The diagnosis can refer to:
- behavioral manifestations
- internal phenomena involving deficits, anxiety, idiosyncratic ideation, and mood
- character structure: the enduring network of traits and dispositions of the personality
- psychotic or organic features

The pathological context is related to diagnosis. The pathological process in which the presenting problem is embedded should constitute a major part of the diagnostic picture.

more general kind of impotence, such as an inability to complete projects, develop or advance a career, or achieve fulfillment in a wider range of endeavors. Further, the passive-aggressive characterological context may reveal the motive to frustrate and assert individuality in a passive, covert way that provides additional meaning to the presenting impotence system. A phenomenon of depression may be either a consequence or contributing feature that is appropriate to diagnose as well. In order to consider further the relationship between diagnosis and prognosis, the organization and description of the diagnostic nomenclature is presented in the following chapter, along with a compilation of the diagnostic nosology.

SUMMARY

The subtle interplay between symptoms and the various levels of personality disturbance were discussed in this chapter. Whenever the interaction of these diagnostic dimensions becomes apparent from the results of testing, it is valuable for the psychologist to integrate them into the diagnostic formulation. Thus, it is frequently useful to detail the context of character in which symptoms occur, even clearly neurotic ones, as well as any underlying psychotic or organic phenomena. It is beneficial to describe the interplay and joint occurrence of any or all of these diagnostic levels as they contribute to personality functioning. Such a formulation enables a clear appreciation of the complex connections that influence the appearance of symptomatology. The interplay between the various levels of personality, and the extent of the relative impact of each, contribute to the prognostic formulation as well as to a choice of intervention strategy. Table 14.1 presents the major features of the diagnostic principles covered in this chapter.

15

Diagnosis and Prognosis
Diagnostic Nosology

The following discussion of the various diagnostic definitions can be viewed in terms of the diagnostic principles set forth in the previous chapter. Although the *Diagnostic and Statistical Manual of Mental Disorders (DSM-III* and *DSM-III-R)* is considered, the nosology presented here also retains those categories that traditionally have been useful in clinical practice.

DSM-III AND *DSM-III-R:* THE DIAGNOSTIC AND STATISTICAL MANUAL

Periodic and extensive revisions of diagnostic terms, definitions, and groupings that appear in each edition of the *Diagnostic and Statistical Manual* reveal the shifting nature of diagnosis as well as the changing emphasis and de-emphasis placed on some categories at different times. These fluctuations are responses to alterations in conceptions about diagnosis and nomenclature, the influence of research and clinical and scientific observations in relation to dysfunctional behavior, and historical and current influences on diagnostic purposes.

DSM-III and *DSM-III-R* conceptually strive to present diagnostic definitions in descriptive terms that eschew causative and etiological factors. The elimination of some time-honored diagnoses from the nomenclature or their inclusion with other categories reflects observations by some researchers of a declining incidence of patients in these categories. The acute versus chronic dimension of some disorders, for instance, is handled by sorting patients into different diagnostic groupings rather than by the customary use of one category differentiated into subcategories on the basis of duration of dysfunction. For example, an acute schizophrenic reaction or episode is classified outside of the schizophrenia group since, in the approach represented by *DSM-III* and *DSM-III-R*, the duration of overt symptoms for at least 6 months is required for consideration of the diagnosis of schizophrenia. Thus, the schizophrenia diagnosis always reflects greater chronicity in *DSM-III* and *DSM-III-R* than in previous diagnostic systems. In this revision of diagnostic use, what is generally and traditionally regarded as acute schizophrenia would now be classified as a brief reactive psychosis or as schizophreniform personality disorder, depending on whether overt florid symptoms endure for more or less than one week.

A further break in tradition is exemplified by the dropping of the diagnostic category known as "inadequate personality disorder" from *DSM-III* and *DSM-III-R*. In contrast to the traditional categories that have been deleted, however, recent interest and research in several areas have resulted in new inclusions. For example, both the borderline personality disorder and the narcissistic personality disorder have been added as discretely recognized diagnostic entities. Similarly, the section on psychosexual dysfunctions has been greatly expanded in response to current interest and treatment approaches in this area. The diagnosis of minimal brain damage is reclassified in *DSM-III* and *DSM-III-R* as an attentional deficit disorder based on insufficient evidence of positive underlying neurological trauma.

Many of the revisions and alterations that have been cited for illustrative purposes, as well as others in *DSM-III* and *DSM-III-R* that have not been described, are controversial and have been developed too recently to determine whether or not conventional acceptance will follow. The effort represented by the current *DSM* system at introducing order and clarity to the nomenclature is worth becoming familiar with because of the inevitable influence it will have on usage as diagnostic concepts inexorably change. A familiarity with the approach represented by *DSM-III* and *DSM-III-R* will facilitate communication among clinicians, researchers, and referral sources who may be inclined for personal, institutional, or legal purposes to rely on diagnostic formulations that follow the newest trends.

Diagnostic Axes in DSM-III and DSM-III-R

A unique feature of *DSM-III* and *DSM-III-R* is the use of multiple axes. Five axes are proposed, each aiming to reflect a relatively independent dimension of assessment. Only the first two are utilized in the diagnosis of mental disorders, however, with the remainder reserved largely for research purposes. As a result, diagnoses associated with the use of Axis I and Axis II completely comprise the final diagnosis. Within each axis, some ordering of diagnoses can be made to reflect the final hierarchical arrangement of the diagnosis. Although these axes enable a listing of the salient diagnostic components that appear in a patient's functioning, there is an absence of a methodology to formulate the interplay of these components or their relationship to presenting complaints. Thus, the use of two axes does not allow specification of the interrelationship of diagnostic dimensions. Employing two axes merely ensures that consideration is given to the presence of disturbances such as personality disorders—that is, maladaptive character structures—that would otherwise be ignored because of the prominence of more obvious dysfunctions. If additional disorders are present and need to be appended, this can be accomplished by further listing along either of the two relevant axes.

In formulating a diagnosis compatible with *DSM-III* and *DSM-III-R*, the largest proportion of disorders is specified on Axis I. These include the various psychoses, organic disorders, affective disturbances, neurotic disorders, disorders involving substance abuse, psychosexual disorders, adjustment problems, and disorders usually first evident in childhood (such as mental retardation and attentional deficit disorders). Multiple disturbances found to be present should be listed. If no diagnosis is relevant for Axis I or if it is deferred, that also needs to be recorded.

In formulating the diagnostic statement according to *DSM-III* and *DSM-III-R*, Axis II is reserved for specific developmental disorders, such as reading disorder, as well as for the important category of personality disorders. The patient's specific personality disorder is encoded on Axis II, and multiple listings can be made if necessary. If no diagnosis is indicated about a patient from the Axis II categories, this must be stated as well. Thus, a diagnostic formulation such as the following example completes the diagnosis recommended in *DSM-III* and *DSM-III-R*:

Axis I: 295.35 Schizophrenia, Paranoid Type in Remission
Axis II: 301.84 Passive-Aggressive Personality Disorder

Code numbers specified in *DSM-III* and *DSM-III-R* as an aid for statistical and record-keeping purposes are also recorded for diagnoses listed on either axis. In the following discussion, a more detailed consideration of specific diagnoses is offered. This analysis of diagnostic nomenclature reflects traditional use of nosology as it is divided into neurosis, psychosis, and organic impairment. The important diagnoses within these major categories will be delineated in a manner enabling the formulation of a complete, explanatory, diagnostic statement. It should be noted that the descriptive information and categorizations introduced by *DSM-III* and *DSM-III-R* in connection with disorders associated with childhood, substance abuse, and psychosexual problems are useful as a clinical resource for these diagnostic entities.

In connection with the diagnostic format that is introduced in this chapter, the categories of neuroses, psychoses, and organic impairment must be considered in relation to characterological structure as discussed and presented in chapters 12 and 13.

Material pertaining to diagnostic nomenclature is formulated here to maximize its usefulness in the psychological report. This means, in part, that the psychologist working primarily with psychological test data and secondly with social and historical material needs to be realistic about the contribution that can be made by an analysis of protocol data. In diagnosing organic syndromes, for example, it is not possible for the psychologist to differentiate the numerous types of organic syndromes detailed in the current *DSM* nomenclature. Such differential diagnosis is also highly inferential when made by physicians or other mental health personnel. However, access to social, developmental, and historical material as well as additional medical records available to other disciplines often permits more refined formulations in this area.

In order to contribute valuable diagnostic information, the psychologist can discriminate broadly between minimal brain involvement and gross organic disorder. In the case of gross organic impairment, the extent of involvement — whether mild, moderate or severe — can further be offered. Discriminations such as between minimal and gross organic impairment are more realistic for the psychologist to undertake and may reliably be formulated on the basis of response data from graphic material, intelligence test data, and projective material.

Thus, the diagnostic nomenclature and differential diagnostic discriminations must derive from the nature of the data that psychologists utilize. However, diagnostic nomenclature relevant to psychologists may not necessarily correspond with the categories proposed in *DSM-III* and *DSM-III-R*. In the interest of parsimony, the discussion presented in the following section on diagnostic format introduces practical considerations of diagnosis stemming from the protocol data available to the psychologist. These practical considerations include a combination of conventional psychiatric and psychological nosology along with elements of the new nosology considered in the current *DSM* nomenclature.

DEFINITIONS OF GENERALLY USED DIAGNOSTIC TERMS

Neurotic Disorders

In conventional diagnostic usage, the neuroses have been considered disorders in which anxiety is instrumental in symptom formation and usually a palpable experience as well. Symptoms in these neuroses are distressing to the individual and are regarded as alien. Anxiety is always central. In *DSM-III* and *DSM-III-R*, the prominence of the experience of anxiety in several of these neuroses leads to their consideration under the general heading of anxiety disorders. Several frequently seen neurotic categories are encountered in the latest *DSM* system — anxiety disorders, somatoform disorders, and dissociative disorders.

Table 15.1 presents the anxiety disorders of *DSM-III-R*. In the following presentation, this category of anxiety disorders will be described along with reference to some dominant features of these various disorders.

Anxiety Disorders.   Of the anxiety disorders listed in Table 15.1 — including several specific phobic reactions along with panic disorder — the following discussion will focus on those disorders of this anxiety category that have also been understood as among the main diagnostic entities within the neurotic range. These include anxiety neurosis (currently

TABLE 15.1   The Anxiety Disorders of *DSM-III-R*

Anxiety Disorders or Anxiety and Phobic Neuroses

Panic Disorder
- Panic Disorder with Agoraphobia
- Panic Disorder without Agoraphobia

Agoraphobia without history of Panic Disorder
Social Phobia
Simple Phobia
Obsessive-Compulsive Disorder or Obsessive-Compulsive Neurosis
Post-traumatic Stress Disorder
Generalized Anxiety Disorder
Anxiety Disorders Not Otherwise Specified

labeled generalized anxiety disorder), phobic reactions and obsessive-compulsive neurosis. The new diagnoses of panic disorder and post-traumatic stress disorder will also be considered. The remaining central diagnostic entities in the neurotic range, considered in previous *DSM* systems within the neurotic categories are now included in *DSM-III-R* under newer generic categories of somatoform disorders and dissociative disorders. These somatoform and dissociative diagnoses will be presented in the next major section of this chapter. They include the conversion disorders within the somatoform category and the various dissociative disorders in a separate listing. Table 15.2 shows this new *DSM-III-R* organization of the somatoform and dissociative disorders.

GENERALIZED ANXIETY DISORDER. This condition is typically one in which a person experiences free-floating anxiety. The anxiety is not directed to any particular object or situation, but instead overwhelms the person. It is experienced as waves of anxiety which are commonly referred to as an anxiety attack. It should be noted that such occasions of generalized anxiety do not occur without cause, even though the sense is conveyed that the person is somehow mysteriously possessed. In this diagnostic category, it is typical that a specific person or event is associated with the onset of the symptom. Symptoms of the generalized anxiety disorder can include interrupted sleep, edginess, trembling, startle responses, facial strain, muscle aches, racing of the heart, and digestive and breathing difficulties. On the test protocol, anxi-

TABLE 15.2   The Somatoform and Dissociative Disorders of *DSM-III-R*

Somatoform Disorders
- Body Dysmorphic Disorder
- Conversion Disorder or Hysterical Neurosis, Conversion Type
- Hypochondriasis or Hypochondriacal Neurosis
- Somatization Disorder
- Somatoform Pain Disorder
- Undifferentiated Somatoform Disorder
- Somatoform Disorder Not Otherwise Specified

Dissociative Disorders or Hysterical Neuroses, Dissociative Type
- Multiple Personality Disorder
- Psychogenic Fugue
- Psychogenic Amnesia
- Depersonalization Disorder or Depersonalization Neurosis
- Dissociative Disorder Not Otherwise Specified

ety responses may be noticeable in the quality of the patient's relatedness, in the line quality of all graphic materials, and in the presence of shading responses seen on graphic material and inkblots. In addition, anxiety with respect to interpersonal relations may be apparent in projective stories.

PANIC DISORDER.   Newly introduced in the anxiety disorders of *DSM-III* and *DSM-III-R*, panic disorder reflects an intensification of the experience of anxiety with symptoms including dizziness and even faintness, heart palpitations, nausea, choking, and feelings of depersonalization. Aspects of these symptoms may become so intense that the patient experiences fears of becoming crazy or dying. In panic disorder, the exceptional experience of terror that characterizes this disturbance occurs for limited periods of time, surfacing sporadically and unpredictably. Fear and anticipation of the unpredictable advent of panic attacks along with an anguished sense that something is wrong with the person may become associated aspects of this disorder. On the test protocol, impairment may be noted with respect to greater disorganization and intensification of anxiety signs along with themes of dependency, need for acceptance and fears of loss of control, especially with regard to anger.

PHOBIC DISORDERS.   This reaction is a highly disturbing, special anxiety condition. It involves a persistent fear of a specific object or situation, requiring the subject to avoid that object or situation. An irrational element in the fear is generally perceived by the subject. As a result of their symptoms, phobic persons are frequently in greater chaos in terms of practical living than some more severely disturbed persons. For example, phobic people fearful of traveling are sometimes completely precluded from pursuing work or career goals. Because of such severe problems, differential diagnostic questions are often posed between phobic and psychotic conditions. Occasionally, the psychologist will be requested to rule out psychosis in the diagnosis of phobic conditions, especially in cases of agoraphobia, where constriction can become quite extensive and limiting.

To assist with this differential diagnostic question, the psychologist can be guided by the recognition that neurotic phobias are based on displacement of the source of anxiety. The test protocol can then be scrutinized for references made by the subject to irrational fears and displacement sources. Thus, the source of irrational fears needs to be contrasted with psychotic indicators in the protocol in order to differentiate these diagnoses. In addition, the psychologist can contribute valuable information to the referral source whenever displacements can be identified.

Some typical phobias include claustrophobia (fear of being closed in), agoraphobia (fear of being alone or in open spaces where return to familiar surroundings may be blocked), and social phobia (fear of scrutiny by others). Simple phobias involve fear and avoidance of discrete categories of objects or circumstances, such as specific animals, injections, dentists, and so on. In instances of phobia, the person, event, circumstance, or emotional impulse that is the original, actual source of the fear is hidden by displacement. This originally feared source of anxiety is displaced onto a target that becomes the phobic preoccupation. The ensuing anxiety may then appear in relation to any number of potential external objects. This sort of displacement frequently appears in projective stories in an obvious manner. Phobic responses that occur in the protocol, especially if they occur in the later stages of the testing session, can also reflect the subject's difficulty in relating to the psychologist who is administering the test battery. The phobic subject will displace to test stimuli the phobic responses that represent the subject's basic interpersonal difficulty emerging toward the examiner. *DSM-III-R* includes as specific diagnostic categories agoraphobia, social phobia, and simple phobia, as can be seen in Table 15.1.

POST-TRAUMATIC STRESS DISORDER.   Post-traumatic stress disorder has been added to the current nomenclature to include the repetitious reexperiencing of a traumatic circumstance in memories, dreams or feelings with the accompaniment of intense, terrifying anxiety. Withdrawal from interpersonal interactions takes place along with a depleted emotional life. Sleep, memory and concentration become impaired. In the protocol, usual anxiety and panic features may exist, along with impairment of memory features and concentration, especially as revealed in the results of intelligence testing. The important consideration in evaluating the protocol would be to establish the neurotic level of functioning as differentiated from more severe pathology, since the symptom picture is rather specific for the post-traumatic stress syndrome.

OBSESSIVE-COMPULSIVE DISORDER.   This disorder involves recurrent thoughts or ideas (obsessions) or behaviors that must be performed repetitively (compulsions). A typical clinical example of obsessive-compulsive neurosis involves the person who begins to ruminate in a recurrent or persistent manner about any specific doubt. For example, the doubt may refer to whether or not the subject has locked the door. Such rumination and preoccupation constitute the first half of the obsessive-compulsive dyad. Whenever the object of the rumination or obsession becomes overwhelming, the subject acts-out the second part by actually checking on the object of doubt. In the example just cited, the subject would check to see whether or not the door was locked. This obsessive-compulsive experience may persist for a few minutes or it may become a ritualized exercise that can interfere with other activities. In cases that are encountered clinically, it is likely that some patients will tend to demonstrate symptoms that are predominantly of the obsessional type while in others, symptoms are more likely to reflect compulsions. In either case, the obsessions and compulsions are experienced as uncomfortable intrusions. Persons with such symptoms express strong needs for control and demonstrate frequent signs of ambivalence.

On the test protocol, the psychologist frequently sees a major focus on symmetry responses and references to self-doubt, and perhaps also responses reflecting the defense mechanism of undoing. Such indications also reflect the considerable development of a pervasive ambivalence. For example, under the pressure of ambivalence, the subject gives a response and then reconsiders and offers an alternate response, frequently an opposite one. In addition, the self-doubt of the subject is expressed in the graphic material by inordinate attention to detail, indecision or ambivalence, and undoing, commonly expressed, for example, in frequent erasures. An intellectualized approach to test responses can produce a lengthy, detailed protocol reflecting the overinclusive obsessional tendency. Subjects may also compulsively attempt to measure their drawings of geometric figures or make references to how symmetrical the inkblots seem to be — an oblique example of anxiety about performance.

Somatoform Disorders. This grouping of disorders in the neurotic range of disturbance utilize hysterical mechanisms in which a spectrum of bodily reactions or preoccupations appear. These bodily symptoms serve to symbolize conflict or to convert anxiety into a controlled or managed, although maladaptive, form. Of the somatoform disorders listed in Table 15.2, the major entities that will be considered here include conversion disorder, hypochondriasis, and somatization disorder.

CONVERSION DISORDER. In this disorder, anxiety is manifested in a physical symptom such as alterations of functioning involving anesthesia, paralysis, tunnel vision, and even vomiting. All of these physical alterations develop in the absence of any physical basis for the disorder. The purpose of these conversions is to keep an internal conflict out of awareness, thereby constituting the subject's primary gain. At the same time, a secondary gain is achieved through securing the subject's dependency gratification. The psychologist may be able to establish this diagnosis by identifying the feature of *la belle indifference,* in which the subject exhibits a conspicuous lack of concern about the symptom, even though it may consist of an alteration as serious as paralysis of a limb. The psychologist also occasionally needs to differentiate between a hysterical reaction and the malingering seen in psychopathic disorders. The difference in these disorders is that in the behavior of the hysterical person a disregard of logic is exhibited with respect to the symptom, while the malingerer maintains a faithful focus on the logic of the behavior as it concerns the symptom. For example, the patient malingering with a paralysis symptom would consistently maintain the paralysis, and the patient with a hysterical alteration would be more inconsistent; that is, the paralysis can disappear whenever convenient.

On the test protocol, the hysteric patient frequently shows samples of suggestibility, such as in projective stories in the form of dependency themes and ineffective activity related to goal achievement. In addition, a childlike quality is often reflected in response to the inkblots, where, the subject may offer a high percentage of animal images, an impulsive response quality, and an immediate reaction to color stimuli. On the graphic material, the absence of pupils and a "smile of denial" can frequently characterize the figure drawing.

HYPOCHONDRIASIS.   The hypochondriacal patient is somewhat similar to the conversion disorder in having bodily complaints without a physical base that are utilized to manage psychological conflicts and anxiety. The essence of hypochondriasis is the exaggerated reaction to physical sensations and persistent unrealistic fears of having diseases that are not medically supported. In this disorder, the person's life becomes governed by a catalogue of fears in relation to physical disease. Such persons become overconcerned with bodily sensations so that the experience of an ache or pain can generate ruminations regarding a possible fatal disorder. A host of phantom symptoms lacking any medical basis develop and promote a complex history of relationships with various physicians. These particular physicians may be depended upon and also may become victims of the patient's disappointment as disease preoccupations persist.

On the test protocol, similarities to the findings in conversion disorders appear along with an abundance of references to disease and impairments, and anatomical references in response to inkblots are seen. Frequent references to bodily defects also appear in the graphic material.

SOMATIZATION DISORDER.   In contrast to hypochondriacal disorders, persons with somatization reactions actually develop physical problems and physical disturbances. Yet, since these disturbances are psychologically based, positive medical conditions with an organic foundation either can not be established or the somatic complaints and disturbances exceed the medical findings disproportionately. Symptoms range from minor discomforts such as swallowing problems or fainting to more serious difficulties involving cardiopulmonary functioning. A lengthy medical history is typical of patients with somatization disorder. On the test protocol the subject often demonstrates submissive traits of deference and supplication in an attempt to rely on the examiner for leadership. Bodily and anatomical references along with themes of weakness and helplessness frequently occur in response to projective material.

Dissociative Disorders. Another grouping of neurotic disorders in the current *DSM* nomenclature includes the dissociative disorders in which the experience of anxiety is minimized by various types of hysterical mechanisms centering on dissociation. Thus, these neurotic disturbances are known as dissociative disorders, or in keeping with more traditional clinical usage, hysterical neuroses, dissociative type.

Among the dissociative reactions, as listed in Table 15.2, are fugue state, psychogenic amnesia, multiple personality, and depersonalization disorder, to be considered here. In these conditions, altered consciousness and identity are central. Subjects may not have any recall of the time they spent in the altered state. In severe cases, persons have been known to disappear for years. In certain special symptom disorders within the dissociative reactions, such as narcolepsy, the dissociation is accompanied by automatic behavior along with a fugue state and amnesia that may last 10 or 15 minutes. In other severe dissociative disorders, such as multiple personality, dissociation takes the form of more than one identity within the personality.

In *DSM-III-R*, the distinction between multiple personality, psychogenic fugue and psychogenic amnesia relates to the major dissociative focus. In multiple personality, the subpersonalities are aware of the major personality but the major personality remains in the dark regarding the other multiple identities. In psychogenic fugue, there is a dissociation and suppression of the central personality. In the condition of psychogenic amnesia, a loss of memory occurs regarding personal identifying information about the personality. In the depersonalization disorder, a disorientation occurs involving an alteration in the sense of self that is comparable to a detachment of self.

In testing patients with dissociative symptoms, the psychologist needs to differentiate between organic brain syndromes and psychogenic dissociation symptoms. On the test protocol, organic brain syndrome may be ruled out whenever the graphic material is faithfully reproduced, and there is an absence of color distortion on the inkblots and the color determinant is reasonably integrated and not chaotically or arbitrarily used by the patient. Organic features are similarly absent on the figure drawings, although unusual compartmentalizations may be drawn into the figures, representing the dissociations that support reliance on repressive and compartmentalization defenses. On the projective stories, disparate overt and covert motives are attributed to the subject without any apparent logical difficulty.

Organic Impairment Disorders

While *DSM* nomenclature covers a wide range of organic disorders, psychological testing most usefully clarifies the traditional categories of minimal brain dysfunction and organic brain syndrome.

MINIMAL BRAIN DYSFUNCTION. The psychologist can gather response samples throughout the test protocol that suggest minimal brain involvement as the cause of an array of imperfect responses. With graphic material, for example, such imperfections include difficulties with closure, line instability, collision features, pressured line quality, difficulty in maintaining symmetry, or self-doubts expressed by frequent questioning of the examiner about whether designs were copied well. In response to the inkblots, questionable form responses may appear, and arbitrary use of color and poor color integration also may be seen. Impulse features in behavior as well as in protocol responses will be broadly represented. On the figure drawing, the subject's productions may be primitive and childlike. On the intelligence test, highly scattered results are seen. Some subtests remain intact and others will reflect impairment.

GROSS ORGANIC BRAIN SYNDROME. This disorder is often obvious in the patient's responses throughout the test protocol. First, many of the gestalts on the graphic material become confused and lost, and the patient appears to be unable to address the task. Frequently, the psychologist can observe that the patients who do make some effort to address this task become momentarily frustrated and express impulsive anger. Perseveration and perplexity often appear in the test results. On the intelligence test, memory and abstraction impairments are typical and many subtests reflect gross confusion. The figure drawings may appear chaotic, with limbs appearing in inappropriate places. On the inkblots, color also is used inappropriately and chaotically. As a differential diagnostic problem, there is a gross gestalt obliteration in organic cases in contrast with the productions of schizophrenic subjects, who generate distorted and inappropriate ideation as well as form idiosyncracies while maintaining the essence of the gestalt. In the following section, the psychoses are considered and divided into schizophrenic and mood disorders.

The Psychoses

In this section, the psychotic disorders—both thinking and affective disorders—are presented. First, those diagnostic entities of traditional *DSM* nomenclature are provided along with the newer conceptualizations of *DSM-III-R* leading to *DSM-IV*. The newer diagnostic refinements of the latest *DSM* nosology (in *DSM-III* and *DSM-III-R*) concerning schizophrenia are listed in Table 15.3. This table also shows the clinical tradition that developed regarding schizophrenia,

TABLE 15.3 Schizophrenic Disorders Classified in *DSM* Nosology

DSM-III	*DSM-III-R*
Disorganized type	Catatonic type
Catatonic type	Disorganized type
Paranoid type	Paranoid type
Undifferentiated type	Undifferentiated type
Residual type	Residual type

Course of Disorder
Subchronic
Chronic
Subchronic with acute exacerbation
Chronic with acute exacerbation
Remission

DSM-II
Simple type
Hebephrenic type
Catatonic type
Paranoid type
Acute schizophrenic episode
Latent type
Residual type
Schizo-affective type
Childhood type
Chronic undifferentiated type

which culminated in *DSM-II*. Several clinically valuable types or variants of schizophrenia appear in the older *DSM-II* classification. Some of these types of schizophrenia described in *DSM-II* have been eliminated or construed as parts of other diagnostic entities in the newest *DSM-III-R* classification scheme. The following presentation will review several of these older *DSM-II* nosologies that clinicians are most familiar with along with several of the newer *DSM-III-R* types leading to *DSM-IV* conceptions.

Schizophrenia.   Conventional psychiatric nosology with respect to schizophrenia traditionally included four major types.

The Simple Type.   The central characteristic in simple schizophrenia is flattened affect within the context of a thought disorder. Another significant characteristic is the gradual, insidious process of withdrawal and isolation that leads the subject increasingly into an autistic state. The protocol material generally reflects marked unproductiveness, poor form quality, and absence of the use of color on the inkblots. Extremely simple and even sticklike figures appear in the figure drawing, and childlike, incomplete stories are produced. Within this context, geometric gestalts usually are maintained.

The Hebephrenic Type.   This diagnostic entity is chiefly characterized by an interpersonal framework of relating that includes silliness, inappropriate giggling, and sudden, childish embarrassment along with expressions of inappropriate affect. This framework is so consistent that the psychologist can often establish the hebephrenic diagnosis on the basis of the patient's interpersonal behavior during testing. Most of the responses to the test material are influenced by the patient's characteristic immaturity and inappropriateness.

Both the simple and the hebephrenic schizophrenia types are no longer considered as distinct entities in *DSM-III* and *DSM-III-R*, but they are included under the category of either disorganized or undifferentiated schizophrenia.

The Catatonic Type.   A major behavioral polarity exists in this diagnostic type that is expressed through either a catatonic withdrawal or excitement. In the withdrawn state, the patient may become fixed in one position and not move for extended periods of time. The skin acquires a waxy flexibility, and although the subject's physical position may be changed by others, the new position will be maintained in the same bizarre manner. Even in this postural state, the patient can be lucid. The restriction of behavior also produces what appears to be a stupor or mutism. During periods of excitement the subject may be destructive.

On the test protocol, subjects who are catatonic but neither withdrawn nor excited may offer responses that show great instability of impulse control. At the same time, they may show responses characterized by energy flowing back into the body. On the figure drawings, for example, a typical drawing appears bizarre in facial expression and somewhat primitive; it may be centered and placed high on the page, and it may include the subject of the drawing in a full frontal position with arms on the hips. Thus, limbs are formed in a way that brings their return to the body, suggesting a reference to an energy that flows from the arms back into the body. Responses of catatonic patients may also show underlying depressive trends which frequently may be difficult to differentiate from withdrawal behavior. Agitation is usually short-lived in the excited state. Depression and withdrawal are generally more dominant.

The Paranoid Type. The paranoid schizophrenic type is characterized by the presence of delusions that may or may not be crystallized, by feelings of persecution and grandiosity and possibly jealousy, and frequently by auditory or visual hallucinations. The delusional system is based on false, fixed ideas and the system is often so pervasive that it appears in protocol responses. Guardedness, reflecting suspiciousness and mistrust, may also appear and affect protocol responses. Also present may be ideas regarding bodily distortion, religious preoccupations and obsessions with death. Obsessional and intellectual defenses are frequently utilized in this ideational type of schizophrenic disorder. The major defense mechanism employed is projection, by which anger and criticality are transformed to persecutory ideation and inferiority to grandiosity. Transparencies may be seen on figure drawings along with figures drawn in profile, and there may be extensive elaborations of the sensory organs, especially the eyes or ears. Inanimate power influences and themes may be inordinately represented on the inkblots. Delusional material also may be seen in the projective stories. The psychologist can make a contribution to the overall assessment by evaluating the possibility of violent or other dangerous acting-out. It is important to remember that a paranoid person with a delusional system can be reasonable in many spheres of cognitive organization and yet have the capacity to act-out fantasies based upon stimulation of the delusional system.

In the newer conception of *DSM-III-R*, as noted, the simple and hebephrenic types have been deleted as specific entities and the category of schizophrenia includes the disorganized, undifferentiated, and residual types as seen in Table 15.3 In addition, Table 15.4 shows the psy-

TABLE 15.4   Psychotic Disorders Not Elsewhere Classified

DSM-III
Schizophreniform Disorder
Brief Reactive Psychosis
Schizoaffective Disorder
Atypical Psychosis

DSM-III-R
Brief Reactive Psychosis
Schizophreniform Disorder
Schizoaffective Disorder
Induced Psychotic Disorder
   (Shared Paranoid Disorder)
Psychotic Disorder Not Otherwise Specified
   (Atypical Psychosis)

chotic disorders in the newer nomenclature that are not classified or targeted to any particular schizophrenic or mood categories. Among these, for example, is the schizoaffective disorder to be presented in the following section. Within the category of psychosis, this schizoaffective diagnosis can be viewed as a bridge between thought and mood disorders.

Schizoaffective Disorder.   While schizophrenia is formulated predominantly in terms of thinking disorganization and the remaining psychoses are characterized primarily by affective disorganization, there are subjects who do not fit either of these categories. The schizoaffective disorder entity encompasses subjects who display aberrations in thinking as well as in mood. The central phenomenon in this diagnosis is the combination of inappropriate, confused thinking and mood disturbance. The diagnosis is determined by the fact that a definite, disordered mood of depression, excitability, or lability consistently appears. On the test protocol, a mixed picture appears of findings relevant to confused and even paranoid thinking, along with signs of depression or agitation.

Affective Psychotic Disorders.   In this section, the affective psychotic disorders will be presented using the terminology of the older diagnostic nomenclature culminating in the tradition of *DSM-II*. In addition, concepts from the newer diagnostic nomenclature regarding affective disorders will also be represented as drawn from *DSM-III-R*. It should be noted as reflected in Table 15.5 that in *DSM-III-R* all distur-

TABLE 15.5 Mood Disorders in *DSM-III* and *DSM-III-R* Nosology

	BIPOLAR DISORDERS	*DEPRESSIVE DISORDERS*
DSM-III Major Affective Disorders	*DSM-III & III-R* Bipolar Disorder, Mixed Bipolar Disorder, Manic Bipolar Disorder, Depressed	*DSM-III & III-R* Major Depression • Single Episode • Recurrent • Chronic/Melancholic

	(1) Mild (2) Moderate (3) Severe
	(4) With psychotic features
	  • Mood congruent
	    or
	  • Mood incongruent
	(5) In partial remission
	(6) In full remission	

DSM-III
Other
Specific
Affective
Disorders
	DSM-III
	  Cyclothymic Disorder
	
	DSM-III-R
	  Cyclothymia
		DSM-III
		  Dysthymic Disorder
		    (or Depressive Neurosis)
		
		DSM-III-R
		  Dysthymia
		    (or Depressive Neurosis)
		Primary or secondary type
		Early or late onset

DSM-III
Atypical
Affective
Disorders
	DSM-III
	Atypical Bipolar Disorder
	
	DSM-III-R
	  Bipolar Disorder Not Other-
	  wise Specified
		DSM-III
		Atypical Depression
		
		DSM-III-R
		  Depressive Disorder Not
		  Otherwise Specified

bances of affect are grouped together and labeled as mood disorders both with respect to the condition of psychosis as well as nonpsychosis.

PSYCHOTIC DEPRESSION. Typically, psychotic depression is differentiated from nonpsychotic depression by the presence of hallucinatory and delusional phenomena. The main mood, however, is intractable depression. In this sense, psychotic depression resembles the schizoaffective type in structure; there are aberrations in thinking as well as in affect, but the mood of depression strongly predominates. The diagnosis of psychotic depression most resembles the cluster of diagnoses listed under major depression in *DSM-III-R*. This category is the major affective disorder that does not involve bipolar elements.

On the test protocol, hallucinatory and delusional material may infiltrate all of the data. In analyzing the responses, however, the depressed mood will be striking. Features of depression will be seen in the projective stories, in the constriction of the graphic material, and in the significant attenuation of color on the inkblots. The overuse of achromatic color may also be produced in responses to inkblots.

MANIC-DEPRESSIVE PSYCHOSIS. The manic-depressive diagnosis is referred to in the new *DSM* nomenclature as the bipolar disorder within the category of major affective disorders. This listing may be seen in Table 15.5. It should be noted that, in the current nomenclature, bipolar disorders may appear within either psychotic or nonpsychotic psychopathological contexts. When the psychotic level of disturbance is reached, then the bipolar major affective disorder corresponds with the traditional manic-depressive diagnosis.

The major feature of manic-depressive psychosis is the presence of a pronounced mood disturbance in the context of the bizarre and confused thinking which is characteristic of any psychosis. The mood disturbance tends to surface repeatedly and to alternate with periods of remission, and it is characterized by either extreme agitation or depression. Only occasionally is there an alternation between the manic and depressive poles of affect disturbance.

On the test protocol, if the patient has a manic disposition or is in a manic phase, productions are extremely expansive and inaccurate, with limited attention to detail. A vast number of responses and circumstantial details are presented. Expansiveness also is seen in the graphic material, which often has many inappropriate features and numerous additions. On the inkblots, form quality is frequently sacrificed to speed. The emphasis on speed also frequently appears on the subtests of the intelligence scale. This sacrifice of quality for the sake of speed is consistent with the subject's generally superficial approach. The subject may often appear to be project-oriented and absorbed in productions during testing.

The manic-depressive patient who is in a depressed phase usually exhibits responses similar to those seen with psychotically depressed patients. Information pertaining to the length and frequency of periods of depression, as well as age of onset, help in the differentiation between psychotic depression and manic-depressive psychosis. In the latter, periods of depression may be less prolonged, tend to occur repeatedly, and begin at a younger age than in psychotic depression.

Nonpsychotic Mood Disorders

CYCLOTHYMIC AND DYSTHYMIC DISORDER. Another kind of bipolar disorder included in *DSM-III* and *DSM-III-R* is the cyclothymic type. Essentially, this diagnosis involves a mood disorder with periods of elation and depression that are considered less severe than in the bipolar disorder. In the dysthymic disorder, depression is the unipolar dimension to be considered and this diagnosis of the dysthymic type roughly corresponds to the reactive depression of *DSM-II* where the depression was designed in the personality to allay anxiety stimulated by a specific precipitating event. In the dysthymic disorder—in contrast to reactive depression—an additional feature of pervasive pessimism characterizes the personality in a more enduring fashion. The test protocols of the cyclothymic as well as dysthymic personalities will reflect similar profiles to the diagnoses of bipolar and major depression, respectively, albeit on a less severe level.

These diagnostic formulations generally outline the amalgam of diagnostic possibilities with which the psychologist would be required to deal. The various diagnostic entities are presented in discrete form, but findings related to pathology in patients invariably reflect more complex involvements. In formulating a complete diagnostic evaluation, elements from the compilation in this chapter as well as from the discussion of characterology in chapter 13 need to be integrated, in order to enable a more complete indication of the relation between the patient's actual functioning and personality structure. Even in instances where organic impairment strongly influences a patient's functioning, the residual elements of character structure invariably make an impression and need to be diagnostically affirmed so that the full range of the patient's individuality is conveyed.

An example of such a synthesis is the psychologist's final diagnosis. This formulation may begin with a statement of the neurotic or symptomatic behavior of the patient, such as one of the anxiety reactions. It may also reveal to the reader the fundamental character structure in which this symptom problem is embedded; thus, the diagnosis may be extended to become generalized anxiety disorder in an obsessive-compulsive personality. By the same token, the diagnosis of paranoid schizophrenia can be formulated to extend the reader's understanding of the symptom picture by indicating that this symptom problem, too, may be embedded in the context of an obsessive-compulsive character structure.

PROGNOSIS

Once the interrelations of the diagnostic amalgam are understood and formulated, a relevant prognostic statement can be attempted. For example, a psychotically depressed person whose character structure is basically compulsive will have a far different prognosis than a similarly depressed person with an essentially paranoid character structure. The patient with paranoid characterology will become entrenched more readily in externalization, suspiciousness, and manipulative efforts to control others. In contrast, the psychotically depressed person whose character structure is compulsive will be concerned with organization and perfectionistic pursuits, consistent with this characterology.

In prognostic terms, the outlook for the compulsive person with psychotic symptoms of depression is more optimistic than the prognosis for the psychotically depressed person with a paranoid character structure, since paranoid qualities generally have fewer adaptive potentials than do compulsive traits. This reveals the importance of an expanded diagnostic formulation in connection with prognostic statements. Once symptom behaviors upon which diagnoses are based are analyzed with respect to basic character structure, differential prognosis becomes evident.

Intervention strategies correspondingly will be affected and determined by the nature of the diagnosis and prognosis. The prognosis will be either optimistic, fair, or guarded. The attention to basic character structure is important in this respect, because guarded diagnostic and prognostic formulations can only definitively become so when the character structure confirms the limits for growth.

Under conditions specified by the prognosis, the referral source may advise a series of possible intervention strategies. The components of this series of steps may receive different weight and emphasis, depending on the clarity and depth of the psychologist's findings and their effective communication. The strategies can include guidance intervention, psychotherapy, counseling, chemotherapy, residential placement, hospitalization, special educational placement, and other important specialized modalities for rehabilitation.

The choice of treatment strategy relates back to the presenting problem that triggered the referral. At the start, the context of the presenting problem may have been unclear, and the role the problem played in the patient's overall functioning may have been incompletely understood. With the material derived from the analyses composing the psychological test report and its final summary—the diagnostic presentation—the meaning of the patient's disturbed behavior becomes substantially more illuminated. In the available range of intervention strategies such as counseling, therapy, and rehabilitation, a relevant and precise approach can be designed to help the patient.

The essential purpose of the psychologist's entry into the referral sequence is now fulfilled. This sequence starts with the patient's disturbance and the difficulties created among the network of people with whom the patient is involved. With the psychologist's contribution of a refined psychodiagnostic report clarifying the particular dysfunction involved, the entire system can be benefited. The psychodiagnostic report is a valuable document because it offers vital information that ultimately will benefit the patient. Thus, a fundamental theme resonating throughout this volume concerns the importance to the psychologist of developing the necessary professional skill in report construction. The final psychodiagnostic report should reflect the salient issues that have emerged in the protocol. This volume is designed to help both the student and the professional psychologist in this endeavor.

The next chapter is supplementary to the previous chapters that correspond to specific sections of the psychodiagnostic report. Chapter 16 focuses on special requirements in the presentation of intelligence test findings for personnel other than psychologists. A final coda aims at helping the psychologist and student transcend the phenomenon of impasse in formulating and writing psychodiagnostic test reports.

SUMMARY

In this and the previous chapter, the final diagnostic formulation that concludes the psychological report was discussed and related to prognostic and intervention considerations. Principles of diagnosis were delineated in terms of both the acute-chronic dimension and the shifting nature of the diagnosis itself. The multiple features of diagnosis and their interplay were related to the different components of personality functioning that can be summarized in an effective diagnostic formulation. This multileveled diagnostic approach also was discussed as a means of clarifying the role of presenting complaints, and in relation to prognostic and treatment formulations. The nosological system of diagnosis employed in *DSM-III* and *DSM-III-R*, the *Diagnostic and Statistical Manual of Mental Disorders*, was reviewed and a description of the various diagnostic categories as an amalgam of traditional and newer *DSM* usage was compiled.

16

Intelligence Test Reports For Counselors, Teachers, and Parents

This book has been concerned with the formulation of a detailed communication regarding the psychological-psychodiagnostic report that is directed to the needs of mental health practitioners. In this sense, a highly sophisticated presentation of findings characterizes the final report. Referral sources utilizing these kinds of results are likely to be in a position to evaluate and determine the implementation of far-reaching intervention strategies such as medication, hospitalization, or psychotherapeutic approaches.

Weighing these intervention alternatives can require a report that offers a full appreciation of diagnostic issues, a complete exposition of underlying personality factors and their ramifications, and a survey of all salient components of the person's functioning. Decisions among various intervention alternatives are based in part on the findings of the clinical psychodiagnostic report. The entire decision-making process of intervention is likely to involve several persons in a network of mental health practitioners that includes clinical psychologists, psychiatrists, social workers, or other referral sources at a professional level.

Frequently, other mental health personnel may require the expertise of a psychologist for a test evaluation. Referral sources may include parents or teachers who are attempting to manage disturbed, acting-out, or withdrawn children, or guidance counselors who are required to determine special educational placements on the basis of test referrals. Testing may be limited to an intellectual assessment or may include further personality evaluation. An intelligence scale may be administered exclusively, or other test instruments may be added to form a battery of assessment tools. In all of these instances, the extensively analytic, fully written psychodiagnostic report that has been the focus of previous chapters exceeds the needs of these groups.

Referral sources other than the psychologist, psychiatrist, or social worker require more concise writing with fewer technical elaborations and more direct responses to specific referral questions. These persons outside of the mental health field require less analytic and dynamic interpretation. Rather, a more descriptive evaluation of the psychological problems of the subject is needed. In addition, a focus on recommendations for intervention is important. The treatment interventions available may include a new class or school placement, recommendations to a teacher or parent with regard to managing the child and referral to a mental health practitioner for evaluation for possible therapy. The report also may be used to assist a case worker involved with the family's problems. Thus, the perspective of such a report, with its recommendations, differs from the psychodiagnostic report.

Referral sources such as teachers and guidance personnel in schools frequently find it advisable or necessary to communicate with parents about the difficulties that become manifest in school children. Educational personnel are in a position to offer salient information to those responsible for the healthy development of these youngsters. The psychologist who receives such a referral has the opportunity to clarify to school personnel the nature of the child's problem and also to present findings in a way that can invite constructive involvement of the parents. Often, in fact, the psychologist can make direct recommendations to consult with the child's parents. These recommendations include what can be beneficially conveyed to the parents and how the information can be utilized most advantageously.

The audience for the psychologist's report in these circumstances is distinctly different from that for the full psychodiagnostic report. Not only is the training of referral sources quite different in its emphasis and goals, but the needs of such persons in relation to the reporting of test findings are divergent as well. Test referrals related to school problems, however, have the same requirements of meaningfulness and communicative precision in the reporting of test results. In this respect, the construction and writing of the report for this audience must meet the same standards of expression as a report directed to any other referral source.

Yet, the report directed to teachers, guidance counselors, and parents may be different in several important respects from the report sent to mental health clinicians.

The importance of carefully presenting a report to educational personnel or parents is underscored when it is realized that some of the findings conveyed may lead to dramatic consequences, including possible recommendations for neurological evaluations, consideration of treatment referrals, or even consideration of residential placement which would separate the child from the family.

THE INTELLIGENCE TEST REFERRAL

A frequent referral in educational settings is the request for intelligence testing. The assessment of intellectual functioning within the school setting often arises in connection with a child who does not seem to be functioning near his or her apparent potential or whose behavioral disturbance raises questions regarding the most advantageous educational placement. Such a referral may implicitly require guidance or teaching personnel to determine constructive management approaches for the child.

If an intellectual assessment is all that is required, a good deal of material naturally presents itself for the psychologist to report. The major question at this point is to determine what issues need to be focused upon and illuminated and what material is best excluded, considering all that the psychologist may potentially address. Once the scope of the discussion in the report is clear, the psychologist can utilize the following type of structure to present the findings.

Identifying Data

This section of the intelligence test report presents a description of the person tested and the reason for the referral as it has been offered by the referring source. The importance of this section lies in its precise description of the individual being considered and of the nature of the problem that the report will attempt to clarify. Facts and figures about the child's age and grade and other classification data form a natural preamble that can be presented concisely.

Behavioral Observations

This section of the report provides the psychologist with an opportunity to detail what has been noticed about the subject in relation to the test process and in the subject's reactions to various aspects of the testing situation. These observations of the subject's behavior contribute to a clearer understanding of the quality of intellectual functioning in addition to actual I.Q.

For example, if the psychologist notes that the child who was tested needed extensive encouragement or even pressure in order to initiate or persist at the tasks of testing, this helps to make the later findings understandable: for example, that obtained levels of intellectual functioning were quite discrepant from optimal potential levels because of inhibitions in the child's motivation and handicaps interfering with full application of intellectual resources. Consequences in terms of academic performance can be linked to these findings at the levels of behavioral observation and intellectual functioning. The importance of the observational context is that it provides a meaningful basis for suggesting some of the implicit personality problems that may be affecting intellectual functioning.

As another example, the observation that the child responded to questions in a pressured manner, answering questions when it was clear that the subject had no idea about the answer, can later prove helpful in evaluating the child's intellectual functioning. Intelligence test results may be impaired because of reflective abilities that are reduced by anxiety and pressure to perform. This interference, which would be apparent in both intellectual functioning and academic performance, can further be related to factors of level of confidence, standard of performance, overcompliance, interpersonal strain, and so on, depending on the findings derived from testing.

These examples reveal that the observations which are presented should not be random or merely descriptive. Instead, the observations that are pointed out in the report should be limited to those that will relate in a meaningful manner to the findings that will be discussed. This means that in the report the appropriate detailing of the subject's behavior during the test session sets the stage for a clearer understanding of the intelligence test findings to follow.

Test Results

Intellectual Functioning. In most instances, the teacher or guidance counselor making a referral for an intellectual evaluation wants to know the I.Q. of the subject, and it is generally appropriate to report the figures — verbal and performance, if available, as well as full scale — that have been derived from testing. Thus, in this section of the report actual intelligence findings are presented and discussed. The common associations to "high" or "low" I.Q. results and any bias that may be triggered by focus on the number alone can be countered by the presentation of additional information by the psychologist.

There are instances where it is appropriate to report the ranges in which the I.Q.s fall instead of the specific scores obtained. These include occasions during which deviations from standard testing procedures were necessary in the administration of the test. Such deviations may occur when the psychologist tests students with unusually extensive behavioral disturbances, limited proficiency in the English language (such as students in bilingual education programs), and so on. In such cases, reporting the ranges in which obtained intelligence results lie introduces a note of caution in interpreting the quantitative results of testing that is appropriate when standard testing procedures could not be maintained. In circumstances in which parents will be given the report or are likely to have access to it, reporting ranges instead of scores provides a more meaningful indication of intellectual functioning.

Even when scores are reported, as discussed in the chapters on intellectual functioning, the descriptive ranges in which the I.Q.s fall need to be cited in order to provide a more meaningful statement about intellectual functioning. The reporting of the percentile ranks that correspond with the I.Q. figures relate subjects to their standing within their peer groups. They can then be evaluated in the framework of their own age and grade. This wider context avoids some of the stereotyped reactions that may be inadvertently stimulated by an isolated I.Q. figure.

Of even more assistance to the referral source is a careful discussion of the particular strengths and weaknesses that are revealed by the results of intelligence testing. An emphasis on strengths, often forgotten when problems lead to testing referrals, tends to indicate the areas of capability that do exist and reveals the constructive side that the individual has maintained in spite of any difficulties which are present. These strengths should be regarded as forming a foundation for concluding recommendations designed to serve the subject's interests in a manner that can be appreciated in realistic terms by the referral source. The discussion of the subject's varied strengths and weaknesses, abilities, and relative incapacities presents a picture of a complex individual. Providing amplification of the person's functioning nullifies preconceived or stereotyped reactions that occur to actual I.Q. numbers or terminology descriptive of these numbers, such as "low average" or even "very superior intellectual functioning."

The section of the report in which the findings are presented needs to include an estimate of the potential level of intellectual functioning. This estimate helps to indicate components of functioning not readily appreciated solely from the unitary I.Q. If the educational personnel have some idea that the child is either more capable or, alternatively, has been placed in a setting beyond his or her abilities, the estimate of intellectual functioning can help to affirm or revise such ideas. Thus, the subject's range of functioning, from the poorest to highest or potential level, is an important finding to communicate.

In addition, the estimate of potential intellectual level as it contrasts with current, actual levels provides some indication of whether the subject is suffering or experiencing difficulty. Factors relating to either the causes or the consequences of the discrepancy between actual and potential intellectual functioning may be associated with a sense of discouragement, pressure, agitation, or boredom. A sharp discrepancy between currently obtained results and potential levels of intellectual functioning usually signals the presence of disturbance within the child that in some way reflects and is linked with problematic stresses in the environment. Such stresses may be part of the educational placement, which could need revision, or result from disturbances in the home environment. Statements in the report about such possibilities are definitely in order when analysis of the findings point to them.

Just as a discussion of any contrast between current results and the student's potential is useful, a comparison between current results and the findings from any previous testing can be illuminating. A discussion of such a comparison can indicate declines in functioning that are relevant to the referral question as well as the presence of any areas of strength that remain intact or that show continued development. These kinds of comparative results can help in predicting the direction of future functioning as well as in evaluating intervention needs.

After analyzing the subject's intellectual functioning, there is logically an opportunity to describe the emotional and personality context in which intellectual functioning takes place. It is also appropriate and advantageous to discuss the ramifications and consequences of these personality factors, however briefly, to the extent that they can be linked to the referral questions. The important guide in reporting personality functioning in an intellectual evaluation is that the reader of the report will most likely be an educator. The reader may also have the task of communicating findings or recommendations to a parent. Therefore, clinical detail needs to be presented in simpler statements in which pathological ramifications are conveyed understandably.

When behavioral problems are part of the circumstances that triggered the test referral, a more complete presentation of personality operations may be useful. This discussion can be placed in an additional, discrete section of the report. Even when referral interest is more limited to concerns about intelligence, however, it may be appropriate to report some personality findings. These findings can be included in a logical way in the same section of the report as the intelligence results and should be explicitly and logically tied to clinical observations as well as to analysis of the person's intelligence.

Personality Functioning in the Intelligence Test Report. Whether briefly or more extensively incorporated, some consideration of the patient's personality functioning may be included in the report. An attempt should be made to maintain a logical and explanatory connection between these findings and those for intellectual functioning.

An example of this kind of linkage may be seen in the instance of a child demonstrating impulsive behavior that precludes adequate reflection. The child's concept formation, within the range of intelligence that applies, may be found to be impaired. Test results may reveal a nonreflective quality in handling verbal material, with resultant lowering of verbal intelligence in comparison with skills in performance areas. In performance subtests, a speed approach, a quick capacity to analyze, and good coordination skills may accompany the impulsive style, leading frequently to successful handling of performance items. Such an action-oriented subject, functioning well in visual and manual areas, cannot slow down sufficiently to exercise reflection consistent with intellectual potential. Thus, the emphasis on verbal and reflective skills in the classroom can produce frustration manifested in motoric overactivity, behavioral acting-out, and difficulty in completing work. In this illustration of an impulsive personality tendency, the pattern of intellectual functioning that includes a deficient verbal area along with an academic handicap relates to an underlying acting-out disturbance that, when reported, enhances understanding of the basis for the subject's classroom difficulties.

In another example, testing might reveal intellectual functioning to be well below estimates of potential, and the psychologist may relate this impairment to a state of depression. The depression might be associated with lethargic passivity at the behavioral level, which interferes with utilizing high-level conceptual and expressive skills. In such cases, academic performance shows a decline.

Still another example might involve test results that reveal the way in which an advancing state of inner confusion makes it increasingly difficult for the subject to understand directions, deal with material that requires abstraction, and focus attentively on what is being presented. This constellation of difficulties deriving from inner confusion contributes to impaired intellectual functioning. This inner confusion also interferes with effective classroom and academic participation consistent with the educational failures that have occurred. Connecting this subject's educational difficulties with the resultant pattern of intellectual functioning that is obtained as well as with the personality disturbance in which confusion is central increases the likelihood of effective intervention. Wording in the report that utilizes terms such as confusion or emotional agitation are more appropriate in a communication to a teacher than terms such as psychosis. This is particularly apparent if it is remembered that a conference with a parent may ultimately be required.

After personality features are clarified, the communication from the psychologist should include an indication of the stresses that contribute to the findings of impairment on the intelligence test and in academic performance. Through analysis of the personality context, the examples just presented suggest ways in which intellectual functioning can be understood and related to the academic problems that originally stimulated the referral.

With the addition of some description of relevant personality variables, the communication from the psychologist lends itself to further indications regarding the advisability of individual treatment, a family consultation, social services for the family, or recommendations pertaining to revisions in the student's educational placement. Such conclusions can be indicated in the section related to findings, but they also should pointedly be presented in the final section of the report, called "Summary and Conclusions."

Summary and Conclusions Section of the Report

This last section of the report should present only the essential findings about the person who was tested, so that the issues raised by the referral question can be satisfied by a reading of this section alone. The summary nature of the results presented in this section will offer a response to the referral question that is relatively brief because of the absence of supportive discussion and analysis; however, the fundamentals that are included will reveal the major points and conclusions cogently.

The implications regarding intervention possibilities that follow from the summarized findings also need to be presented. For example, such intervention recommendations might be a referral for a neurological evaluation if organic impairment was reflected in the data, or administration of a fuller psychological battery to ensure an exacting investigation of any problems that the intelligence testing may have revealed. Another example of a recommendation would be to suggest a review of the child's educational placement in keeping with the level of intellectual functioning or potential as determined by testing. The report may advise that an educational battery be administered by an educational specialist to determine the areas and components of educational disability. It may be recommended that the teacher further encourage the student's participation, or that the teacher put less pressure on the student to be productive.

The report should also recommend, if appropriate, that school personnel or the teacher confer with the parents, and should include the way in which the findings and recommendations can be conveyed to the parents and the points to be made in such a conference. This recommendation can be cast in terms that clarify to the parent the child's current intellectual functioning with regard to a particular ranking (percentile) showing where the child stands in relation to others of the same age. It could, perhaps, be added that potentially greater accomplishment would be possible if it were not for certain areas that need improvement. These areas can be detailed and the steps to assist with such improvement can be suggested to the parents in language that is simple, clear, and unthreatening. For instance, if problems of withdrawal or distractibility play a role in school difficulties, the parents need to be counseled about this part of the problem. Improvement may develop following the parent conference or through personal counseling for the child. The psychologist can present these recommendations as they seem appropriate, or as alternatives.

LANGUAGE IN THE INTELLIGENCE TEST REPORT

The consideration of possible recommendations emphasizes the requirement of clear communication in meaningful, nontechnical terms that will present the human qualities of the subject and relate them to statements easily absorbed by parents. In fact, the entire report as it is addressed to teachers, counselors, or guidance personnel is best served if technical concepts are as unencumbered as possible. For example, simple terms reflecting complex diagnostic issues can include confusion, sadness, discouragement, loneliness, fear, or panic. These kinds of simple terms that are associated with serious or moderate underlying personal pathology can be related to causes of the disruption in learning, working, conceptual thinking, interpersonal relating, or attendance.

To explore the issues of schizophrenia, depression, or phobias in terms of intrapsychic, interpersonal, and impulse and control factors, as well as in terms of a sense of identity and all other applicable psychological dimensions, is excessive and would obscure the points that are appropriate to make. Therefore, it is better to replace any full discussion of these psychologically relevant issues with simpler, more immediately descriptive terminology that an educator can make use of.

In a similar vein, concepts having to do with impulsivity and acting-out can be indicated simply by use of these descriptive terms without the support of a discussion of the nature of anxiety. What can be stated is that the child who is impulsive cannot slow down enough to be more thoughtful, conceptual, and logical, and that such a problem is caused by a specific tension involving a parent, sibling, etc. Ideas concerning judgment and self-confidence also can be conveyed in similarly descriptive terms by focusing on the test results through examples from the protocol or behavioral observations. Restricting the discussion to this level avoids the unnecessary addition of the particular underlying network of internal factors that, if explored, would confuse the client rather than illuminate the questions concerning the referral.

In parts of the report in which intellectual functioning is discussed, findings of mental deficiency, learning disabilities, and organic impairment also need to be presented with minimal emphasis on underlying technical considerations. A descriptive analysis that clarifies what the subject can and cannot be expected to do and that states what treatment and further assessments are advisable is more helpful than a technically worded discussion of brain functioning. Expressions such as "neurological impairment," "incapacities in specified intellectual areas," and "disabilities related to specific academic areas" are preferable to statistical or pessimistically colored terminology. Clear inclusion of areas of strength that the subject's protocol presents is advisable and beneficial. Reporting these positive areas enables a sense of appreciation and sensitivity to be conveyed to both the child and parent.

The kind of report that has been discussed in this chapter is less technical than a full psychodiagnostic report; nevertheless, the findings need to be conveyed with care. Often the so-called simpler, less technical report for the less sophisticated referral source becomes more difficult to compose than the complex and extensive psychodiagnostic report. To write simply, clearly, and plainly to individuals such as teachers and parents who know the tested individual well can be especially challenging to the psychologist. In fact, the challenge in this "simpler" work can readily lead to impasses and blockages in formulating and in writing the report, a circumstance that presents the writer with an especially disruptive experience: writing block, procrastination, and anxiety about professional functioning.

The final chapter of this book is presented in the form of a coda—a relevant but new theme on taking steps to overcome writer's block. Information that is particularly useful to establishing or reestablishing the flow of composing the test report is provided. Many students find that even after completing their professional studies and after writing numerous reports under supervision, they experience disruptive writing impasses in spite of the extent of their preparation. The question may be asked, "What are the special problems that the professional psychologist or psychology student encounters that create impasses generating the phenomenon of difficulty in psychological report writing?"

SUMMARY

This chapter has considered the special requirements involved in preparing an intellectual evaluation and test report for nonprofessionals and for personnel in educational settings. Since the readers of such reports may include guidance counselors, teachers, or parents, the discussion presented the distinct treatment necessary for the construction of this document. Such treatment includes a descriptive analysis in clear and nontechnical language, integrating the subject's behavior and intellectual and personality functioning. The aim of reports for personnel in fields other than mental health, however, is primarily concerned with intellectual findings. Thus, a major focus of this chapter concerned how to effectively present I.Q. scores to teachers and parents. A final summary of the report was described which emphasizes the importance of including recommendations for intervention and describing how these were derived, and how to convey them in an appropriate, sensitive, and effective manner.

CODA
Overcoming Impasses in Report Writing

The student or professional who has administered the required test battery may often experience great difficulty with initiating the writing up of findings. Similarly, within the process of composing the report, stumbling blocks to continuity and completion lead to procrastination and undue delay. In this chapter such blocks and impasses are discussed and approaches that can assist in preventing this kind of writing block are offered. The discussion orients the reader to the effective reporting of results in written form with a minimization of procrastination and blocks.

It is understandable that psychologists and students may have particular difficulty in the composition of psychological reports, in contrast to other written material such as book reviews, papers, patient process notes, and experimental reports. In all of these, the student and the professional psychologist can prepare written material in a relatively straightforward manner, and usually, findings can be integrated more easily than in a psychological report. In contrast, the psychological test report demands obvious professional expertise and authoritative determinations that are based upon an arduous integration of complex data.

Because of the demands placed on the writer by the requirements of the written psychological report, the student may experience conflict in the assumption of authority, which has several correlates. These include insecurity of role, surfacing of inadequacy feelings, the emergence of doubts about the efficacy of such reporting itself, and fundamental questions about the actual validity of the tests. These elements are derivative features of the writer's concern with professional role and status. It should be remembered that in clinical and applied psychological practice, the only technological or concrete apparatus visible to the patient as well as to the psychologist is the test materials. Therefore, problems of assuming an authoritative stance and position of expertise become exacerbated by the demands of utilizing the test technology as well as by internal pressures of self-doubt.

The anxiety generated by the need to use this technology and by the internal pressures of self-doubt is expressed in various ways. For example, when this sort of tension is high, the writer can become confused with respect to whom the report is directed: is it written solely with the patient's interest in mind, or is it written in order to gain favorable responses from supervisors or other referring personnel? Some writers may become anxious because they need to produce each report in a form resembling a literary masterpiece. Thus, generally speaking, the writer's problem can concern a confusion about whether the focus of the report is on the patient, the supervisor, the referrer, or oneself.

This kind of confusion constitutes a major impasse in writing psychological reports. Lack of clarity regarding to whom the report is directed introduces anxiety about the appropriate role for the writer to assume. It can become nearly impossible to formulate ideas and communications to which the writer feels committed because of uncertainty about the report's aim and audience.

RESOLVING THE ROLE-ANXIETY DILEMMA

The anxiety associated with anticipated reactions to a report can be caused by the presence of several individuals who may read or evaluate it. All those who have something to do with the final report, including the writer, are viewed as split off from each other and having divergent interests. These divergent interests or parts are further evaluated in positive and negative terms. For example, the patient, who is placed in a pathological role, may represent the bad part. The writer of the report, in order to avoid identification with the bad part—the patient—may need to construct a report that will please the supervisor, professional colleague, or the referral source. The writer imagines, therefore, becoming the good part and gaining acceptance by the supervisor or fellow professionals. Accomplishing this goal can satisfy yearnings to be seen in purely good terms and to be praised. The difficulty in writing the report under such fantasy circumstances is that the report must become a praiseworthy document.

In order for the writer to overcome such unnecessary psychological conflict, it is helpful to consider the report a unifying mechanism in the overall referral context. This means that the report is a cooperative representation of the alliance among patient, referral source or supervisor, and writer. In this conception, there are no competing interests or divergent representations of good and bad. There is, instead, the goal of seeking the truth as closely as possible.

In order to defuse further the psychological obstacles that report writers experience, it is important to recognize the value in the psychological test report of clarity and simplicity and the way in which the report itself becomes a new and useful learning vehicle for the referring source or supervisor as well as for the writer.

THE SUPERVISOR'S ROLE

The supervisor or referral source or other professional colleagues who come into contact with the report are often viewed as being all-knowing and judgmental. In the model of supervision that follows from this view, an uninitiated student works with a thoroughly wise and critically evaluative teacher. This oversimplified perspective leads to considerable tension about writing reports and produces inevitable blocks. Often, the same naive perspective is applied between the tester and the referral source. The actual context of supervision, referral, and professional communication is quite different; in fact, supervision is a sharing condition in which a process unfolds and informs both people involved. The student as well as the professional psychologist need to focus on the central concern in supervision: the creation of a report about a patient's functioning. The construction of the final report, in all its phases, constitutes an enormously valuable learning opportunity that is every bit as helpful to the supervisor or referring person as it is to the writer and patient. Thus, the report reflects a cooperative effort among all concerned: the writer, the supervisor or referring person, and the patient.

In the anxiety experienced about the evaluation as one reflecting the division of good and bad with respect to patient and psychologist, it has been pointed out that the patient can readily be viewed as bad. To counteract this distortion, it must be remembered that the patient does not provide problems, bad material, or terrifying pathologies. The patient provides only samples of behavior. The instructive nature of the report and the process of creating it are in part dependent upon the fact that the patient's responses and samples of behavior are neither right nor wrong, but only instructive and potentially interpretable. Therefore, in the supervisory effort, or in the direct communication between writer and referral source, the major consideration is what is to be learned. The supervisor and the writer share in uncovering what is to be learned and in placing it in communicative terms.

The professional psychologist who works without external supervision can experience the same problem of self-doubt as the supervised psychologist. This problem can be based on the psychologist's inner conflict between the creative writer self and the critical, evaluative, supervisor self. These two aspects of self can become separate from each other and experienced as distinct, opposing forces that generate tension. Thus, in the absence of external supervision one's own evaluative impulses and needs, if severe, can be the determining factors that compel the writer to strive toward the composition of a masterpiece, thereby impeding the writer's progress. Such needs for perfection usually generate fear of writing the report and procrastination, and the patient's interests can then become compromised. The psychologist needs to bear in mind the fundamental importance of the alliance with both the patient and the referring source. An attitude of alliance can enable the psychologist to prepare a report that is appropriate and beneficial as a professional communication, corresponding to a milieu of learning and instruction.

Taking steps to alleviate role anxiety and the sense of external and internal divisions helps to resolve one major writing impasse. Then, the writer's primary effort is to maintain a sharing alliance in order to create a report that will generate a learning climate because of the particular cooperative attitude of the writer with all other components of the referral process — patient, supervisor, referral source, and so forth.

THE ACTIVE-PASSIVE DILEMMA

Another major problem that can interfere with efforts to compose a report is the passivity phenomenon that occurs in the face of demands that are inherent in the task of writing. Such demands include the need to organize and put into words the meaning of a body of data that has been compiled. In addition, the passivity of the writer can be reinforced by the sense that the referral source awaits the completed report. When the writer of the psychological report views this task exclusively in terms of fulfilling requirements, the demand quality of the situation can become exaggerated. In such a case, the given body of data that needs to be interpreted becomes viewed as being vast, and the awaiting referral source is transformed into an urgent, impatient source.

Under these conditions, the passivity experienced by the writer is actually an example of the previously mentioned anxiety concerning self-doubt, role tension, and separateness from the referral and testing process. An apparent paradox in connection with this anxiety is that the psychologist's objectivity is increased by becoming involved and allied with the entire referral process. Conversely, the psychologist's objectivity is decreased and anxiety is increased by remaining separate. The resolution of this paradox resides in understanding that a report fostering a learning climate can only be constructed when the focus on good-bad distinctions is removed.

The role played by the psychologist in the sharing endeavor of the test referral process has numerous implications. This sharing reflects the elimination of psychological impasses, it attests to the psychologist's involvement, and it permits the psychologist to be objective in the interests of the patient. All of these factors enable the psychologist to contribute to the overall learning climate of this sequence of events.

Only when the psychologist is allied with the patient and the sequence of factors within the referral can the psychologist trust the data. If the psychologist is separate from the patient and is automatically inclined to maintain divisions, then the psychologist will find it more difficult to trust personal impressions. In such a case, self-doubt is raised with respect to the psychologist's expertise and contribution, and the data can become suspect.

The psychologist or student who is aware of such issues is not afraid of the data, can discuss impressions raised by the data whatever their implications may be, and can calmly withstand the reactions of those who eventually read the report. Criticisms or disagreements are seen as factors in a learning situation in which the data is the source of knowledge. For example, suppose a patient who is tested generates responses throughout the protocol reflecting suicidal ideation. Even though the patient may not appear to be overtly depressed and all of those familiar with the patient do not recognize suicidal indications, the psychologist can nevertheless stand firmly with the data and also with the patient. The psychologist supports the patient's experience even when it cannot be clearly verbalized and when others cannot see it. Support means only seeing the experience, integrating it, reporting it, and learning about it.

Thus, the inertia, lethargy, fatigue, and passivity that are major obstacles to report writing can be at least in part resolved by grasping and appreciating the writer's role in the sequence of the referral process and in contributing to the learning climate.

APPRECIATING LIMITS

The nature of the data that are obtained by means of psychological testing has numerous implications and ramifications. The task for the writer is to decide the central ideas, hypotheses, and conclusions. The communication of conclusions encapsulates what is to be learned from the data for the benefit of the patient and those in the referral process.

Equally important to beginning the write-up is to determine when it is appropriate to stop. Any protocol can be analyzed further and utilized to draw additional information and stimulate further speculation. The aim of the report, however, is to provide specific information about the patient that ultimately will be helpful in understanding and planning for that patient. An excessive supply of information interferes with the patient's interest to the same extent as insufficient information.

An additional feature of the information derived from the data is that it is inferential. The psychologist is uniquely trained to organize inferences in order to form a coherent and understandable discussion. It should be noted, however, that there are degrees of inference. For example, it is frequently tempting to speculate on a patient's early history, relationships, and traumas, based upon what seem to be logical connections to current data. The psychologist needs to appreciate that the report is a psychological evaluation containing diagnostic and personality information, not a psychohistory or psychosocial compendium. Philosophical speculations and psychohistorical reconstructions can easily create a condition in which the writer of the report unwittingly exploits the patient.

In contrast to the writer's personal interests, the report is exclusively about the patient: current functioning, personality structure, anxiety, symptoms, behavior, intelligence, emotional integration, and cognitive control. To know when to limit speculation and to adhere to the data, bearing in mind the interest of the patient, is a reflection of the extent of the maturity of the psychologist or student. This level of maturity, of course, changes and develops over time. It is not the case that the writer of a report is simply mature or immature; rather, a writer's degree of maturity is reflected in a sense of alliance with the entire referral process, from which is also derived a greater facility in writing the report.

The understanding and appreciation required in the construction of the psychological report involve a connection with the patient's interests that develops out of continuing effort, supervision, and the writer's authentic striving to create and participate in a climate of learning. Psychological report writing constitutes an important training for this kind of development in the psychologist. The increasing capacity to contribute to the patient's welfare results from repeated exposure to a wide array of testing situations, each offering a unique opportunity to learn about the meanings of personality structure, diagnosis, behavior, and anxiety. It is a learning endeavor in which patients contribute arrays of response samples to the psychologist's fund of information and experience.

Psychological report writing can benefit patients; it can also contribute to the development and growth of psychology students as well as professional psychologists. As knowledge and capacity deepen through the experience of report writing, the psychologist's subsequent ability to contribute to the referral sequence and to the patient's ultimate interests is enhanced.

RECOMMENDED READINGS

Clinical Applications of Psychological Tests

Allison, J., Blatt, S. J., & Zimet, C. N. (1968). *The Interpretation of Psychological Tests*. New York: Harper & Row.

Arnold, M. B. (1962). *Story Sequence Analysis*. New York: Columbia University Press.

Beck, S. J., Beck, A., Levitt, E., & Molish, H. B. (1961). *Rorschach's Test: Vol. 1 Basic Processes* (3rd ed.). New York: Grune & Stratton.

Bender, L. A. (1938). *Visual Motor Gestalt Test and Its Clinical Use*. New York: The American Orthopsychiatric Association.

Benton, A. L. (1955). *The Revised Visual Retention Test: Clinical and Experimental Applications*. New York: The Psychological Corporation.

Blank, L. (1965). *Psychological Evaluation in Psychotherapy*. Chicago: Aldine.

Caligor, L. (1957). *A New Approach to Figure Drawings*. Springfield: Charles C. Thomas.

Exner, J. E. (1974). *The Rorschach: A Comprehensive System*. New York: Wiley.

Hammer, E. (1958). *The Clinical Application of Projective Drawings*. Springfield: Charles C. Thomas.

Klopfer, B., Aimsworth, M. D., Klopfer, W. G. & Holt, R. R. (1954). *Developments in the Rorschach Technique: Vol. 1. Technique and Theory*. New York: Harcourt, Brace & World.

Machover, K. (1949). *Personality Projection in the Drawing of the Human Figure*. Springfield: Charles C. Thomas.

Murray, H. A. (1943). *Thematic Apperception Test*. Cambridge: Harvard University Press.

217

Phillips, L., & Smith, J. G. (1953). *Rorschach Interpretation: Advanced Technique*. New York: Grune & Stratton.

Piotrowski, Z. A. (1957). *Perceptanalysis*. New York: Macmillan.

Rapaport, D., Gill, M. M., & Schafer, R. (1970). *Diagnostic Psychological Testing*. New York: International Universities Press.

Rorschach, H. (1951). *Psychodiagnostics*. New York: Grune & Stratton.

Schafer, R. (1973). *Clinical Application of Psychological Tests*. New York: International Universities Press.

The Clinical Interview

Bird, B. (1955). *Talking with Patients*. Philadelphia: Lippincott.

Blum, L. H. (1972). *Reading Between the Lines: Doctor-Patient Communication*. New York: International Universities Press.

Console, W. A., Simons, R. C., & Rubinstein, M. (1976). *The First Encounter: The Beginnings in Psychotherapy*. New York: Aronson.

Deutsch, F., & Murphy, W. F. (1955). *The Clinical Interview* (Vol. 1). New York: International Universities Press.

Gill, M., Newman, R., & Redlich, F. G. (1954). *The Initial Interview in Psychiatric Practice*. New York: International Universities Press.

Mackinnon, R. A., & Michels, R. (1971). *The Psychiatric Interview in Clinical Practice*. Philadelphia: Saunders.

Pruyser, P. W. (1979). *The Psychological Examination*. New York: International Universities Press.

Stevenson, I. (1971). *The Diagnostic Interview* (2nd ed). New York: Harper & Row.

Sullivan, H. S. (1954). *The Psychiatric Interview*. New York: W. W. Norton.

Reality Testing and Cognitive Functioning

Ausubel, D. P., & Kirk, D. (1977). *Ego Psychology and Mental Disorder: A Developmental Approach to Psychopathology*. New York: Grune & Stratton.

Hartmann, H. (1951). *Ego Psychology and the Problem of Adaptation*. New York: International Universities Press.

Jacobson, E. (1967). *Psychotic Conflict and Reality*. New York: International Universities Press.

Rapaport, D. (Ed.). (1951). *Organization and Pathology of Thought*. New York: Columbia University Press.

Vaillant, G. E. (1977). *Adaptation to Life*. Boston: Little, Brown.

Intellectual Functioning

Hunt, J. McV. (1961). *Intelligence and Experience*. New York: Ronald Press.

Matarazzo, J. D. (1972). *Wechsler's Measurement and Appraisal of Adult Intelligence* (5th enl. ed.). Baltimore: Williams & Wilkins.

Wechsler, D. (1972). *The Measurement and Appraisal of Adult Intelligence* (5th ed.). Baltimore: Williams & Wilkins.

Zimmerman, I. L., & Woo-Sam, J. M. (1973). *Clinical Interpretation of the Wechsler Adult Intelligence Scale.* New York: Grune & Stratton.

Anxiety

Freud, S. (1936). *The Problem of Anxiety.* New York: W. W. Norton.

Izard, C. E. (1972). *Patterns of Emotions: A New Analysis of Anxiety and Depression.* New York: Academic Press.

Lader, M. H., & Marks, I. (1971). *Clinical Anxiety.* London: Heinemann.

May, R. (1950). *The Meaning of Anxiety.* New York: The Ronald Press.

Impulse Versus Control

Abt, L. E., & Weissman, S. L. (Eds.). (1965). *Acting Out.* New York: Grune & Stratton.

Izard, C. E. (Ed.). (1979). *Emotions in Personality and Psychopathology.* New York: Plenum.

Lion, J. R. (1974). *Personality Disorders: Diagnosis and Management.* Baltimore: Williams & Wilkins.

Saul, L. J. (1971). *Emotional Maturity: The Development and Dynamics of Personality and Its Disorders.* Philadelphia: Lippincott.

Wishnie, H. (1977). *The Impulsive Personality: Understanding People with Destructive Character Disorders.* New York: Plenum.

Defensive Structure

Freud, A. (1966). *The Ego and the Mechanisms of Defense* (rev. ed.). New York: International Universities Press.

Laughlin, H. P. (1970). *The Ego and Its Defenses.* New York: Appleton-Century-Crofts.

Sjöbäck, H. (1973). *The Psychoanalytic Theory of Defensive Processes.* New York: Wiley.

White, R. B. (1972). *Elements of Psychopathology: The Mechanisms of Defense.* New York: Grune & Stratton.

Interpersonal Behavior and Character Structure

Deutsch, H. (1965). *Neuroses and Character Types: Clinical Psychoanalytic Studies.* New York: International Universities Press.

Erikson, E. H. (1963). *Childhood and Society* (2nd ed.). New York: W. W. Norton.

Erikson, E. H. (1968). *Identity, Youth and Crisis.* New York: W. W. Norton.

Reich, W. (1949). *Character-Analysis* (3rd ed.). New York: Farrar, Straus & Giroux.

Shapiro, D. (1965). *Neurotic Styles.* New York: Basic Books.

Diagnosis

American Psychiatric Association. (1980). *Diagnostic and Statistical Manual of Mental Disorders* (3rd ed.). Washington, DC: Author.

American Psychiatric Association. (1987). *Diagnostic and Statistical Manual of Mental Disorders* (3rd rev. ed.). Washington, DC: Author.

Burton, A., & Harris, R. E. (1955). *Clinical Studies of Personality.* New York: Harper.

Choca, J. (1980). *Manual of Clinical Psychology Practicums.* New York: Brunner/Mazel.

Costello, C. J. (Ed.). (1970). *Symptoms of Psychopathology: A Handbook.* New York: Wiley.

Gardner, R. A. (1979). *The Objective Diagnosis of Minimal Brain Dysfunction.* Cresskill, NJ: Creative Therapeutics.

Kellerman, H., & Burry, A. (1989). *Psychopathology and Differential Diagnosis: A Primer. Volume 2. Diagnostic Primer.* New York: Columbia University Press.

Lezak, M. D. (1976). *Neuropsychological Assessment.* New York: Oxford University Press.

Pruyser, P. W. (Ed.). (1976). *Diagnosis and the Difference It Makes.* New York: Aronson.

Small, L. (1973). *Neuropsychodiagnosis in Psychotherapy.* New York: Bruner/Mazel.

Strahl, M. O., & Lewis, N. D. C. (Eds.). (1972). *Differential Diagnosis in Clinical Psychiatry: The Lectures of Paul H. Hoch.* New York: Science House.

Report Construction

Klopfer, W. G. (1960). *The Psychological Report.* New York: Grune & Stratton.

Noland, R. C. (1970). *Research and Report Writing in the Behavioral Sciences.* Springfield: Charles C. Thomas.

Tallent, N. (1976). *Psychological Report Writing.* Englewood Cliffs, NJ: Prentice Hall.

Index